Exploring AND Upgrading Your PC

French text by Anatole d'Hardancourt
Illustrations by Joël Bavagnoli and Kristof Chemineau
Translated by François Coulombe
Contributors: Gary Masters, Richard King
Editor: Barbara Gordon
Proofreader: Taris Duffie
Indexer: Matthew Spence
Cover Designer: Joanna Kim Gladden

10 9 8 7 6 5 4 3 2 1

Exploring AND Upgrading Your PC

SYBEX

Contents

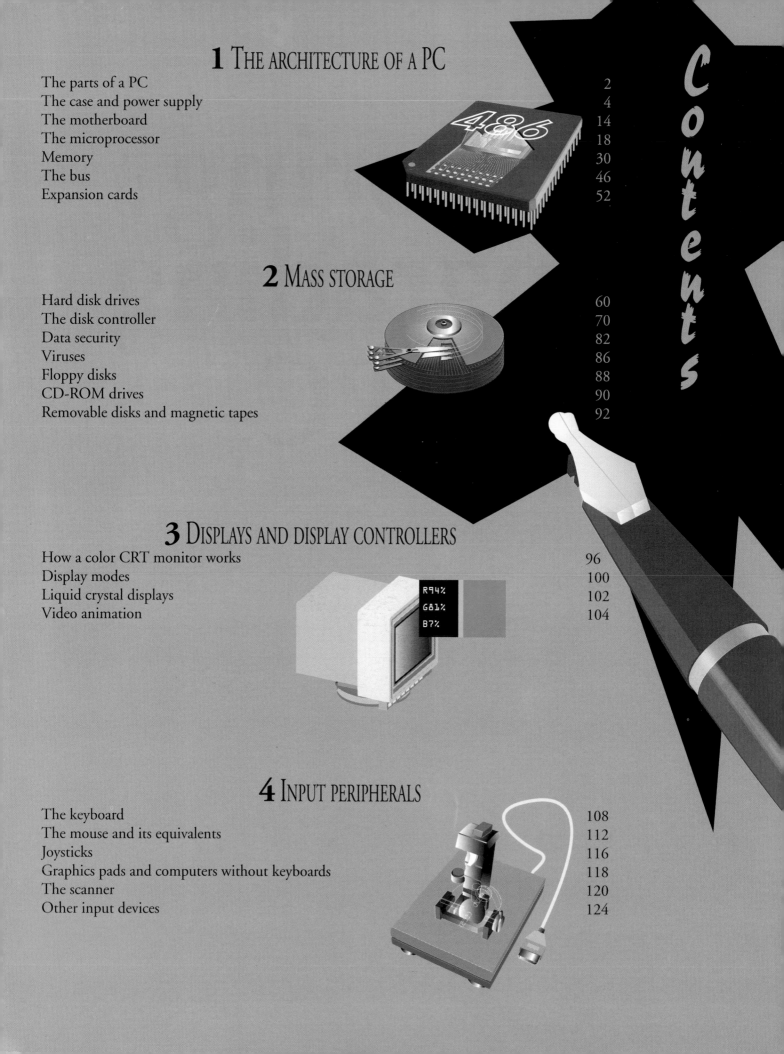

1 THE ARCHITECTURE OF A PC

The parts of a PC	2
The case and power supply	4
The motherboard	14
The microprocessor	18
Memory	30
The bus	46
Expansion cards	52

2 MASS STORAGE

Hard disk drives	60
The disk controller	70
Data security	82
Viruses	86
Floppy disks	88
CD-ROM drives	90
Removable disks and magnetic tapes	92

3 DISPLAYS AND DISPLAY CONTROLLERS

How a color CRT monitor works	96
Display modes	100
Liquid crystal displays	102
Video animation	104

4 INPUT PERIPHERALS

The keyboard	108
The mouse and its equivalents	112
Joysticks	116
Graphics pads and computers without keyboards	118
The scanner	120
Other input devices	124

5 PRINTED OUTPUT

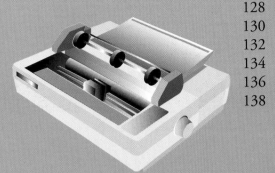

Dot-matrix printers   128
Laser printers   130
Inkjet printers   132
Color printers   134
Imagesetters and film recorders   136
Rendering grayscale and color   138

6 TELECOMMUNICATIONS AND NETWORKS

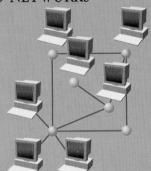

Local area networks   142
Modems and digital telephone networks   148
Wide area networks   152
Using a network   154

7 SOFTWARE

Organization of a PC's software   160
Starting up a PC   162
Applications   166

8 MULTIMEDIA

What is multimedia ?   170
Multimedia PC configuration   172
A multimedia application   174

After having written many books on how to use microcomputers, we've learned that many of the questions readers ask could be answered easily if they simply understood how the hardware works. For example, knowing how data is written on the hard drive makes it easier to understand the precautions you need to take to avoid accidental data loss. Also, it's easier to recover the data lost during such an accident when you understand how the data is organized on the disk. Moreover, many problems encountered by users are caused by minor events that seem unrelated to the problem. For example, a computer located under a desk that is hit by the user or a vacuum cleaner on a daily basis or a computer located in an unventilated area can suddenly break down. A PC with a defective power supply can produce irregular voltages that will lead to data loss. We can certainly provide strict guidelines to follow to avoid such problems. But it's better to understand the cause of them, and that is possible only if you know how the various parts of the computer work.

People who are buying PCs have other concerns. Nowadays, you can buy a computer in a department store, the same way you buy shoes or furniture. The information available in such a store is often limited to a few lines of advertising listing the machine's characteristics. How many buyers of PCs with "expandable" memory found out later that they had to discard the memory already in their PC before they were able to add more? How many bought a "local bus" PC only to find out that it wasn't compatible with the accelerated video card they needed? How many brought home a "486" machine only to find out that any manufacturer can give this name to its processor—even if its performance is less than half that of a "real" 486?

This book's objective isn't to show you how to *use* a computer. Instead, it is designed to help you understand exactly how a computer works so that you might *better* use it.

And, if a picture is worth a thousand words, we're confident that the hundreds of beautiful and richly detailed illustrations produced by Joël Bavagnoli are the best way to achieve our goal.

We would like to thank Intel and Toshiba for their help. Many thanks also to the translators and editors of the international versions, whose contributions helped us realize this book.

The architecture of a PC

• The parts of a PC 2

• The case and power supply 4

• The motherboard 14

• The microprocessor 18

• Memory.................................... 30

• The bus 46

• Expansion cards 52

The parts of a PC

A PC consists of a case of core electronic components connected to various *peripherals*, accessories that let users send data to the computer (*input*) or receive information from the computer (*output*). Although PCs vary in shape, size, capacity, speed, and price, they all include elements that enable them to perform these essential tasks: 1) receive data, 2) save it, 3) manipulate it in various ways, and 4) generate a result. Computers receive most data from either the keyboard or a disk. Information is usually saved on a floppy diskette or on a hard disk. Data is manipulated and changed (*processed*) by the microprocessor, and the resulting output is either displayed on a monitor or printed on paper. Although many computers include additional components—such as scanners, modems, magnetic tape drives, sound cards, and so on—every computer has at least the basic elements shown in this illustration.

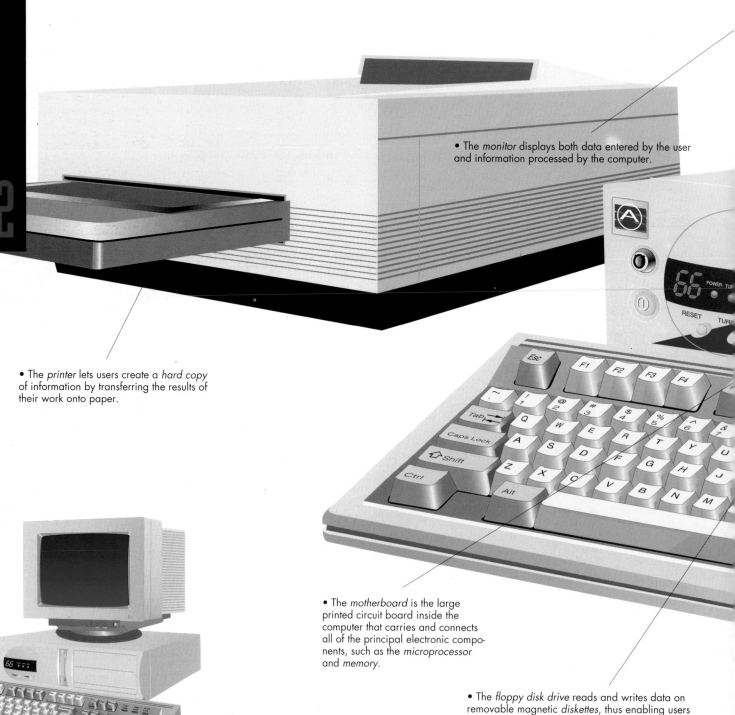

• The *monitor* displays both data entered by the user and information processed by the computer.

• The *printer* lets users create a *hard copy* of information by transferring the results of their work onto paper.

• The *motherboard* is the large printed circuit board inside the computer that carries and connects all of the principal electronic components, such as the *microprocessor* and *memory*.

• The *floppy disk drive* reads and writes data on removable magnetic *diskettes*, thus enabling users to transfer information between computers, make copies of data for backup purposes, and install new programs.

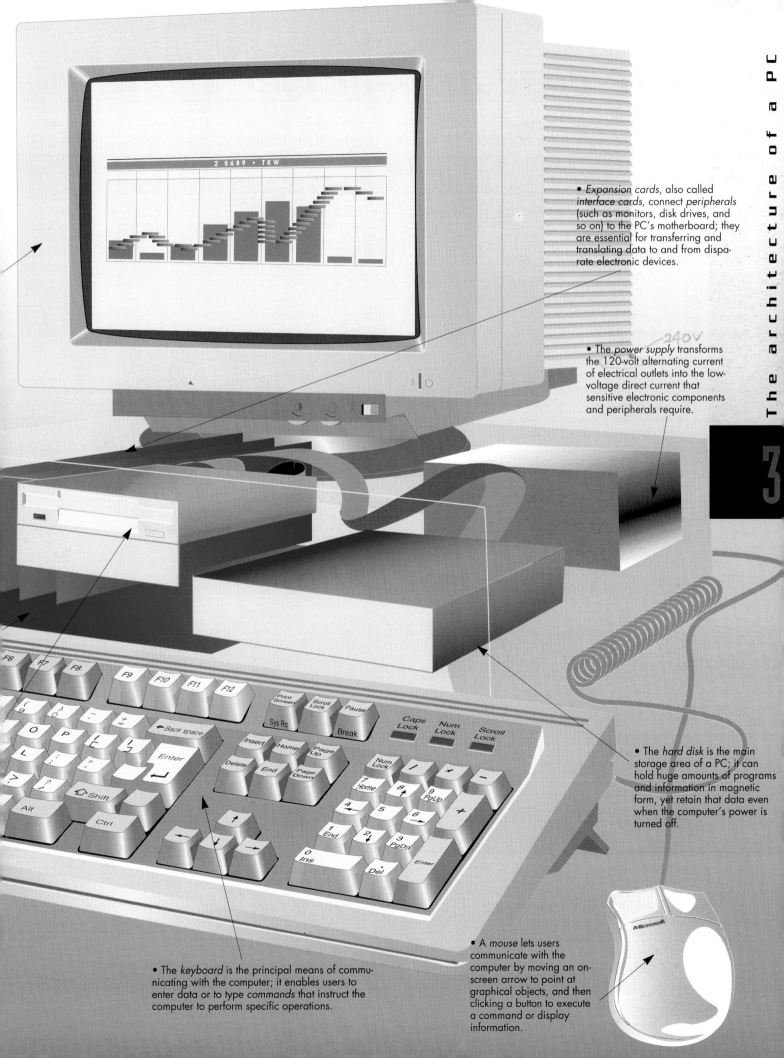

2 5689 · TKW

• *Expansion cards*, also called *interface cards*, connect *peripherals* (such as monitors, disk drives, and so on) to the PC's motherboard; they are essential for transferring and translating data to and from disparate electronic devices.

• The *power supply* transforms the 120-volt alternating current of electrical outlets into the low-voltage direct current that sensitive electronic components and peripherals require.

240V

3

• The *hard disk* is the main storage area of a PC; it can hold huge amounts of programs and information in magnetic form, yet retain that data even when the computer's power is turned off.

• The *keyboard* is the principal means of communicating with the computer; it enables users to enter data or to type *commands* that instruct the computer to perform specific operations.

• A *mouse* lets users communicate with the computer by moving an on-screen arrow to point at graphical objects, and then clicking a button to execute a command or display information.

The case and power supply

The design of a computer's case (or *system unit*) is far from being its most important characteristic, even though it may be the most noticeable feature for the novice. However, the design does influence many important details: ergonomics, expansion possibilities, and ventilation issues, for example. Although some large manufacturers use custom-made cases designed specifically for their PCs, most brands of computers (and nearly all of the less expensive compatible PCs called *clones*) use identical generic cases. Since most computers include the same basic components, the size and shape of cases are fairly standard.

Case design

PCs can be classified into three general categories according to the design of their cases:

• The *desktop* (horizontal case) PC. These cases come in two heights: standard (6") and mini, or slim-line (4"). Lengths and widths can vary widely: from 20" x 16" for the largest (often called "Standard AT cases" because they are the size of the modern PC's ancestor, the IBM AT) to 14" x 12" for smaller "mini-ATs."

• The *tower* (vertical case) PC. These cases are usually 7" wide and 16" deep (mid-tower), but their height can vary from 12" (mini-tower) to 24" (full tower). Even larger models, commonly used as *network servers* for many users, also exist.

• *Portable* PCs. Portable computer cases are horizontal and are 3/4" to 1-1/2" thick. The length and width are usually equal to or smaller than the size of a standard 8-1/2" x 11" sheet of paper. The three main types of portables are *laptops* (13 pounds), *notebooks* (6 pounds), and *sub-notebooks* or *handbooks* (4 pounds or less).

• Mid-tower case

• Mini-tower case

• Mini-AT case

• Portable

• Full tower case

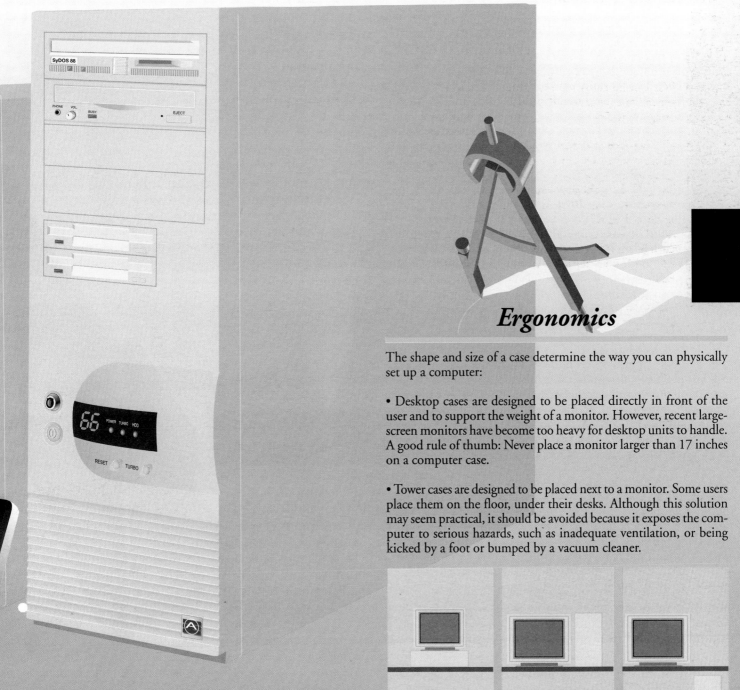

Ergonomics

The shape and size of a case determine the way you can physically set up a computer:

• Desktop cases are designed to be placed directly in front of the user and to support the weight of a monitor. However, recent large-screen monitors have become too heavy for desktop units to handle. A good rule of thumb: Never place a monitor larger than 17 inches on a computer case.

• Tower cases are designed to be placed next to a monitor. Some users place them on the floor, under their desks. Although this solution may seem practical, it should be avoided because it exposes the computer to serious hazards, such as inadequate ventilation, or being kicked by a foot or bumped by a vacuum cleaner.

Expandability

One of the most important characteristics of a PC is its *expandability,* its potential to increase the computer's power and functionality by adding new, specialized components. There are two types of add-on components:

• Expansion cards: *memory* cards to increase the computer's capacity to run programs, *sound* cards to take full advantage of software with speech or sound capabilities, *modem* cards to use telephone lines to communicate with other computers and networks, *interface* cards for adding new drives, and so on.

• Peripherals: additional hard disk drives, floppy disk drives, compact disc (CD-ROM) drives, printers, and so on. These peripherals are usually installed in internal compartments called *bays,* which can either be open at the front of the case (so that a person can insert a diskette or compact disc) or completely enclosed in the cabinet like some hard disk bays (because those drives are never *physically* accessed by a user).

The size of the case determines the number of expansion cards and peripherals that can be added to the system. In full-size PCs, expansion cards are inserted into slots perpendicular to the motherboard. Often, as many as eight cards can be installed directly on the motherboard. Standard desktop PCs can also accommodate four peripherals (floppy and hard disk drives, CD-ROM drives, magnetic tape drives, etc.), while full-size tower cases let you install as many as nine peripherals. In the smaller slim-line cases, in which vertical space is restricted, expansion cards must be installed parallel to the motherboard with a special connector.

In this limited configuration, you can rarely install more than two cards or internal peripherals at one time.

Portables use smaller expansion cards and special peripherals about the size of a credit card, called PCMCIA cards. The expansion possibilities of portable computers are limited by the number of connectors built into the case and by the thickness and number of their individual PCMCIA card slots.

• Peripherals

• Expansion cards

Full-Tower

Ventilation

The proper ventilation of modern PCs is an important consideration. The reliability of a computer depends, in part, on its operating at an ideal, relatively cool temperature. Modern microprocessors and interface cards can generate a lot of heat, and the design of the system case directly affects ventilation and how cool the computer remains:

• The less free space there is in the interior of a case, the more heat tends to build up. Therefore, larger cases are generally safer, and powerful computers that can accommodate many interface cards *require* larger cases.

• Although most power supplies include fans to cool their internal transformer and dissipate heat generated by the other electronic components, tower cases also use convection (the natural upward movement of hot air) to help keep the system cool.

Some users buy special stands that let them place horizontal desktop cases in an upright position. This is not recommended, because floppy and hard drives can warp and become unreliable when used in the vertical position.

The expandability of a PC is determined not only by the number of available expansion slots or the configuration of its connectors. A computer must also have a large enough power supply (measured in *watts*) to run all of the installed peripherals. Furthermore, some peripherals and expansion cards are incompatible, or must be physically reconfigured to work together correctly. Therefore, installing many expansion cards and peripherals in a system can sometimes be as confusing as a Chinese puzzle box!

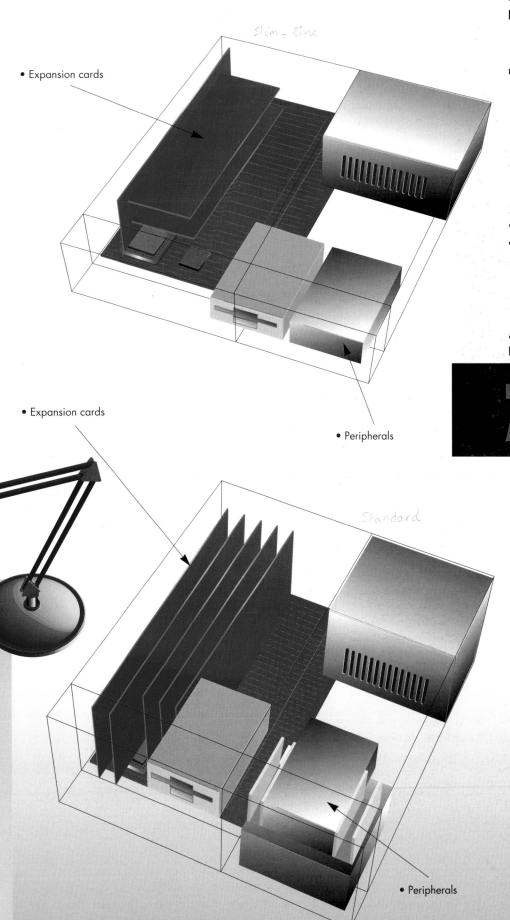

Slim-line

• Expansion cards

• Peripherals

7

Standard

• Expansion cards

• Peripherals

The front panel

The front panel of a PC includes control switches, indicator lights, and drive-bay openings that let you install and use peripherals requiring direct access. All modern PCs have the same elements; only the number of drive-bay openings varies, depending on the size and shape of the case.

• The power switch lets you turn on the computer. When working, be sure not to turn off the power before you save your data on disk, or you'll lose your data. (See the warning on the facing page.) If you use a disk cache program, you need to wait a second or two after saving your data before it's safe to turn off the computer.

• The reset button is useful for re-starting the computer when it locks up and refuses to respond to your commands. This button didn't exist on many earlier models of PCs.

• The turbo button is used to slow down (or speed up) the computer to make it run at a different "clock" speed (measured in millions of cycles per second, or megahertz). The ability to reduce a computer's speed was once essential for ensuring software compatibility, but programs now take into account the computer's speed and adjust themselves accordingly. In fact, although the button is still there, many modern computers have the turbo function completely disabled. On most cases, the computer's current clock speed is shown on an LCD display at the top of the case.

• The security lock prevents unauthorized people from using a computer by disabling the keyboard. The computer can still be turned on, but the keyboard is inactive.

• The hard disk light goes on whenever data is being written to or read from the disk.

• Hard drives and 1.44MB/720KB floppy disk drives can be installed in 3.5-inch drive bays. Tower PCs may have several 3.5-inch bays, some of which may not even have front-panel openings because they are meant to accommodate only hard disks.

• Compact disc (CD-ROM) drives and 1.2MB/360KB floppy drives can be installed in 5.25-inch bays. 5.25-inch bays can also be used for 3.5-inch drives by attaching special "rails" to the sides of the drive to enable it to fit the larger opening.

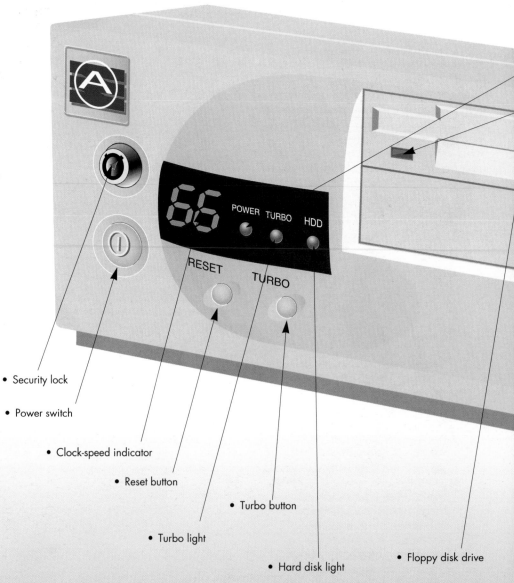

• Security lock

• Power switch

• Clock-speed indicator

• Reset button

• Turbo light

• Turbo button

• Hard disk light

• Floppy disk drive

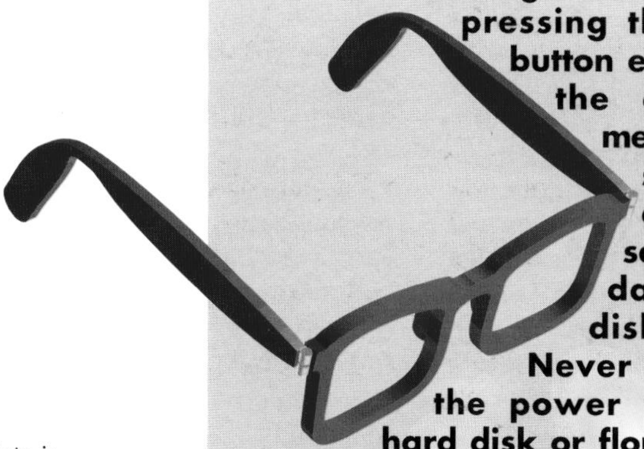

9

Turning off the PC or pressing the reset button erases all the data in memory; be sure to always save your data on a disk first. Never turn off the power when a hard disk or floppy disk drive light is on! Also, never press a floppy diskette's eject button while the drive light is on. By following these simple instructions, you reduce the risk of losing data or, worse, damaging your disks beyond repair.

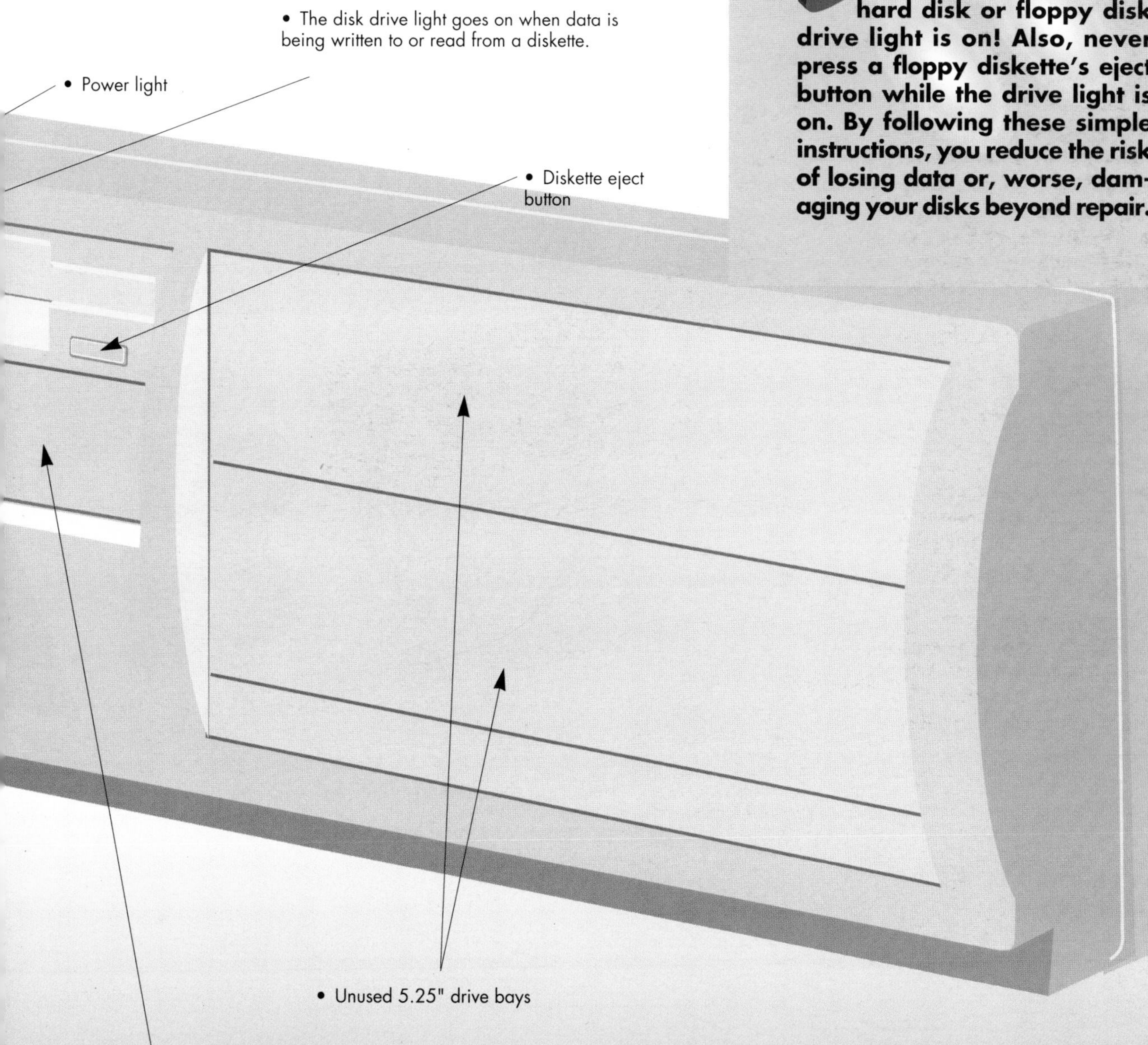

• The disk drive light goes on when data is being written to or read from a diskette.

• Power light

• Diskette eject button

• Unused 5.25" drive bays

• 3.5" floppy disk drive bay (some PC cases have two bays)

The back panel

The back of the case is reserved for the various connectors and ports needed to operate the PC. Their number and layout varies according to the case itself and the number of expansion cards currently installed. The power supply and its corresponding connectors are always at the left side of a desktop case and at the top of a tower case. The vent for the power supply's cooling fan is also located on the back panel and must *never* be obstructed by any object!

• The male power socket supplies electricity to the computer and must be connected to the wall's power outlet with a heavy-duty cable. The female power socket provides an alternate back-panel AC power source into which most people plug the monitor, using a special adapter. This enables the

PC's main power switch to also control the monitor, thus eliminating the risk of having the screen remain on after you've turned off the PC.

• A voltage selector, usually located near the power sockets, lets you match the computer's power supply to your country's voltage and frequency standards. It is usually set properly when you buy the computer, so you don't have to touch it unless you move to a country that uses a different power standard.

• The right side of the back panel contains the slots through which peripherals access expansion card connections, such as ports

for the monitor, printer, mouse, and so on. Note that some slots are covered by a flat metal plate. These slots either contain no expansion cards or contain cards that don't have exterior connectors, such as disk drive controllers.

• Some computers include a special round PS/2 mouse port. If yours does not, simply plug the mouse into a free serial port. A computer can also include a special bus adapter card, as shown in the illustration.

• The connector for the keyboard cord is also on the back panel. It's usually a round 5-prong connector.

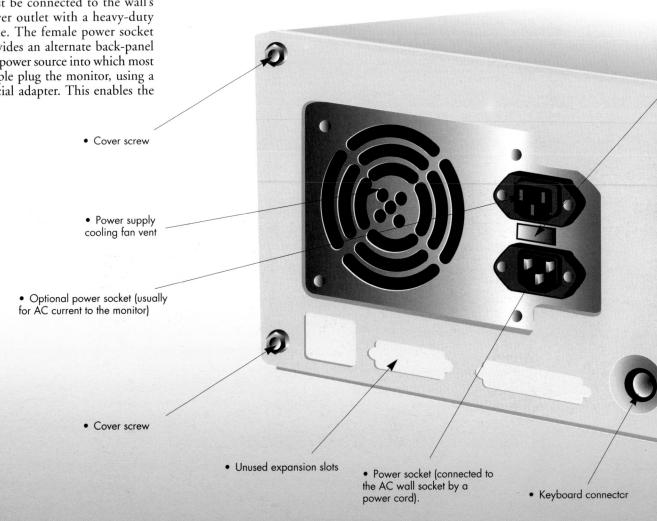

• Cover screw

• Power supply cooling fan vent

• Optional power socket (usually for AC current to the monitor)

• Cover screw

• Unused expansion slots

• Power socket (connected to the AC wall socket by a power cord).

• Keyboard connector

You never have to change the setting of the voltage selector unless you take the computer to another country that uses a different AC voltage standard. It is absolutely essential that you set the voltage properly when you leave *and also when you come back.* Write a note and tape it to the computer, because this bit of forgetfulness can lead to serious damage, especially if the selector is set for a lower voltage than the wall socket supplies. Fortunately, laptop and notebook computers are usually equipped with automatic voltage selectors that eliminate this potential risk.

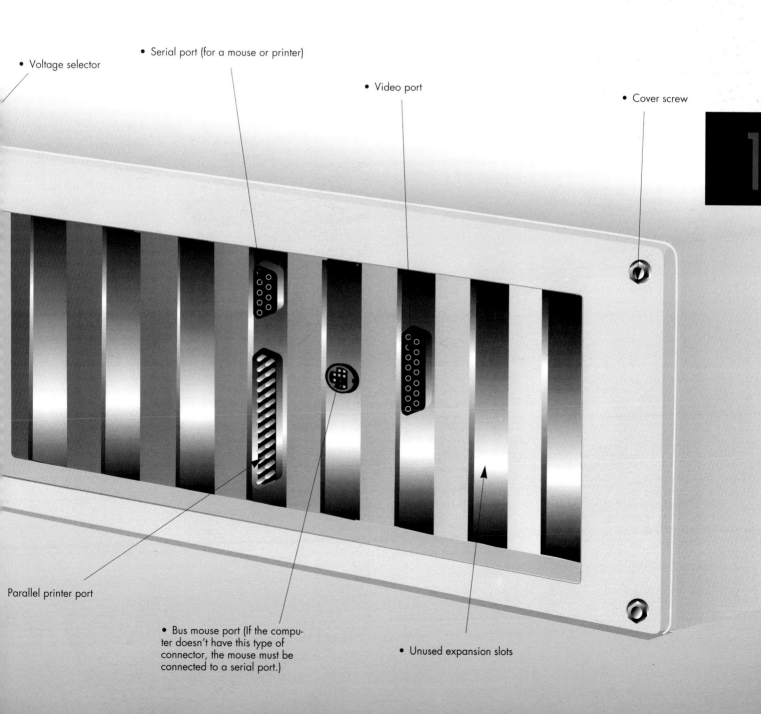

• Voltage selector

• Serial port (for a mouse or printer)

• Video port

• Cover screw

Parallel printer port

• Bus mouse port (If the computer doesn't have this type of connector, the mouse must be connected to a serial port.)

• Unused expansion slots

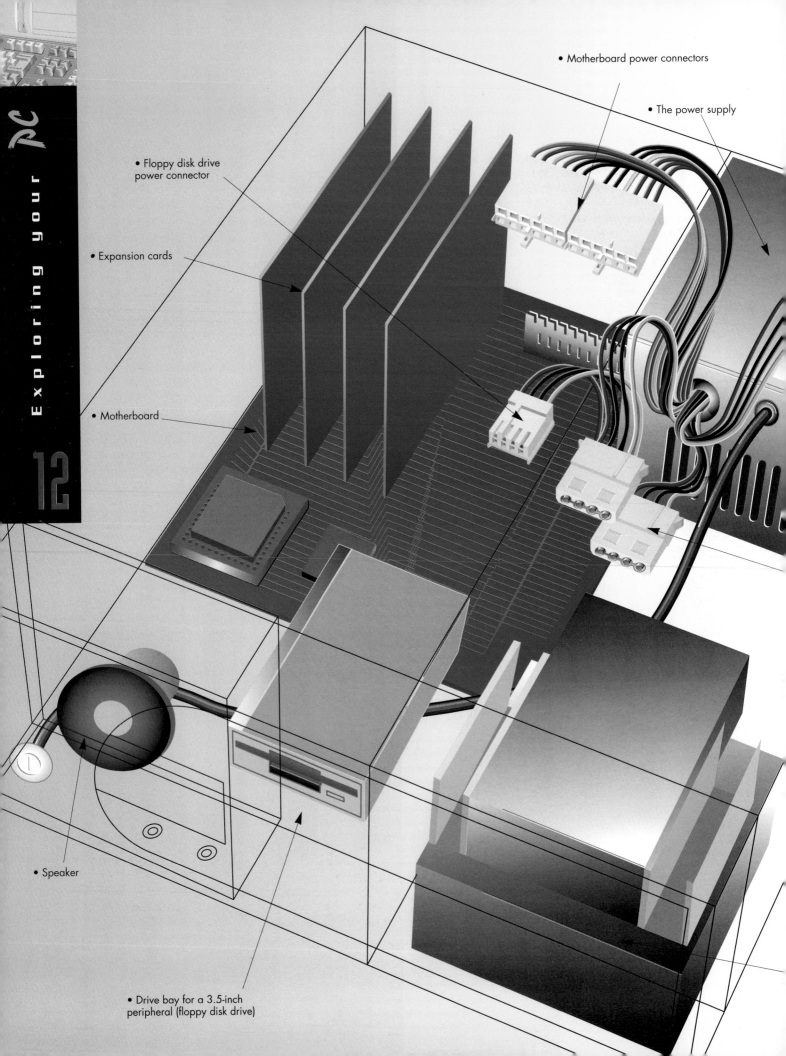

• Motherboard power connectors

• The power supply

• Floppy disk drive power connector

• Expansion cards

• Motherboard

• Speaker

• Drive bay for a 3.5-inch peripheral (floppy disk drive)

Inside the case

The PC's external cover is fastened to a chassis (an interior metal frame) by several (usually 4 to 6) screws located on the back panel. When you remove the cover, you can easily locate the motherboard (the large circuit board that holds the expansion cards), the power supply, and the disk drives.

• The motherboard is fastened to the chassis with screws or plastic clips so that the expansion cards are lined up with the slots on the back panel. The keyboard connector is also lined up with its corresponding opening. Most modern motherboards use a standard layout so that users can easily replace components when upgrading. On machines made in the 1990s, for example, it is usually a simple matter to change the processor, install new memory, or change a BIOS chip.

• Hard and floppy disk drives are fastened to the frames of their corresponding bays. (Special adapter rails let you use a 3.5-inch hard drive in a 5.25-inch bay.) Although drives are nearly always positioned horizontally, some cases do allow them to be installed vertically. Note, however, that drives should *never* be installed upside down.

• The PC's speaker is located behind the front panel and is connected to the motherboard. The quality of the sound it produces is quite poor, but it is adequate for emitting beeps that notify the user of an error, the end of an operation, and so on.

• The power supply provides direct current (5 volts and 12 volts) to the motherboard and disk drives through three types of connectors. Two 6-wire connectors supply power to the motherboard. They plug into the board side by side, with the black wires of each connector next to each other. If you ever need to replace a power supply, be careful not to reverse these connectors; they are not notched (*keyed*) to prevent incorrect attachment. Each power supply has several 4-wire connectors (the number of connectors available is proportional to the unit's overall power capacity). The smaller 4-wire connectors power floppy disk drives, and the larger ones are used for hard disk drives and other peripherals. If you want to install a new drive but have no free connectors, you can use a Y-cable to split a connector into two separate plugs, but doing so may overload the power supply.

The life expectancy and reliability of a computer's electronic components depends on the power supply providing quality, spike- and interference-free current. The generated current, measured in watts, must be sufficient to power all the installed components and peripherals. Two hundred watts are adequate for most standard computer configurations.

Y-cable (split)

• Power connector for additional peripherals

• Power connectors for 5.25-inch peripherals and all sizes of hard disk drives

2 volts DC
Ground
+ 5 volts DC

• Drive bay for 5.25-inch peripheral (can accommodate a 3.5-inch drive with special adapter rails)

Peripherals such as floppy disk drives or tape drives are housed in many different-sized cases. They are usually referred to by the size of the media (disks) used in them. Regardless of the case size, a 3.5-inch peripheral always has a 4" x 1" front panel, and a 5.25-inch peripheral always has a 5-7/8" x 1-5/8" front panel.

13

The motherboard

The motherboard is the most important part of a PC, completely determining the computer's internal architecture. This circuit board is created for a specific type of processor working at a set frequency, and its design determines the maximum amount of internal and cache memory that can be installed on the computer. The number and type of expansion cards that can be used depends on the number of slots on the motherboard and the type of bus it uses. Usually, all the computer's main components—the processor, the memory, the bus, the clock, the keyboard controller, etc.—are located on the motherboard. However, in some PCs, the processor and memory are placed on special expansion cards, called *daughterboards*, to facilitate upgrades.

Anatomy of a motherboard

The microprocessor executes all program instructions and is truly the heart of the computer. Early PCs could use only one model of processor and could not be upgraded. Modern motherboards, however, can be modified to accommodate different models of processors and operate at different frequencies. Some are even designed to be able to accommodate processors still on the drawing board!

Jumpers (small removable plugs that connect specific pins on the motherboard) let you change the motherboard configuration to match the processor and other components installed on the system, such as the amount of cache memory, the clock speed and type, the amount of RAM (random access memory), the type of video display card, and so on.

To maximize your investment in your computer, be sure to choose a PC with a motherboard that lets you upgrade the processor. There are two ways to upgrade the processor. Some motherboards include an empty socket into which you can plug an additional *overdrive* processor that replaces or complements the original processor to provide the enhanced performance of a more powerful processor. With other motherboards, you can simply replace the processor with a more powerful model. The second option requires more planning by the manufacturer, but these motherboards are more economical to upgrade—overdrive chips are generally more expensive than the corresponding microprocessors.

• The "real-time" clock is the calendar and watch of the computer. It lets the PC keep track of the current date and time.

• Keyboard controller

• These jumpers indicate the type of processor installed on the motherboard.

• Microprocessor   CPU
see page 29

• These connectors are attached to switches and usage lights on the front panel, such as the power light, reset button, keyboard lockout, "turbo" button and light, and so on.

• Speaker connector

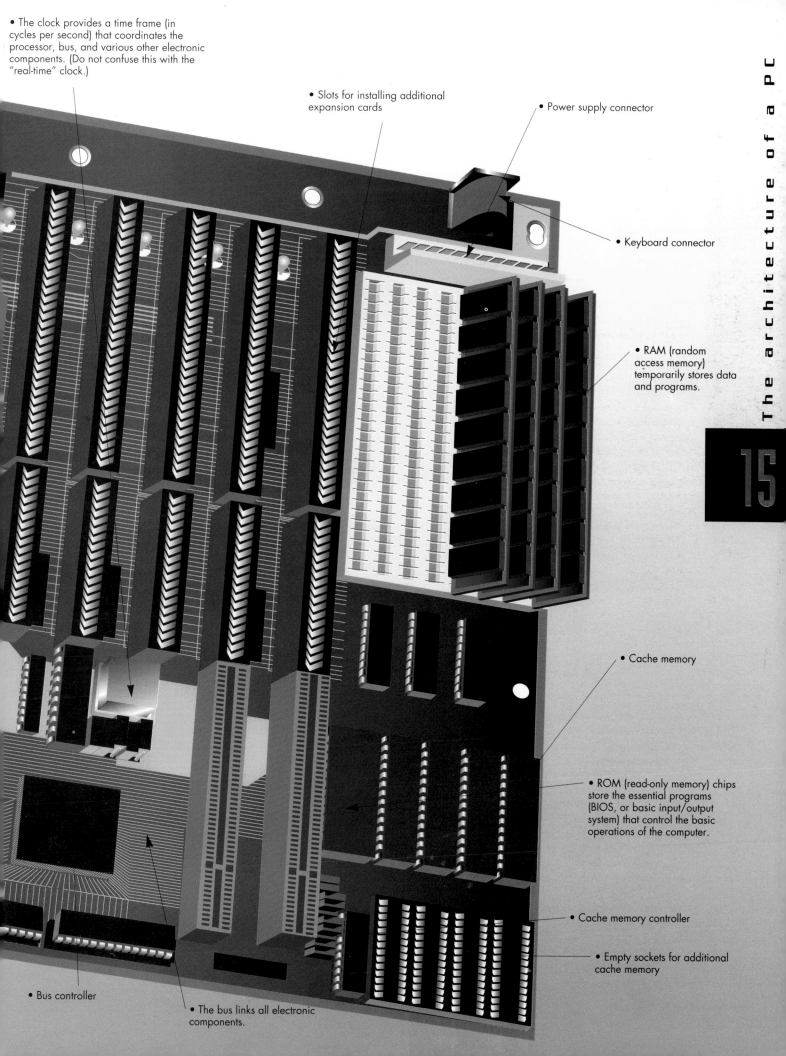

• The clock provides a time frame (in cycles per second) that coordinates the processor, bus, and various other electronic components. (Do not confuse this with the "real-time" clock.)

• Slots for installing additional expansion cards

• Power supply connector

• Keyboard connector

• RAM (random access memory) temporarily stores data and programs.

• Cache memory

• ROM (read-only memory) chips store the essential programs (BIOS, or basic input/output system) that control the basic operations of the computer.

• Cache memory controller

• Empty sockets for additional cache memory

• Bus controller

• The bus links all electronic components.

The printed circuit

The motherboard is a *printed circuit* board into which circuit designs are etched through a series of photochemical processes. Originally, printed circuit boards were resin plates covered with a copper film onto which an electronic circuit was "printed." Electronic components were then soldered onto the circuit. If you look closely at a modern motherboard, however, you'll notice that some of the components' pins don't seem to be connected to the circuit or even to match the soldered holes on the bottom of the board. In fact, there are several layers of copper embedded in the resin, each layer consisting of a distinct circuit. Those layers (circuits) are linked through holes filled by plugs with an interior copper lining. These plugs connect each component with the correct embedded circuit.

Top

Underside

• These pins look like they aren't connected to anything.

RP3

MC74F244N
XXAB9248

Limiting circuit length helps prevent interference that can result in the loss of data.

Many motherboards have four layers of circuits; some have as many as seven layers.

The "unused" holes at the bottom of the motherboard are simply connections between different layers of circuits. They do not indicate missing components.

Some electronic components, however, are simply soldered onto the motherboard's surface.

MC74F244N
XXAB9248

• Circuits etched into different layers are connected through holes drilled in the board.

Those additional layers allow the engineers who design the boards to solve circuit-crossing problems more easily. On a board that has only one metallic surface, an electronic circuit must be designed so that the copper wires never cross each other. By increasing the number of layers, this problem is lessened and connections between components can be greatly shortened. Limiting the length of the circuitry is important for reliability, because the frequencies used by those circuits are in the same range as radio and television frequencies. For example, in many PCs data is exchanged between the microprocessor (CPU) and memory at 66 MHz, very near the frequency of an FM radio station and in the range of VHF television.

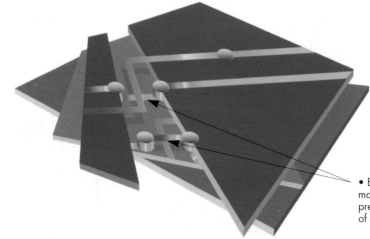

• Example of a bridge made possible by the presence of different layers of circuits

The jumpers

The same motherboard can be used in several different configurations: at 25 or 33 MHz; with a 486 SX, 486 DX, or 486 DX/2 processor; including a cache memory of 64 KB, 128 KB, or 256 KB; and so on. To adapt the board to these various configurations, *jumpers* are used. Jumpers are two- or three-hole connectors that connect pins on the motherboard. The locations of the jumpers are labeled JP and followed by a number, as in JP1, JP2, and so on.

In this illustration, JP1 is set to ON, or SHORT, which means that the jumper is closing the circuit between the pins. JP2 and JP3 are set to OFF, or OPEN. Because there is no jumper bringing the pins into contact with each other, the circuit remains open.

When a jumper must be removed, it is usually placed on a single pin so it won't get lost.

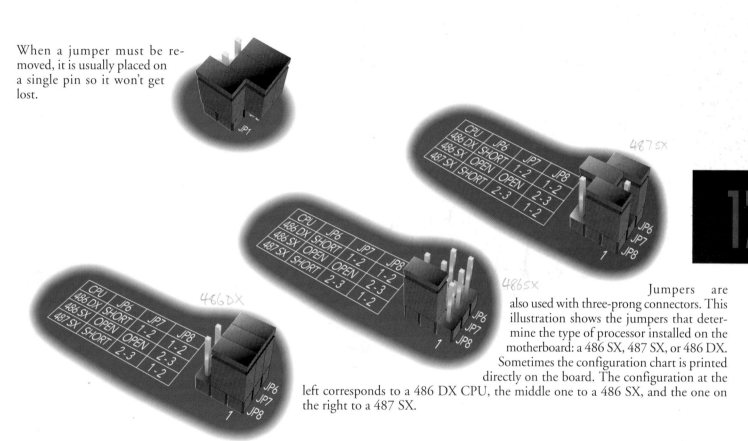

Jumpers are also used with three-prong connectors. This illustration shows the jumpers that determine the type of processor installed on the motherboard: a 486 SX, 487 SX, or 486 DX. Sometimes the configuration chart is printed directly on the board. The configuration at the left corresponds to a 486 DX CPU, the middle one to a 486 SX, and the one on the right to a 487 SX.

CPU	JP6	JP7	JP8
486 DX	SHORT	1-2	1-2
487 SX	OPEN	OPEN	2-3
486 SX	SHORT	2-3	1-2

DIP switches

In some cases, jumpers are replaced by blocks of sliding, or flip-flop, DIP switches. These blocks are labeled SW and followed by a number, as in SW1, SW2, etc. Each DIP switch is set to either ON or OFF.

An individual DIP switch is designated by its block number followed by its position within the block. For example, the fourth switch of block 2 is called SW2-4. The configurations in the illustration are referred to as follows:

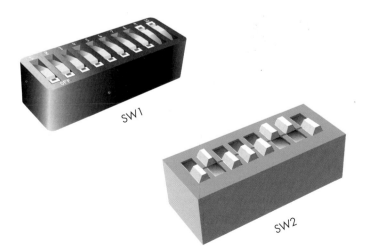

SW1	1-1	1-2	1-3	1-4	1-5	1-6	1-7	1-8
	OFF	OFF	OFF	OFF	OFF	OFF	ON	ON
SW2	2-1	2-2	2-3	2-4	2-5	2-6	2-7	2-8
	OFF	ON	OFF	OFF	OFF	ON	ON	OFF

The microprocessor

The microprocessor is the heart of the computer. A PC's performance depends in large part (but not solely) on the capability and speed of the microprocessor. In a computer, the microprocessor isn't really visible, because it is enclosed in a ceramic or resin case. This case is sealed and can't be opened without destroying the microprocessor.

The microprocessor itself consists of a silicon chip on which tiny circuits are etched through a photochemical process. Those circuits are the equivalent of millions of transistors.

A PC's microprocessor (not the case!) is only about 3/8" by 9/16", yet more than 160 electrical contacts radiate from its perimeter. Because these contacts are so tiny, the microprocessor must be set in a much larger case. Different types of cases are used for microprocessors in modern PCs.

The PGA (pin grid array) case is a ceramic square of between 1-3/4 and 2-3/16 inches, with a thickness of 1/10 of an inch, and has a varying number of pins—either 168, 169, or 273. The microprocessor is located in the center, and its electrical contacts are connected to the case's pins. The case is protected by a soldered brass plate and is designed to be inserted into a socket soldered on the motherboard.

PQFP (plastic quad flat package) and SQFP (small quad flat package) cases are plastic squares of between 1-3/16 and 1-3/8 inches into which the microprocessor is embedded. Their pins, which are extremely small, are located only on the sides. This type of case

is designed to be soldered directly onto the motherboard's surface and is generally used in portable computers.

A microprocessor in a PGA ceramic case for insertion into a socket

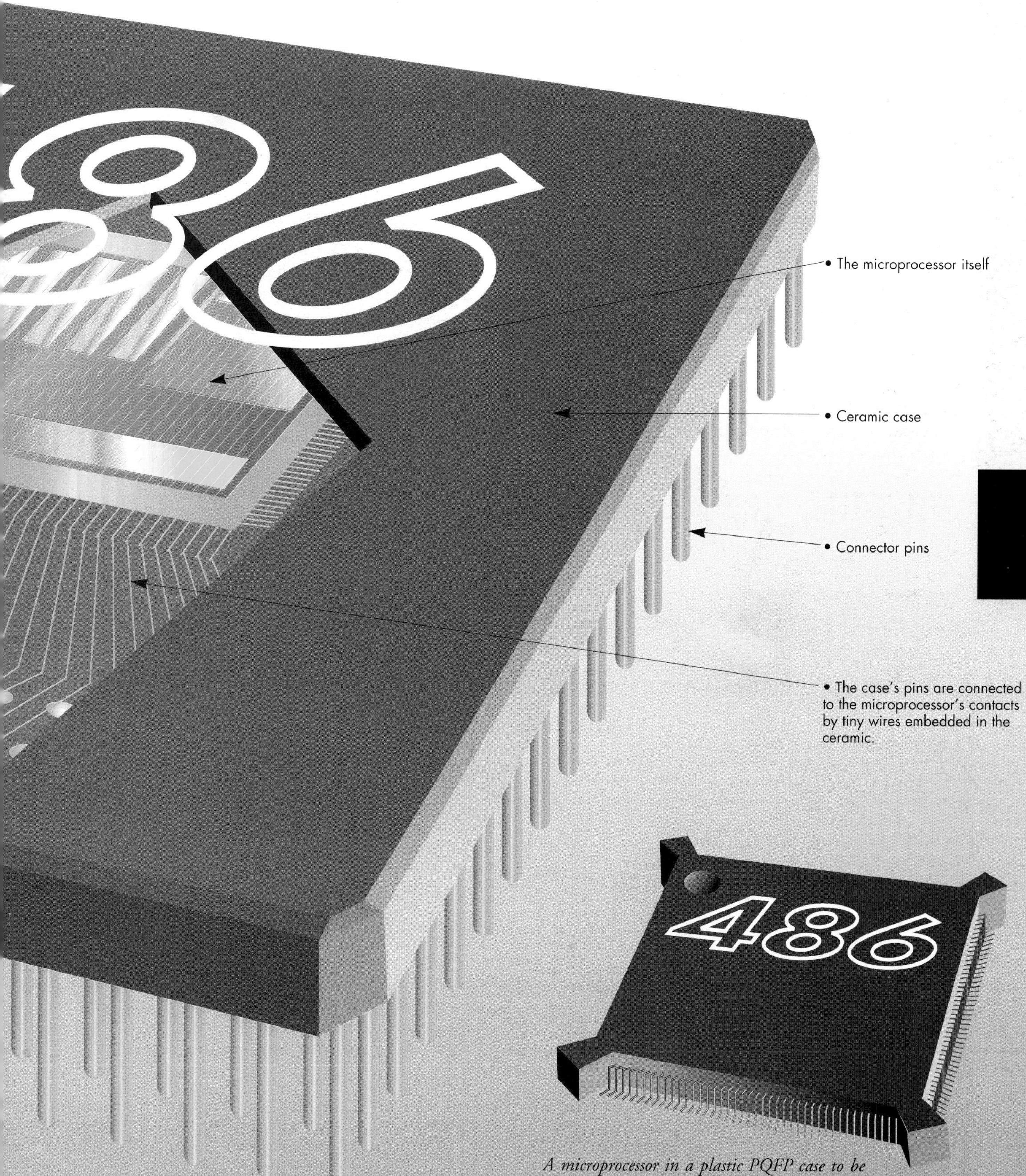

• The microprocessor itself

• Ceramic case

• Connector pins

• The case's pins are connected to the microprocessor's contacts by tiny wires embedded in the ceramic.

A microprocessor in a plastic PQFP case to be soldered directly onto the motherboard

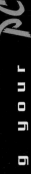

The different models of microprocessors

The first microcomputer to be called a PC (personal computer) was introduced by IBM in 1981. It used the 8088 microprocessor manufactured by Intel. Later models were built around increasingly powerful microprocessor—the 8086, 80286, 80386, 80486, and Pentium. New PCs usually include either a 486 or a Pentium microprocessor. There are, however, many other versions of processors in the PC world—special processors to speed arithmetic calculations, called *math coprocessors;* enhancing speed-up chips, called *overdrive processors;* and dozens of Intel-compatible clone processors made by manufacturers such as Cyrix, AMD, and IBM.

Processors are distinguished from each other by the following criteria:

• Their architecture: the presence and size of cache memory, the inclusion of a floating-point math coprocessor, etc.

• The size of data that can be manipulated at one time: 16 bits, 32 bits, or 64 bits. The word *bit* means *binary digit*. It's the smallest piece of information the computer can use—1 or 0, True or False, etc. A single character usually can be represented with 8 bits.

• The size of the external bus; that is, the width of the path data uses to go to other components. For example, with a 64-bit bus, 8 characters can be sent simultaneously, while a 16-bit bus requires four separate operations to perform the same data transfer.

• Maximum addressable memory, which limits the amount of memory that can be installed in the computer.

• The internal and external clock frequency; that is, the speed at which the processor itself works and the speed at which it can communicate with the other components.

The following processors are commonly used in PCs:

• The 386 SX and DX are rarely found in new machines, because other processors are more powerful yet cost about the same. Still, millions of older PCs use these chips. The 386 SX model has a 16-bit external bus, while the 386 DX has a 32-bit bus. The 387 SX and 387 DX math coprocessors, which assist the main microprocessor in numerical computations, have the same bus structures. They greatly improve the performance of calculation-intensive computer applications, such as CAD (computer assisted design) and computer-generated graphics programs.

• The 486 DX is the most popular processor in today's PCs. It has a 32-bit bus and is distinguished from the 386 DX because it includes an internal cache memory controller and a built-in floating-point math coprocessor.

• The 486 SX is the entry-level processor of the Intel line and can be found in the less expensive models of PCs. It has exactly the same internal structure as the 486 DX processor, except that its floating-point math coprocessor is disabled.

• The 486 DX/2 is identical to the 486 DX except that it includes a clock-frequency doubler that enables it to work twice as fast

Model	Maximum clock speed (MHz)	Internal data bus width (bits)	External bus width (bits)	Addressable memory (MB)
386 SX	25	32	16	16
386 DX	50	32	32	4096
486 SX	25	32	32	4096
486 DX	50	32	32	4096
486 DX/2	66/33	32	32	4096
486 DX/4	100/33	32	32	4096
Pentium	100	64	64	4096

Comparison chart of the major PC processors

Relative computing power of the major microprocessors used in PCs

internally. However, because its external data exchange occurs at the original *undoubled* speed, performance gains are variable. (They depend mainly on the efficiency of the cache memory controller with the program being used.)

• The 486 DX/4 has a clock-frequency tripler—not *quadrupler*, as you might guess. Its internal clock speed can be 75, 83, or 100 MHz.

• The Pentium is distinguished from the preceding processors by many important features. It has a clock speed of 60 or 66 MHz. (Intel has also announced models that will run at 90 and 100 MHz.) It uses a 64-bit bus and includes two processor units that can work simultaneously. It also has two separate cache memories for instructions and data.

In addition to the microprocessor, many other components are available for improving the performance of a PC (as long as the motherboard is designed to accommodate them):

• The 487 SX is a "math coprocessor" used to complement the 486 SX chip. In fact, it is nothing more or less than the original 486 DX chip with its pins set up differently! Its installation completely disables the computer's original 486 SX, the presence of which, however, is still required. Considering that the original 486 SX is actually a 486 DX with its math unit disabled, it appears that Intel has created a clever way to get users to install two processors per PC !

• Overdrive chips are processors that enhance the per-

formance of a PC. However, they must be installed in special sockets, which not all motherboards have. The DX overdrive chip accomplishes the same tasks as the 487 (by deactivating the main processor) but also includes a clock-speed doubler. It is actually identical to a 486 DX/2 but requires a special socket (an added pin prevents its installation in the 486 DX socket).

• The Pentium Overdrive (also known as the P24T chip) is a 64-bit Pentium that has only a 32-bit *external* bus. (This enables manufacturers to reuse older 32-bit 486 motherboard designs instead of designing completely new 64-bit boards.) The P24T is meant to disable the original processor when installed in motherboards that include a special "Pentium Ready" socket.

Main processor	Overdrive or coprocessor	Installation process	Resulting equivalence
486 SX	487 SX	Addition	486 DX
486 SX	Overdrive 486 SX	Addition	486 DX/2
486 DX	Overdrive 486 DX	Addition	486 DX/2
486 DX/2	Overdrive Pentium	Replacement	Pentium 32 bits
486 DX/4	Overdrive Pentium	Replacement	Pentium 32 bits

Upgrading capabilities of Intel processors

The architecture of a microprocessor

The microprocessor of a PC consists of several specialized units that work together seamlessly. Different models of processors, however, may not include all of these units. For example, the floating-point math coprocessor (the unit that performs complex arithmetic computations) isn't active on the 486 SX chip. (Although the unit is on the microprocessor, its operation is disabled.) Also, the 486 DX/2 and DX/4 chips include a clock-speed doubler or tripler that's not found in the 486 DX. (This frequency multiplier lets the microprocessor run internally two or three times faster than it communicates with the other components, such as memory.) This illustration shows the individual units that comprise a 486 DX microprocessor.

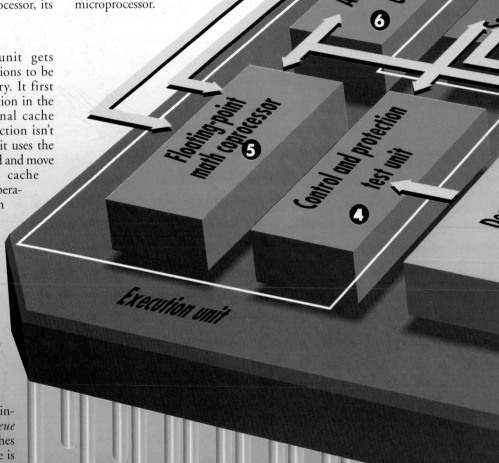

Arithmetic/logic unit (ALU) **6**

Segmentation unit

Floating-point math coprocessor **5**

Control and protection test unit **4**

Decoding unit

Execution unit

1 • The *pre-fetch* unit gets ("fetches") the instructions to be executed from memory. It first searches for an instruction in the processor's fast internal cache memory. If the instruction isn't there, the pre-fetch unit uses the bus interface unit to read and move the instruction into cache memory. During this operation, instructions from successive memory locations are *also* read and placed in the processor's cache memory. When a new instruction is needed, it is then likely to be immediately available in the CPU's fast, internal cache memory (as long as some other operation hasn't changed the content of the cache memory).

2 • The pre-fetch unit puts an instruction in an instruction *queue* (sort of a pipeline) and then fetches the next one. Because the queue is always kept full, the central operating unit almost never has to wait to execute instructions. Only rarely does a situation occur in which a group of instructions executes so quickly as to deplete the queue. On the other hand, if instructions take longer than usual to execute, the queue fills up, and the pre-fetch unit suspends operations until space frees up to hold new instructions.

3 • The decoding (interpretation) unit translates the instructions in the queue into a format that the operating unit can understand and then sends them to the control unit.

4 • The control and protection test unit oversees the execution of instuctions. In particular, it checks to see that all accesses to memory are valid so that memory conflicts don't arise.

5 • If it's not disabled (as in the case of the 486 SX chip), the floating-point math unit executes all appropriate floating-point calculations.

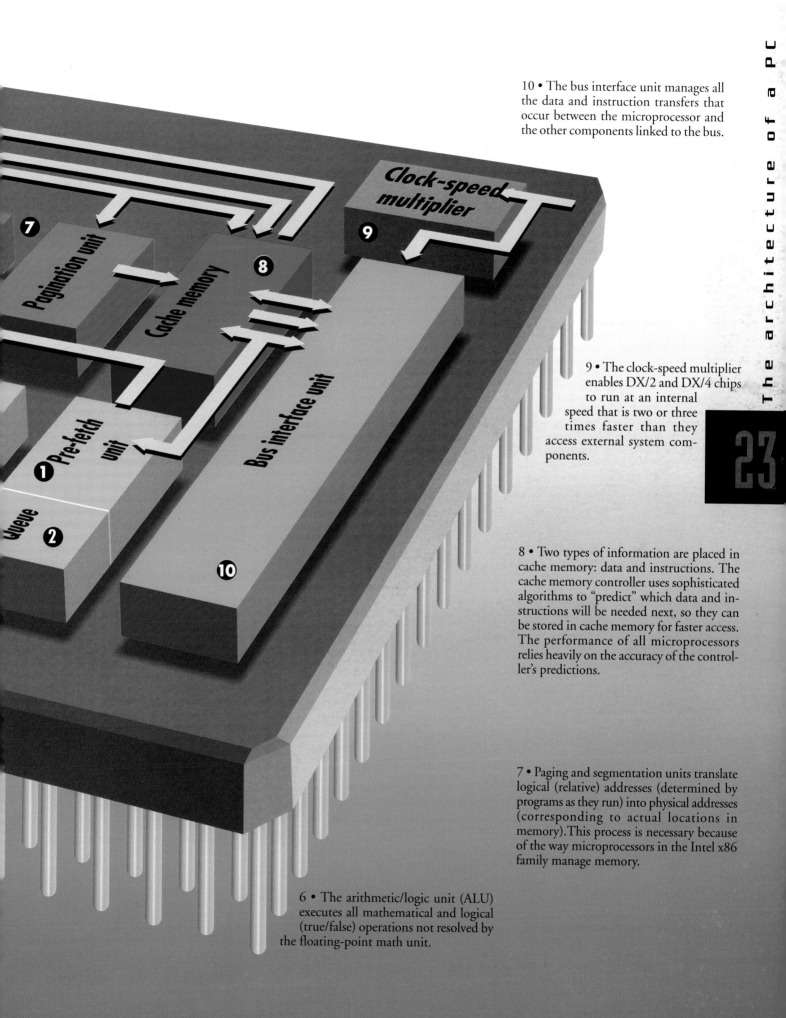

10 • The bus interface unit manages all the data and instruction transfers that occur between the microprocessor and the other components linked to the bus.

Clock-speed multiplier

7

Pagination unit

8

Cache memory

9

1 Pre-fetch unit

Bus interface unit

Queue **2**

10

9 • The clock-speed multiplier enables DX/2 and DX/4 chips to run at an internal speed that is two or three times faster than they access external system components.

23

8 • Two types of information are placed in cache memory: data and instructions. The cache memory controller uses sophisticated algorithms to "predict" which data and instructions will be needed next, so they can be stored in cache memory for faster access. The performance of all microprocessors relies heavily on the accuracy of the controller's predictions.

7 • Paging and segmentation units translate logical (relative) addresses (determined by programs as they run) into physical addresses (corresponding to actual locations in memory). This process is necessary because of the way microprocessors in the Intel x86 family manage memory.

6 • The arithmetic/logic unit (ALU) executes all mathematical and logical (true/false) operations not resolved by the floating-point math unit.

Execution of an addition instruction

The execution of a basic operation, such as adding two numbers, is actually a complex process that illustrates the fundamental operating mechanisms of a PC's microprocessor. The following example is somewhat simplified, but it will give you a good idea of how a 486 microprocessor really works. This example executes three basic instructions:

1. Get a number in memory and place it in one of the microprocessor's *registers* (small, temporary, on-chip storage areas).

2. Get a second number and add it to the first, storing the result in the same register.

3. Write the resulting number into the computer's main memory.

1 • The pre-fetch unit knows the memory location of the next instruction to be executed. However, it first searches the processor's cache memory to see if the instruction is already in the chip.

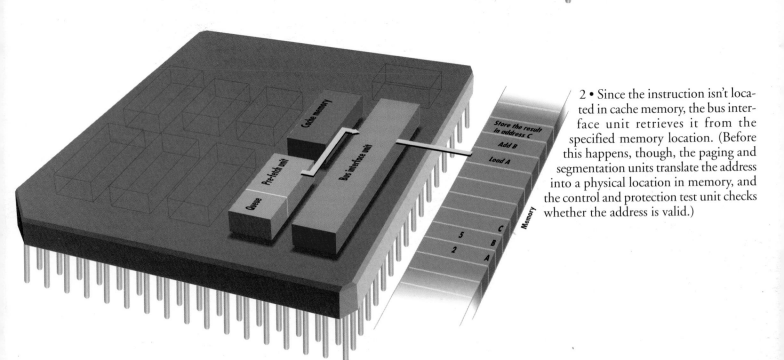

2 • Since the instruction isn't located in cache memory, the bus interface unit retrieves it from the specified memory location. (Before this happens, though, the paging and segmentation units translate the address into a physical location in memory, and the control and protection test unit checks whether the address is valid.)

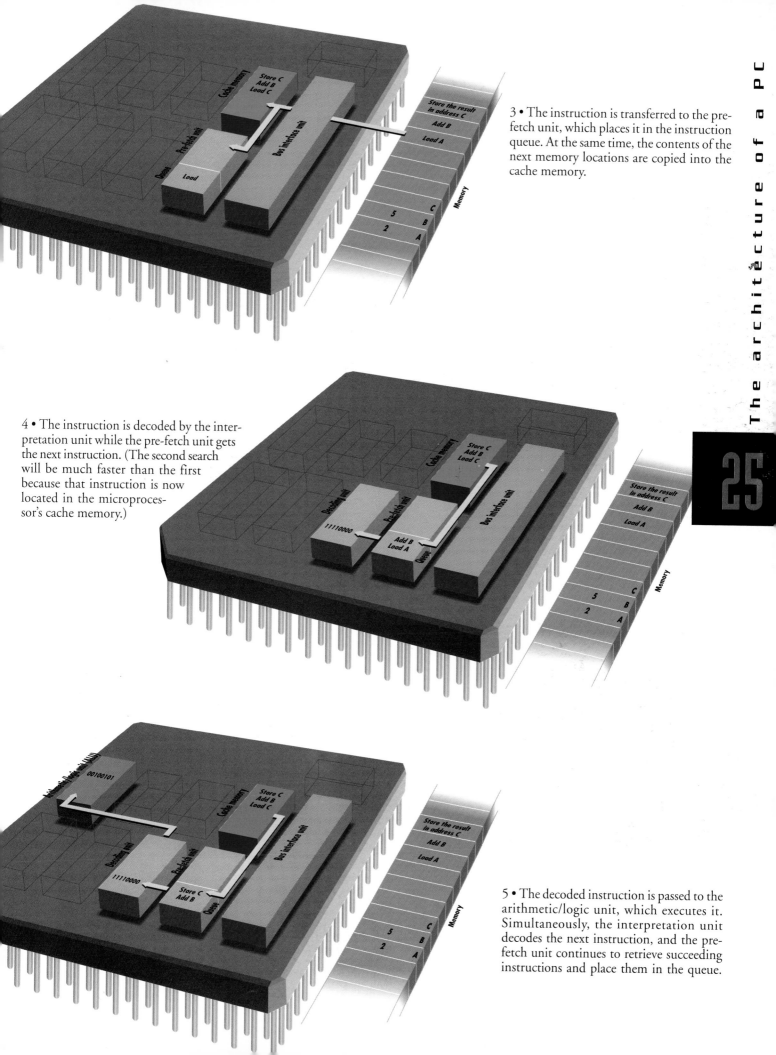

3 • The instruction is transferred to the pre-fetch unit, which places it in the instruction queue. At the same time, the contents of the next memory locations are copied into the cache memory.

4 • The instruction is decoded by the interpretation unit while the pre-fetch unit gets the next instruction. (The second search will be much faster than the first because that instruction is now located in the microprocessor's cache memory.)

5 • The decoded instruction is passed to the arithmetic/logic unit, which executes it. Simultaneously, the interpretation unit decodes the next instruction, and the pre-fetch unit continues to retrieve succeeding instructions and place them in the queue.

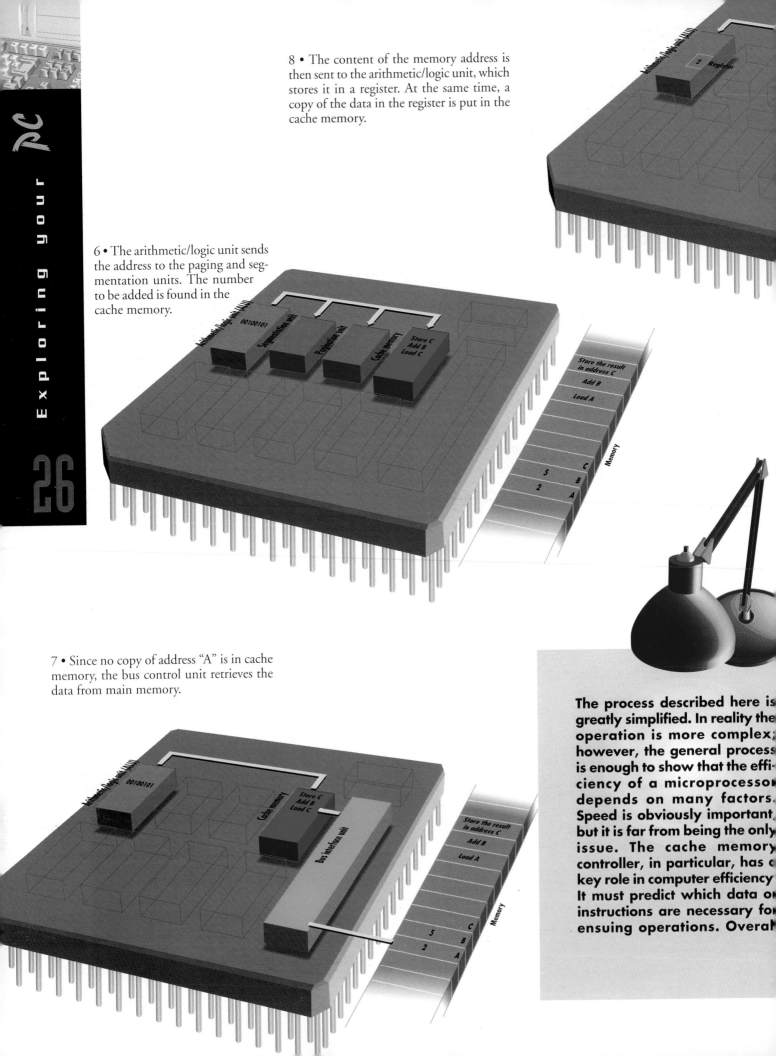

8 • The content of the memory address is then sent to the arithmetic/logic unit, which stores it in a register. At the same time, a copy of the data in the register is put in the cache memory.

6 • The arithmetic/logic unit sends the address to the paging and segmentation units. The number to be added is found in the cache memory.

7 • Since no copy of address "A" is in cache memory, the bus control unit retrieves the data from main memory.

The process described here is greatly simplified. In reality the operation is more complex; however, the general process is enough to show that the efficiency of a microprocessor depends on many factors. Speed is obviously important, but it is far from being the only issue. The cache memory controller, in particular, has a key role in computer efficiency. It must predict which data or instructions are necessary for ensuing operations. Overall

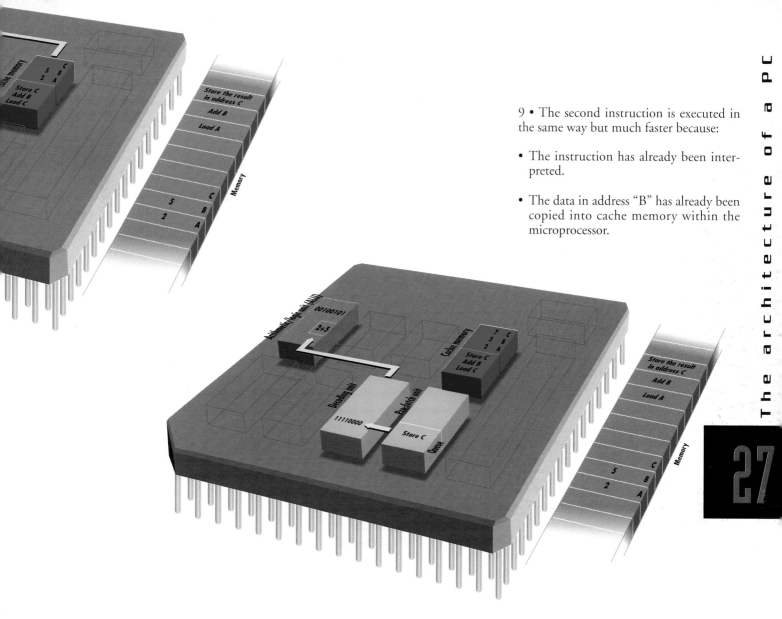

9 • The second instruction is executed in the same way but much faster because:

• The instruction has already been interpreted.

• The data in address "B" has already been copied into cache memory within the microprocessor.

performance actually depends on the percentage of information that winds up in cache memory, since access to that memory is much faster than access to the computer's main memory. The way programs are written is also important. If numbers that need to be added are located in addresses that are far apart, it is likely that the second number won't be accessible in cache memory when it is needed.

10 • The third instruction is executed. The result of the addition, now held in the microprocessor's register, is copied to address "C" of main memory—and *also* into cache memory. This way, if the data in address "C" of memory is needed for an ensuing operation (which is likely to happen), it is quickly available on board the microprocessor. Note that if the data must be used *immediately*, the access will be instantaneous since it is also still in the microprocessor's register.

Replacing a processor

Intel, the manufacturer of most PC processor chips, designed them so they can be replaced by the user to improve the computer's performance. This is an attractive alternative to replacing the entire motherboard. Replacement processors are called *overdrive* chips. Before you install one, however, you must consider these important factors: choosing the right replacement chip, cooling it, and handling it safely when doing the swap. Be aware that the options available to you will vary according to the design used by your motherboard's manufacturer.

Choosing the right replacement. Each overdrive chip is specially designed to replace a specific processor. It is important that you choose the one made for your original processor. However, in many cases, the motherboard's manufacturer may provide alternative solutions.

Addressing cooling problems. Overdrive chips are more powerful than the processors they replace and, therefore, often require more power and emit more heat. Though power consumption usually isn't a big problem (the most power-hungry chip, the Pentium, uses only 16 watts), cooling can be a major concern. Because overheating can cause data loss or even destroy the processor itself, you

should protect your investment by installing a heat-sink (cooling fins) or a small fan directly on the processor.

Handling the replacement carefully. A microprocessor's many, small, fragile pins make the removal or installation of chips a risky operation. The pins bend easily, so be careful not to force a chip into its socket. Handle a processor as though it cost more than its weight in gold—it does!

Another important point is the orientation of the processor. Because a processor is square, you might be confused as to which direction it should face. Inserting a new processor in the wrong position can lead to irreversible damage.

Choosing a replacement processor

An overdrive chip can be installed on computers using the following processors: 486 SX, 486 DX, 486 DX/2, and 486 DX/4.

The 487 SX math coprocessor can be installed on 486 SX computers with motherboards that are equipped with a special socket. (The original processor remains in its current position, but the new chip disables it and takes over all its duties.) As already explained, it is no more or no less than a full 486 DX chip with a slightly different pinout configuration. In fact, this processor has only one additional pin, an electrically inactive dummy pin that serves as a "key" to prevent positioning mistakes. The pin also prevents the installation of a 487 SX coprocessor in the socket intended for the 486 SX.

The overdrive chip for the 486 DX can be installed on computers equipped with a 486 DX or SX processor and a motherboard with a special overdrive socket. (The original processor will remain in its current position, but it will be disabled.) This overdrive chip is the equivalent of a clock-doubled 486 DX/2. It also has an additional pin to prevent installation mistakes.

On most newer PCs, an original 486 DX processor can be replaced directly by a DX/2 chip, as long as the jumper configuration on the motherboard is also modified. This solu-

tion is more economical than using an overdrive chip, because you can reuse the original processor on another computer (or resell it!). Certain motherboards can accept a 486 SX, a 486 DX, or a 486 DX/2. Also, overdrive chips cost between 20 and 50 percent more than the equivalent processor. Therefore, if the motherboard of your computer is equipped with a 33 MHz 486 DX but can accept a 66 MHz 486 DX/2 chip, it is in your best interest to *replace* the processor rather than *add* a 486 DX overdrive chip. (In theory, only overdrive chips are available in the retail market, while other processors are reserved for computer manufacturers. Don't believe it. One quick look at a direct-market magazine or hardware catalog will show you that *all* processors are readily available in the marketplace!)

A computer equipped with a 486 DX/2 or DX/4 usually can accept a Pentium overdrive chip that disables the original processor. This 64-bit Pentium, which has four rows of pins on each side rather than three, uses a 32-bit external bus so it can communicate with circuitry and components originally designed for a 486.

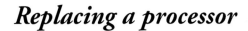

• Processor installed in a Zero Insertion Force (ZIF) socket

Removing and inserting a processor

When removing and inserting processors, first make sure you are completely grounded. Second, make sure you have the chip oriented correctly with respect to its socket. Third, insert it carefully and slowly—the pins are extremely fragile!

Because a processor is square, you may be confused as to which direction it should face. In fact, the carrier has a clipped corner marked with a round dot. This corner must match up with the pin marked number 1 on the motherboard. Sometimes letters are also inscribed on the motherboard. In that case, be sure the clipped corner is in the A1 position. (The safest procedure is to note the positioning of the clipped corner on the original processor *before you remove it*.)

Because overdrive chips were designed to be installed by nontechnical users, Intel took additional precautions by using an asymmetric pinout design that lets the chip fit in only one way. This also prevents users from installing an overdrive chip or a math coprocessor by itself. Motherboard manufacturers quickly bypassed this restriction by installing special sockets that can use a 487 SX chip without a corresponding 486 SX.

Problems arising from the removal and replacement of processors (i.e., the breaking or bending of pins) led to the development of new types of sockets that make the handling of processors easier and safer. These advanced designs are called Low Insertion Force (LIF) sockets and Zero Insertion Force (ZIF) sockets. Most new motherboards include ZIF sockets. However, even if you have an older motherboard, you can install a ZIF socket yourself—between the original socket and the replacement microprocessor.

A ZIF socket is easy to spot. It's usually blue, and it has a lever on one side. Pulling up the lever lets you effortlessly remove one processor and install another.

Pressing down the lever locks the new processor into place and ensures perfect contacts between the pins and socket.

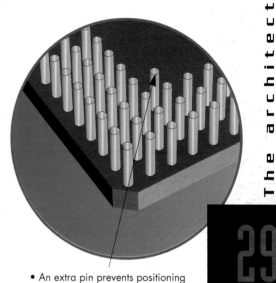

29

• An extra pin prevents positioning mistakes.

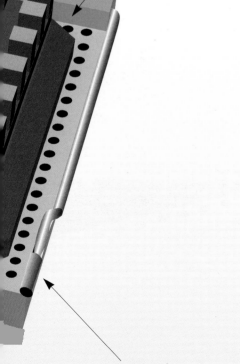

• Locating the A1 corner

• Locking lever

Cooling

To avoid overheating, you can always add a heat-sink to the processor. In fact, overdrive chips have built-in heat-sinks. If you choose a standard processor (for example, a DX/2 to replace a DX), it is in your best interest to add a separate heat-sink. Each chip requires its own type of heat sink, but all are easily installed—either by gluing them onto the processor or by attaching them with clips.

The best way to cool a processor is to attach a small, specially made fan to it. The fan needs to be hooked up to a free connector on the power supply. If no connectors are available, you will need to use a Y-cable (*see page 13*).

• A processor equipped with a heat-sink and a fan

Memory

The computer stores the programs it works with and their data in memory. There are two kinds of memory: *primary* or *main memory,* and *secondary memory* or *mass storage.* Mass storage, generally magnetic media such as floppy diskettes, hard disks, or tapes, is used to store data and programs on a long-term basis, because what is stored there remains even when the computer's power is turned off. However, access to this type of storage is relatively slow. When the computer is powered up, programs and data are copied to main memory. This is the memory usually referred to when people use the term "memory." Information is stored in memory as bits (binary digits)—1's and 0's—the smallest piece of computer data. There are two types of main memory—read-write memory (random-access memory, or RAM), which can be both read and modified, and read-only memory (ROM), which can be read but not modified.

Read-write memory (RAM)

Bits are stored in read-write memory (RAM) chips as electrical charges in tiny capacitors. A charged capacitor represents a 1; an uncharged capacitor a 0.

Unfortunately, capacitors naturally lose their charges unless they are frequently recharged through a process called *refreshing.* Memory that needs periodic refreshing is called dynamic RAM, or DRAM. The PC's main memory consists of DRAM.

Dynamic RAM consists of black plastic chips with a row of pins on each side. They may be inserted into sockets or soldered directly onto a printed circuit board.

Each chip can store a specific number of bits, the most common capacities these days being 1 and 4 megabits.

Most of the time, the computer manipulates a number of bits at a time—this group of bits is called a *word.* Early PCs manipulated 8-bit words (also called *bytes*). As it happens, 8 bits are what it takes to encode one character of text, so the byte has become the usual measure of a computer's memory capacity. This terminology is imperfect, because modern PCs manipulate 32-bit words—4 bytes!—at a time.

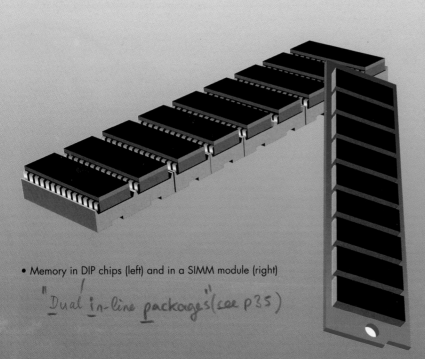

• Memory in DIP chips (left) and in a SIMM module (right)

"Dual in-line packages" (see p 35)

• Most motherboards include eight SIMM slots.

Memory chips are usually inserted into the computer in groups of nine. The ninth chip in the group stores the *parity bit* and serves as a control to ensure that the other eight chips hold the correct values. Most PCs use small, 9-chip carrier modules called *SIMMs* (single in-line memory modules) for their RAM memory.

In computers that manipulate 32-bit words (386s and 486s), those SIMMs must always be installed in groups of four. A group of four SIMMs is called a *memory bank*. The center illustration shows a fully *populated* (filled) first memory bank (bank 0) and four empty SIMM slots (an unpopulated bank 1).

Instead of using groups of 4 SIMMs of 8 or 9 bits, newer PCs use 32- (4 by 8) or 36- (4 by 9) bit SIMMs. These SIMMs make memory installation more convenient because they don't need to be grouped in banks (except in 64-bit Pentium computers, in which they need to be grouped in banks of 2).

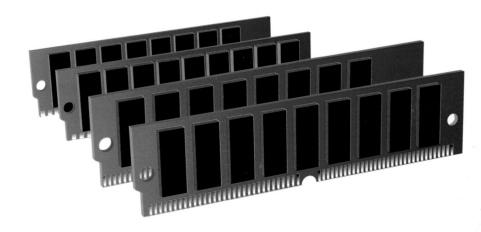

• Memory SIMM modules of 8 bits, 9 bits, 32 bits, and 36 bits

Other types of read-write memories

31

DRAM (dynamic RAM) memory is used in every PC. However, there are many other types of RAM memories:

SRAM (static RAM) retains its contents without needing to be refreshed and is also much faster than dynamic memory. Not surprisingly, it is also much more expensive.

VRAM (video RAM) is specialized fast-access memory used to efficiently store and display graphical images.

CMOS (complementary metal oxide semiconductor) memory is found in every modern PC. It is RAM connected to a battery so that it permanently retains its contents, even when the computer's power is shut off. CMOS maintains vital information about the configuration of the computer—the number and types of hard and floppy disk drives, the amount of memory available, the current date and time, and so on. (CMOS is the name of the technology used to create chips that consume very little electrical power.)

1 kilobit is equal to 1,024 bits. 1 megabit is equal to 1,024 kilobits. The number 1,024 is not chosen at random—it corresponds to 2^{10}, a number easily manipulated by computers, which compute in base 2. Thus, in computing, the prefix *kilo* always represents *1,024* units and the prefix *mega* always represents *1,048,576* units.

How memory operates

As mentioned on the previous page, dynamic memory consists of tiny transistors that hold binary information as electrical charges. This information is grouped into units called *words*. Computers using 486 processors manipulate 32-bit words, and those equipped with Pentiums use 64-bit words. Those words are organized and accessed through a system of addresses. Thus, to write a word in memory, current must be sent to the transistors corresponding to a specific address. To accomplish that, an electrical charge is sent through a control line in the memory chips. Transistors are electronic entities that close an electrical line when they are activated by a current. (Contrary to what you'd think, a line is referred to as *closed* when a current passes through it.) After the transistors

that correspond to the chosen address are activated, current is sent through the data lines to those transistors that must hold a value of 1 (i.e., that must be charged).

Unfortunately, transistors lose their charges soon after they stop receiving current. That's why a special circuit, called the *refresh circuit*, constantly reads the contents of memory and then immediately rewrites it to maintain the charges on all transistors.

Because of this continual recharging process, this type of memory is called *dynamic* memory, or DRAM. Obviously, as soon as the computer's main power is turned off, all transistors lose their charges, and the

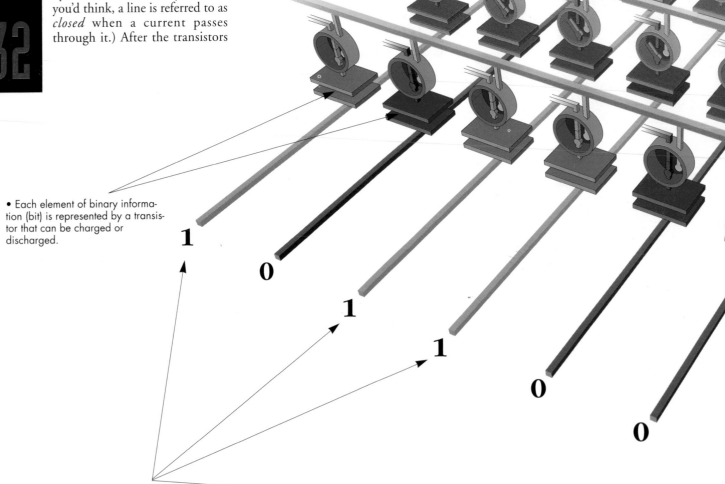

• Each element of binary information (bit) is represented by a transistor that can be charged or discharged.

• Current is sent to charge the transistors on the data lines that correspond to bits having the value of 1.

contents of memory are lost. When the power is turned on, all DRAM memory chips hold only zeros.

Some computers also use *static* memory (SRAM) chips, which don't require refreshing. They are much faster than their DRAM counterparts, but they are also much more expensive.

Reading the data in memory is similar to writing it. The transistors corresponding to the addresses to be read are activated, thus permitting current to run through the data lines. The transistors that represent bits having the value of 1 are discharged through the data lines. Data is then immediately rewritten by the refresh circuit so that the content of an address isn't modified because it was read.

• The transistors corresponding to other addresses are deactivated, preventing current from running through the data lines.

• The transistors corresponding to this address are activated, permitting current to run through the data lines.

1

How memory is organized

Although computers with 486 processors manipulate 32-bit words and computers with Pentium processors manipulate 64-bit words, memory size is still measured in bytes (8-bit words). The main reason for this is that a byte can hold all the data needed to represent any text character. A 486 computer with 4 megabytes of memory will have access to more than four million 8-bit words or one million 32-bit words. All of these words are stored and accessed through a system of addresses that mark their locations in memory. Pentium and 486 computers have 32 address lines. Since each line can accept two values (1, activated, or 0, not activated), the computer has access to 4,294,967,296 (2^{32}) unique addresses. This number is a purely theoretical limit; no microcomputer could be manufactured with enough connectors to install that much memory.

Because a processor must manipulate 32- or 64-bit words, certain restrictions apply to the way memory is organized. Specifically, the amount of memory installed must be equal to a whole number of words. For example, if you install 8-bit SIMM modules in a computer with a 486 processor, you must always install them in groups of four (four 8-bit SIMMs create 32 bits of addresses). Most motherboards have eight SIMM slots, grouped in two *banks* of four. Each bank must include four SIMM modules of identical capacity. (One bank can remain empty.) Note, however, that some 486 computers and all Pentium computers include slots for *32-bit* SIMM modules. On a 486 you may therefore install any number of this type of SIMM, while on the Pentium you must install the 32-bit SIMMs in pairs.

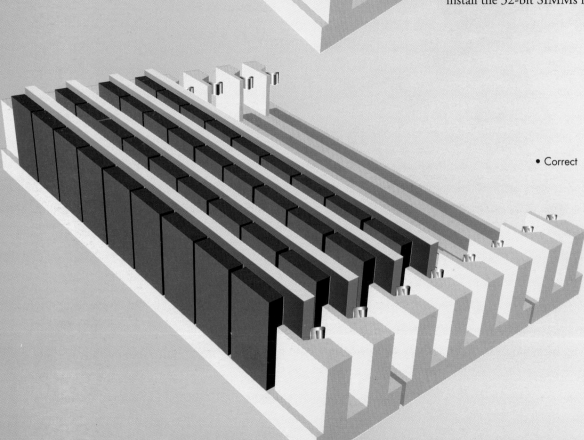

• Correct

• Correct

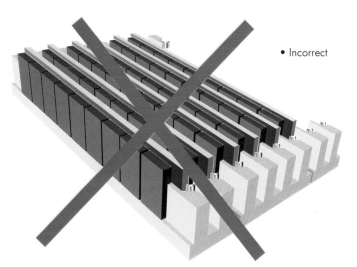

• Incorrect

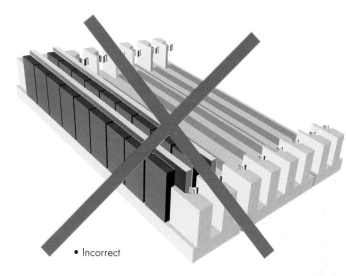

• Incorrect

Parity checking

SIMM modules are manufactured with different capacities—some have 8 or 9 bits, while others have 32 or 36 bits. An 8-bit SIMM can store exactly the same amount of data as a 9-bit SIMM; the ninth bit serves only as a means of checking the integrity of the other 8 bits. 36-bit SIMMs store 32 bits of data and 4 parity bits (one per group of eight bits). Parity checking consists of adding the values of the eight bits and storing either a 1 (if the result is even) or a 0 (if the result is odd) in the ninth bit. (The opposite storage scheme can also be used: *Even parity* refers to an even sum being stored as a value of 1; *odd parity* refers to an odd sum being stored as a value of 1.) When a system uses parity checking, if a bit accidentally changes, the error is immediately apparent because the parity bit doesn't match the result. It might seem that this method of ensuring data integrity isn't very reliable—if a second bit changes value, the parity bit will show a correct value. However, if the chance of an error occurring in one bit is one in a thousand (for example), the chance of two bits being incorrect is one in a million. So practically speaking, this method of checking data integrity is indeed dependable.

• The sum of the bits equals 4. Assuming that even parity is used, the parity bit has a value of 1.

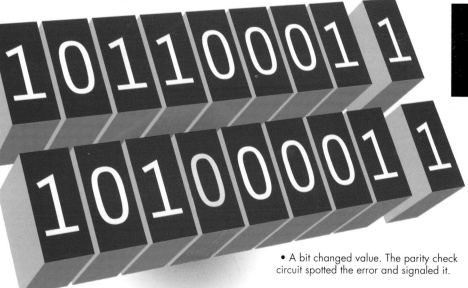

• A bit changed value. The parity check circuit spotted the error and signaled it.

35

On older computers, memory was composed of separate chips called DIPs (dual in-line packages). Eight or nine chips (depending on whether the computer used parity checking) constituted a bank. This configuration was perfectly adapted to computers that manipulated 8-bit words. With AT-type computers that handled 16-bit words, chips had to be installed in groups of 16 or 18. If the system of DIP memory chips had been used with the Pentium, groups of 64 or 72 chips would need to be installed when upgrading memory. The use of SIMM modules lowers this number to 2. Unfortunately, there's also a downside to SIMMs. With DIP chips, defective memory could easily be replaced with a single, inexpensive chip. Nowadays, an entire SIMM module must be replaced. Given the prices of today's SIMMs ($700–$1000 for a single 32-bit 16 MB SIMM), one might look back longingly at the good old days, when replacing memory cost $5–$10 a chip!

How a processor accesses memory

Data being manipulated by the microprocessor can't remain in the processor, because the capacity of its *registers* (internal data storage areas) is extremely limited. A 486 processor has only about ten 32-bit registers. This limited data-storage space forces the microprocessor to make many data exchanges with external memory during the course of operations.

In the microprocessor section you learned that the processors must search memory for instructions to be executed. Those data exchanges slow down processing speed and must be optimized. This is parti-cularly true when the microprocessor is clock doubled or tripled. The CPU is then running two or three times faster internally, but its data exchanges with memory still occur at the CPU's base speed. For example, a 486 DX/4 has an internal clock speed of 99 MHz, but its memory access still occurs at 33 MHz.

A technique called *caching* is used to solve this problem. This consists of including in the microprocessor a storage area containing copied elements that will eventually be used by the processor. Thus, if the processor needs the content of a memory address, it can obtain it immediately as long as it's been copied (during the execution of the previous instructions) into cache memory. The effi-cacy of this system depends on the ability of the *cache controller* to predict the memory addresses the processor will need to access.

In addition to the computer's data trans-mission speed, the CPU's exchange of data with memory is also slowed by limitations of the physical *access time* of the memory chips themselves. This is the actual time required to move the contents of an address to the *bus* and send it to the processor. The price of memory is inversely proportional to a chip's access time. DRAM chips with an access time of between 60 and 100 ns (nano-seconds, or billionths of a second) are often used for internal memory in today's PCs. Access time isn't the only factor that delays memory access; loading time also slows data exchange. When memory can't supply data fast enough to the CPU, the processor must pause for a clock tick, creating a nonpro-ductive *wait state*. A single wait state (latency period) delays data exchange rates by 50 per-cent. To avoid this problem, most compu-ters install *secondary cache memory*, which consists of extremely fast (20 ns) static memory. On PCs using this type of memory, between 64 KB and 512 KB of cache memory can be installed, but 256 KB is considered to be the most efficient configu-ration. The following diagrams show how the secondary cache works.

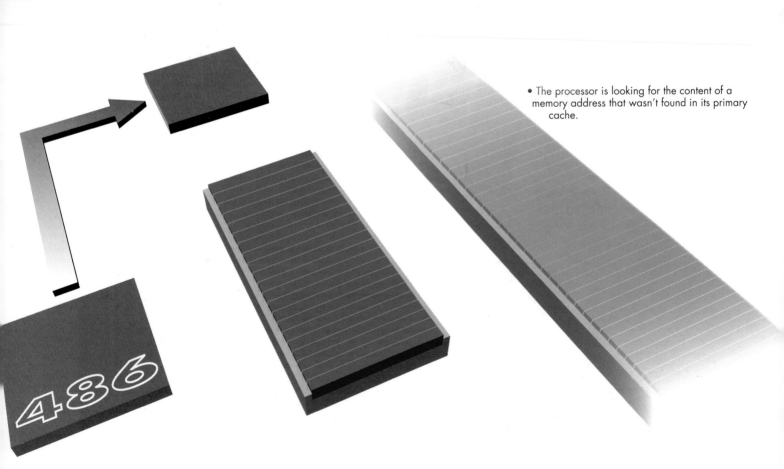

- The processor is looking for the content of a memory address that wasn't found in its primary cache.

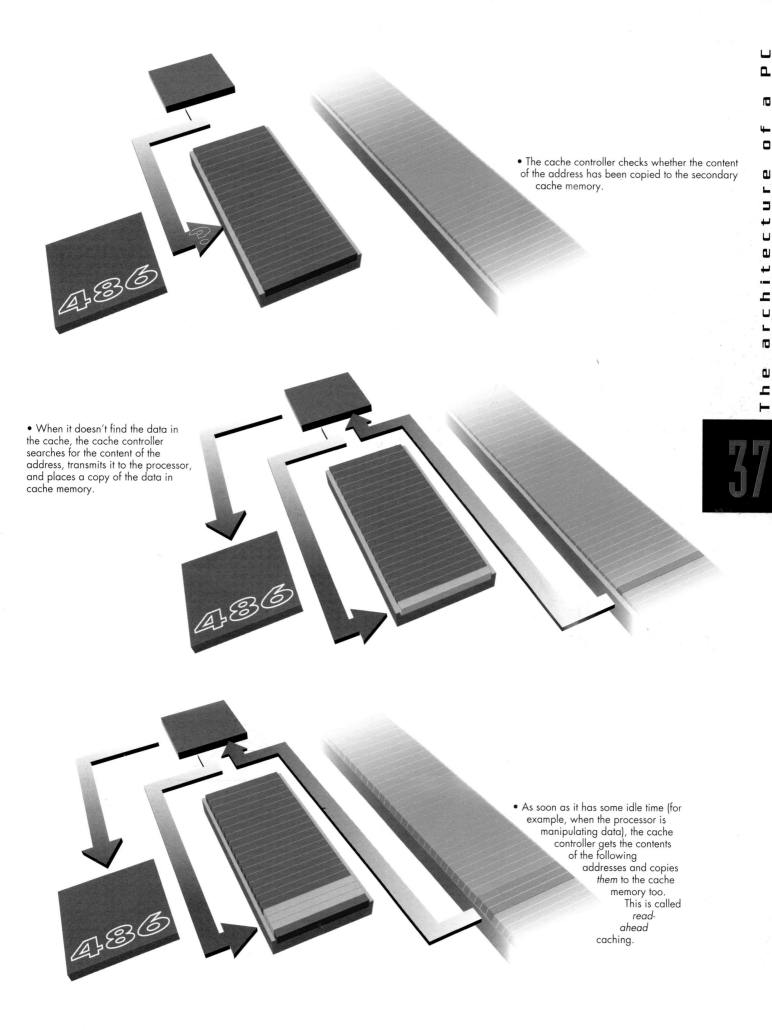

• The cache controller checks whether the content of the address has been copied to the secondary cache memory.

• When it doesn't find the data in the cache, the cache controller searches for the content of the address, transmits it to the processor, and places a copy of the data in cache memory.

• As soon as it has some idle time (for example, when the processor is manipulating data), the cache controller gets the contents of the following addresses and copies *them* to the cache memory too. This is called *read-ahead* caching.

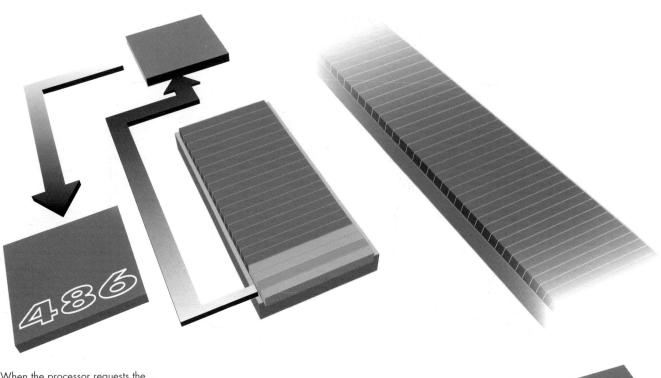

• When the processor requests the contents of the next addresses, the cache controller provides them immediately.

• When cache memory is full, the oldest contents are erased.

• If the processor requests the contents of addresses that go beyond what the cache holds, the cache controller repeats the previous retrieval process.

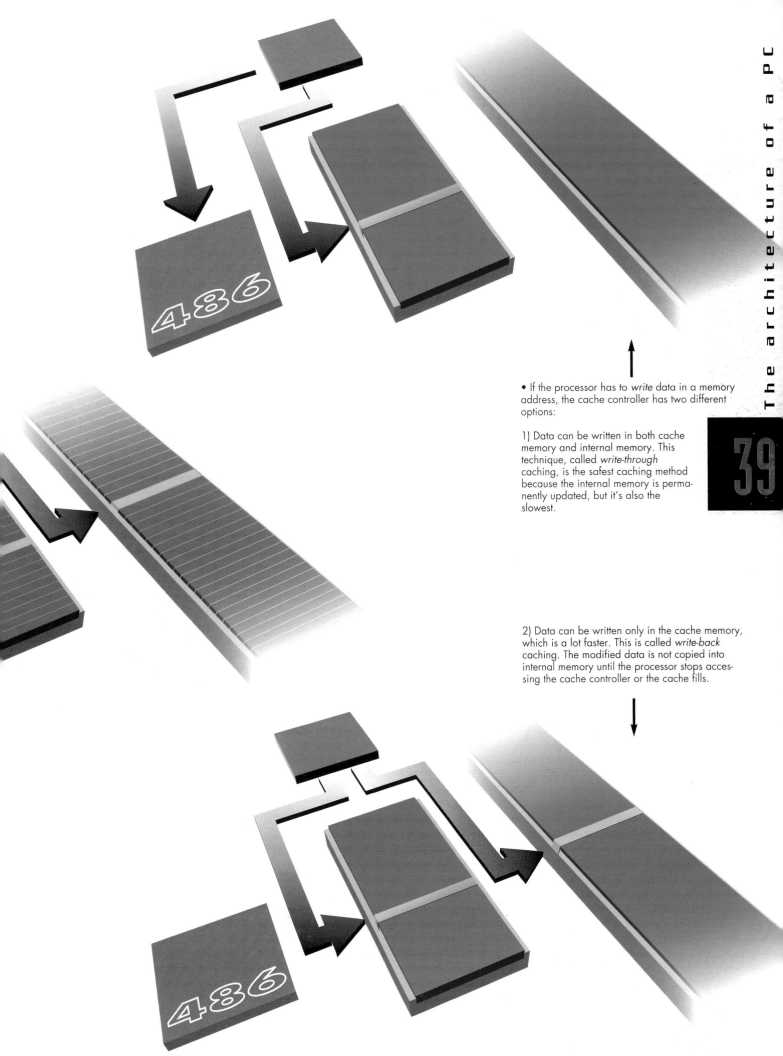

• If the processor has to *write* data in a memory address, the cache controller has two different options:

1) Data can be written in both cache memory and internal memory. This technique, called *write-through* caching, is the safest caching method because the internal memory is permanently updated, but it's also the slowest.

2) Data can be written only in the cache memory, which is a lot faster. This is called *write-back* caching. The modified data is not copied into internal memory until the processor stops accessing the cache controller or the cache fills.

Virtual memory

Often computers include another type of memory called *virtual memory*. Virtual memory isn't another kind of memory chip; instead, it is a technique that simulates the presence of additional memory without the expense of additional hardware. This technique, which is similar to the one used for cache memory, sets aside a protected area on the hard drive to temporarily store data that won't fit into main memory.

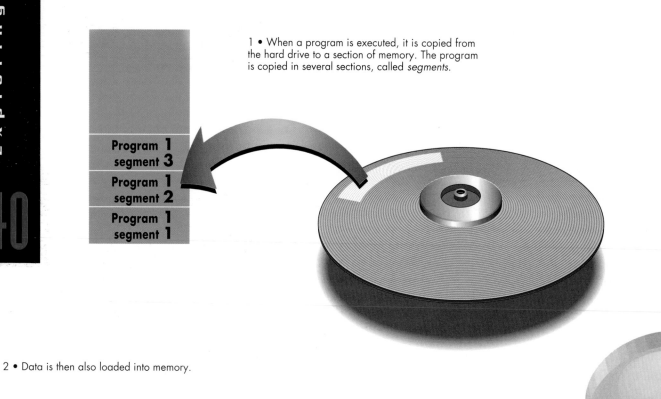

1 • When a program is executed, it is copied from the hard drive to a section of memory. The program is copied in several sections, called *segments*.

Program 1 segment 3
Program 1 segment 2
Program 1 segment 1

2 • Data is then also loaded into memory.

Data

Program 1 segment 3
Program 1 segment 2
Program 1 segment 1

Using virtual memory has an upside and a downside. A megabyte of hard disk space is much less expensive than a megabyte of DRAM, and this technique lets you run programs that require huge data files without needing to purchase a lot of additional memory chips. On the other hand, the constant data exchange between memory and hard

41

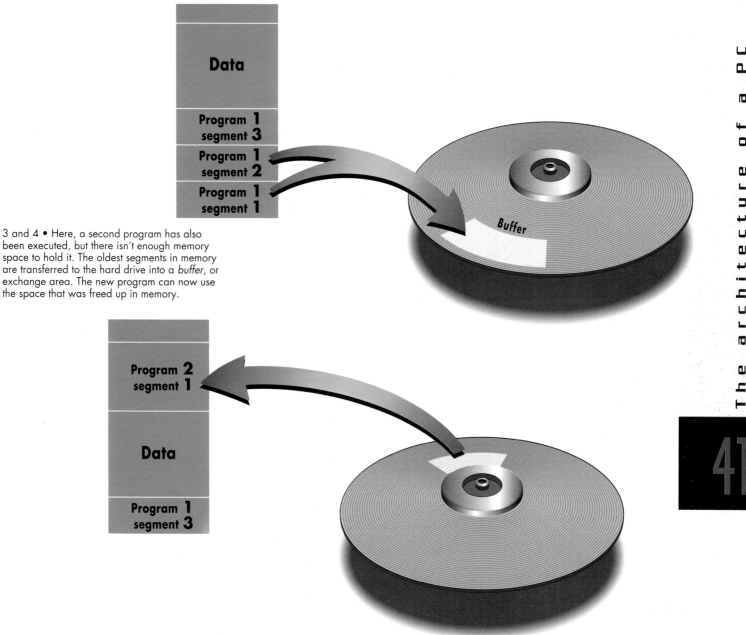

3 and 4 • Here, a second program has also been executed, but there isn't enough memory space to hold it. The oldest segments in memory are transferred to the hard drive into a *buffer*, or exchange area. The new program can now use the space that was freed up in memory.

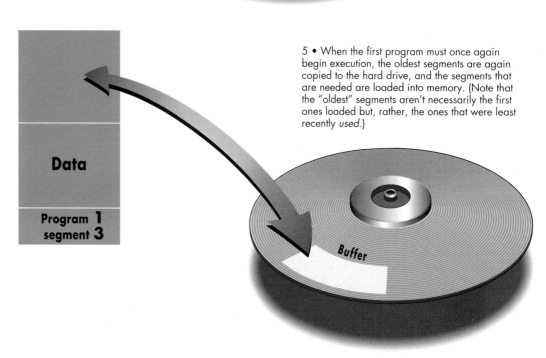

5 • When the first program must once again begin execution, the oldest segments are again copied to the hard drive, and the segments that are needed are loaded into memory. (Note that the "oldest" segments aren't necessarily the first ones loaded but, rather, the ones that were least recently *used*.)

drive slows down the execution of the programs. Furthermore, some programs internally manage the selective loading of their segments. (Those programs "know" that sometimes certain segments should be unloaded even if they aren't the *oldest* ones.) The use of virtual memory can therefore disrupt the program's execution.

Upgrading your PC's memory

If you want to add memory to your PC, you first need to verify your computer's current configuration. Next, you need to determine which upgrades are possible and what type of memory chips to buy. Then, you must physically install the chips, taking every precaution to insert and position them properly.

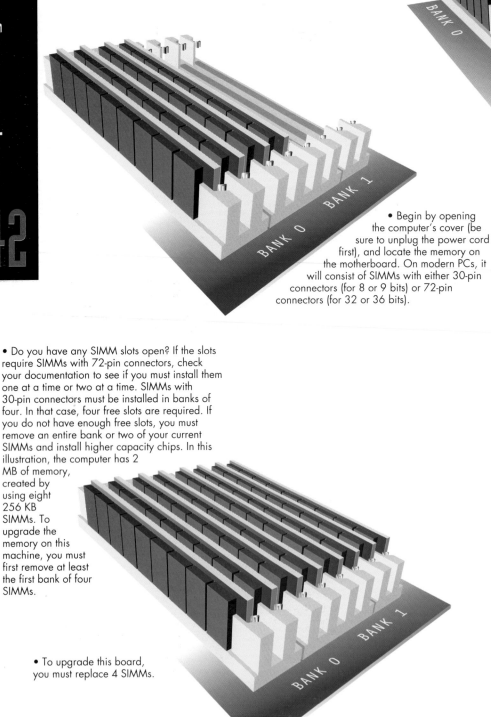

• Begin by opening the computer's cover (be sure to unplug the power cord first), and locate the memory on the motherboard. On modern PCs, it will consist of SIMMs with either 30-pin connectors (for 8 or 9 bits) or 72-pin connectors (for 32 or 36 bits).

• Do you have any SIMM slots open? If the slots require SIMMs with 72-pin connectors, check your documentation to see if you must install them one at a time or two at a time. SIMMs with 30-pin connectors must be installed in banks of four. In that case, four free slots are required. If you do not have enough free slots, you must remove an entire bank or two of your current SIMMs and install higher capacity chips. In this illustration, the computer has 2 MB of memory, created by using eight 256 KB SIMMs. To upgrade the memory on this machine, you must first remove at least the first bank of four SIMMs.

• To upgrade this board, you must replace 4 SIMMs.

When buying a PC, it is extremely important to consider not only the *amount* of memory installed but also the type, number, and capacity of the SIMMs used. It is particularly important that the computer have free SIMM slots to enable you to upgrade memory later without having to remove existing chips. Always be wary of the memory

• Determine your chips' memory access time by checking your PC's documentation or by examining the chips themselves. (The last number stamped on the chip is usually the access time. The smaller the number, the faster the chip.) Although you can add faster memory, it won't make your computer run faster. However, you mustn't use slower memory chips than those already installed.

• "Keyed" (notched) modules prevent incorrect positioning.

Antistatic wrist band

43

• Insert a SIMM at a 30-degree angle, being careful to position the module correctly in the slot (a notch prevents positioning errors), and then move it to a vertical position. It will click into place. Never put SIMMs of different capacities in the same memory bank.

capacities advertised by computer dealers. Video display memory (DRAM or VRAM) should be listed separately. The most common memory installations are powers of 2 (4, 8, or 16 megabytes). If a dealer advertises 5 megabytes of "memory," chances are that it's 4 megabytes of main memory plus 1 megabyte of video memory.

16000 KB OK

• When you boot the computer, it automatically detects the amount of memory installed and displays the results on screen. Always pay attention to the boot messages, and be sure that the proper amount of memory is displayed.

Read-only memory

As mentioned at the start of this section, computers also use another type of memory called ROM (read-only memory), which can be read but not modified. All computers have this type of memory—it contains the basic programs that control the hardware. These programs constitute the PC's BIOS (basic input-output system). Although the BIOS consists of several elements located in different chips, you can easily update the BIOS by changing the main BIOS component, a single DIP chip inserted directly on the motherboard. (Note: If you do update your BIOS, be sure to upgrade the keyboard controller chip at the same time.)

There is also a separate BIOS on the video controller card, as well as on certain other expansion cards.

ROMs are created with programs already embedded in them, using a process called *burning*. While this technique simplifies the mass production of PCs, it makes the development and fine-tuning of the included programs more problematic. During its development phase, a program often has to be modified. If thousands of components had to be produced (and paid for) every time there was a modification, it would be impos-

Shadow ROM

The PC's ROM contains the basic programs that control the operation of the computer. These programs are therefore used very often. Unfortunately, ROM has a disadvantage: it's slower than RAM. To address this shortcoming, a technique was developed that

• When booting, the contents of ROM are copied into RAM.

improves the PC's speed by copying the contents of ROM into RAM as the computer boots. This creates what is known as *Shadow ROM*. Then, each time a BIOS function needs to be used, it is read from the Shadow ROM on the much faster RAM chips. Some BIOSes also include a *cache BIOS* option that copies the programs into cache memory; this speeds BIOS access times even further.

sible to manufacture computers at affordable prices. To this end, another type of chip, called a PROM (programmable ROM) is often used. Whereas information in a ROM is represented by conductors (holding the 1 values) and insulators (holding the 0 values), all values on a PROM are initially set to 1. When a program is ready to be inserted, the PROM is placed on a special device and varying voltages burn the conductors that represent the chosen addresses, thus setting them to 0.

The process of burning programs into PROM isn't reversible. To get around this problem, engineers created another type of chip, called an EPROM (erasable programable read-only memory). This type of memory can be erased with a device that emits ultraviolet rays, thus enabling the chip to be reused.

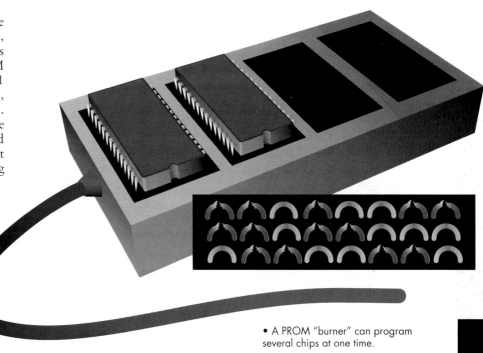

• A PROM "burner" can program several chips at one time.

PCMCIA *memory boards*

Notebook and subnotebook computers have little space for additional memory cards. A special *bus* standard, called PCMCIA, has been created to solve this problem (see the next section for a detailed look at buses). One of the advantages of PCMCIA is that it uses tiny connectors, which enables manufacturers to make expansion boards the size of a credit card. Available boards include RAM cards, which expand read/write memory, and ROM cards, which contain various application programs and replace disk-based programs.

Some PCMCIA cards contain *nonvolatile* RAM, the contents of which aren't lost when the power is turned off or when the computer is disconnected. Those cards can replace floppy disks because they have the advantages of higher storage capacities and a much faster access time. Many other peripherals (such as modems and hard drives) are also available as PCMCIA cards.

• BIOS functions are then executed from RAM.

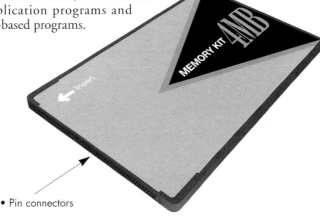

• Pin connectors

• PCMCIA memory expansion card (credit card size)

The bus

Up to this point, we've described several of the components that make up a computer, and we have shown how the processor communicates with the cache memory controller and with internal memory. But nothing has been said about the underlying circuitry that makes this communication possible. We know that data is put into memory at specific addresses. But *how* is an address sent from the processor to memory, and *how* is the data contained at that address sent back to the processor? These processes involve the *bus*, one of the fundamental elements of the architecture of a PC. In fact, the PC's bus is the most defining part of its architecture: Whereas expansion cards and memory can be added, and the type of processor or its frequency can be changed, the bus can never be changed.

What is a bus?

A bus is simply a group of electrical circuits that allow the transmission of signals between the different components of the computer. Those circuits include:

• Data lines

• Address lines

• Control lines (for the signals that tell the parts of the system what to do)

A bus is distinguished by the number and disposition of its electrical lines, or circuits.

Older PCs had an 8-bit bus with only 8 data lines. The most common buses today have 16 data lines, first introduced with IBM's PC AT.

A bus is also distinguished by its operating frequency. The IBM AT bus originally operated at 6 MHz, but its speed was later increased to 8 MHz, and then to 12 MHz on some computers. Buses introduced since the AT have even higher operating frequencies.

The bus controller

The operation of the bus is supervised by a special circuit called the bus controller. The bus controller manages each component's access to the bus and prevents conflicts between components that want to access the bus at the same time.

Expansion slots

A bus not only allows communication between components on the motherboard but also allows the addition of entirely new components to the system. It does this by providing several *slots* into which expansion boards may be plugged. Because these slots are standardized, bus types can be easily recognized. In the illustration, two types of slots can be distinguished:

• 8-bit slots, which are compatible with those of older PCs.

• 16-bit slots, which consist of an 8-bit slot and an additional slot. These are compatible with IBM AT slots.

All these slots are black, which, as you'll see later, is a matter of some distinction.

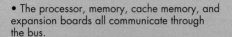
• The processor, memory, cache memory, and expansion boards all communicate through the bus.

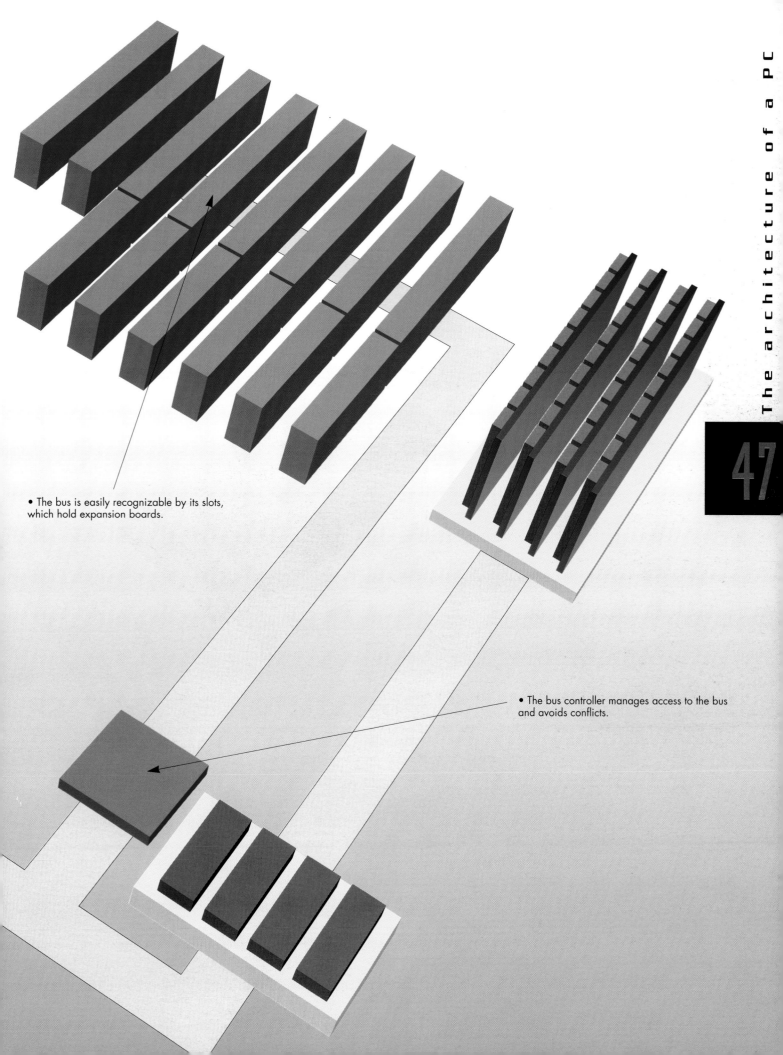

47

• The bus is easily recognizable by its slots, which hold expansion boards.

• The bus controller manages access to the bus and avoids conflicts.

The different bus types

The ISA bus

Under the name *ISA (Industry Standard Architecture)*, the IBM AT bus was for many years the standard for IBM-compatible PCs. Derived from and compatible with the IBM PC bus, the AT's *width* of 16 bits and operating speed of 8 to 12 MHz matched the characteristics of the Intel 286 microprocessor perfectly, and allowed the installation of additional memory on an expansion board plugged into one of the bus slots. The AT bus also worked well with the first 386 microprocessor, the 16-MHz 386 SX. However, the later 386 DX micropro- cessor created a paradoxical situation. While the 386 DX could work with 32-bit words at microprocessor speed (and it was available in 20, 25, 33, and, eventually, 50 MHz ver- sions), the AT's 16-bit bus necessitated two 16-bit operations to transmit each 32-bit word of data. The effective data transfer speed was thus no faster than that of the 386 SX.

ISA bus

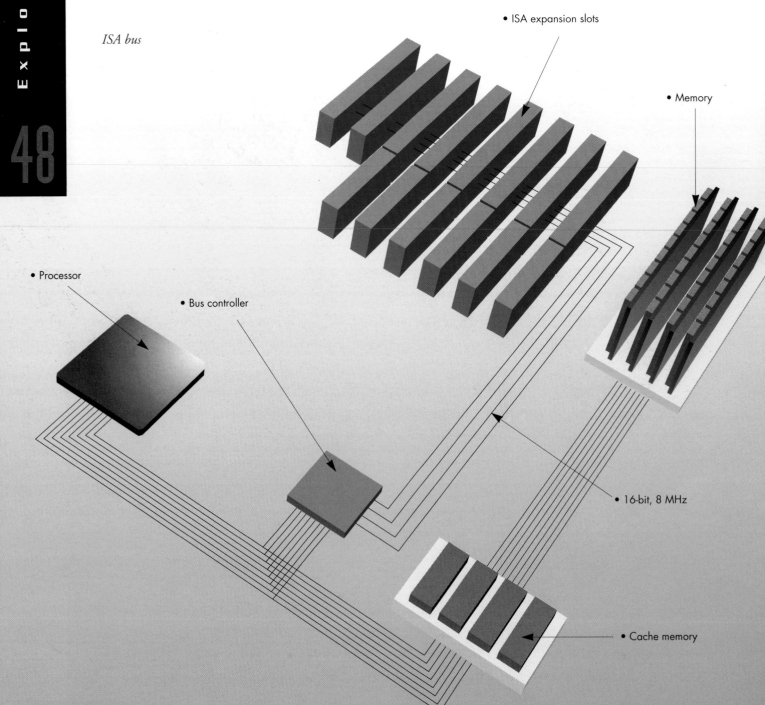

• ISA expansion slots

• Memory

• Processor

• Bus controller

• 16-bit, 8 MHz

• Cache memory

The MCA bus

IBM then tried to impose a new bus standard, called *MCA (Micro Channel Architecture)*. It provided some advantages, but it also had serious drawbacks. MCA uses a 32-bit bus, but its operating speed is clearly inferior to that of modern microprocessors. MCA allows the expansion cards to take control of the bus, making possible direct information transfers between peripherals without involving the microprocessor. This means that information can be transferred from the hard drive to memory while the microprocessor does other things. However, this bus is totally incompatible with the ISA bus. This, combined with IBM's decision to charge a license fee to all PC manufacturers using this architecture, prevented its widespread adoption.

The local bus

To improve the speed of information exchanges between the processor and memory, one solution was to install a bus between only the two components involved in the transfer. This type of bus, called a *local bus,* can run at the same speed as the microprocessor without expensive circuitry because of the short distance involved and the fact that it does not have to interface with any other peripherals. Most PCs sold on the market today have at least one local bus slot.

The EISA bus

To thwart IBM's attempts to control future bus architecture, several manufacturers grouped together to create and promote a new standard, EISA (*Extended Industry Standard Architecture*). The EISA bus has a 32-bit width and a 20-MHz operating speed, and allows the peripherals to control the bus. Furthermore, it is compatible with all ISA expansion cards. However, because the operating speed of the EISA bus was not as fast as that of the microprocessors being sold at the time it was released, sales of EISA were less than the manufacturers had hoped. After all, memory plugged into an EISA slot would be limited to operating at 20 MHz, while the processor itself was running at 33 MHz or faster. The high cost of production further limited its success.

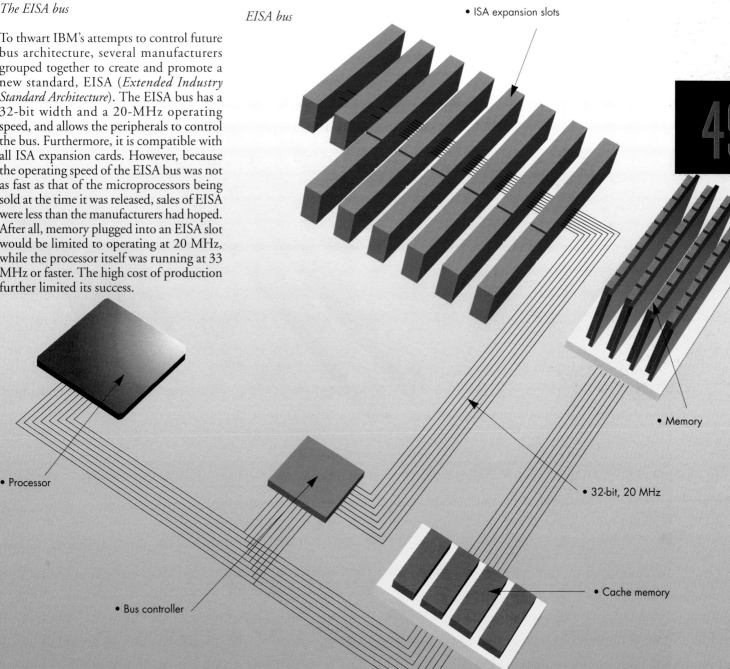

EISA bus

• ISA expansion slots

• Processor

• Bus controller

• Memory

• 32-bit, 20 MHz

• Cache memory

49

The VESA bus

The existence of a local bus quickly gave manufacturers the idea of using it for peripherals that require high information transfer rates. Displays running a graphical interface (such as Microsoft Windows) are among such peripherals. Network interface cards and hard disk drives can also benefit from local buses. (In the case of the hard disk drive, data transfer to and from the platters is still limited by how fast the disk rotates. However, memory installed on the drive's interface card serves as a buffer for the data, permitting data transfer from the processor to the buffer to occur at the speed of the local bus. The contents of the buffer are ultimately transferred to the disk while the processor is busy doing something else.) Initially some manufacturers developed local buses incompatible with products from other manufacturers. But other manufacturers joined together to create the *VESA (Video Electronics Standards Association)* standards, whose prime goal was the installation of a display card on a local bus. VESA slots are easily recognizable by their brown color.

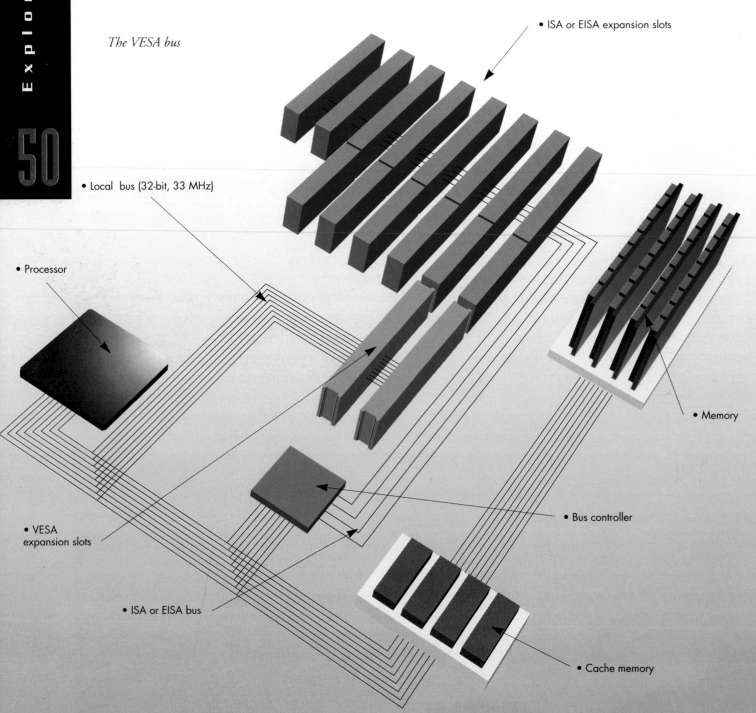

The VESA bus

- ISA or EISA expansion slots
- Local bus (32-bit, 33 MHz)
- Processor
- Memory
- VESA expansion slots
- Bus controller
- ISA or EISA bus
- Cache memory

The PCI bus

The VESA bus unfortunately has its limitations. Because it was developed as an extension to a bus dedicated to communicating with memory, VESA allows for a maximum of only three slots. Furthermore, it's a 32-bit bus with a maximum frequency of 33 MHz, and 64-bit microprocessors running at 100 MHz are already on the market. A newer standard, called *PCI (Peripheral Components Interconnect)*, proposed by Intel, is a 64-bit bus (but can be used as a 32-bit bus, to ensure compatibility with the 486 processor) that currently runs at 33 MHz, though there are already plans for it to run at a higher speed. It is somewhat compatible with the ISA and EISA bus because the bus controller provided by Intel also manages those standards. It allows the peripherals to take control of the bus, and also allows automatic configuration of the expansion cards (a feature called *Plug and Play*). It is, without doubt, the bus of the future. It is easily recognized by its white color.

The PCMCIA bus

The PCMCIA bus was developed mainly for portable computers. Its performance is relatively limited, given its 16-bit width and a 33-MHz upper limit on speed. It has only 26 address lines, which limits its memory space to 64 megabytes, and it won't allow the peripherals to take control of the bus. On the other hand, it has some advantages that particularly suit it for use in portable computers. The main one is its tiny size (the expansion cards that you plug into it are about the size of a credit card). Also, it's the only bus that allows you to connect and disconnect an expansion card without turning off the computer's power.

PCI bus

- ISA or EISA bus
- ISA or EISA expansion slots
- PCI expansion slots
- Memory
- Processor
- ISA or EISA bus controller
- PCI bus controller
- Local bus (64-bit, 33 MHz)
- Cache memory

51

Interface boards

A PC's motherboard usually contains a microprocessor, memory, and the bus, as well as the circuits that connect them. Some motherboards also include a display interface for controlling the screen, an input/output interface for, say, printers or modems, and an IDE or SCSI interface for communicating with a hard disk and other peripherals. At the other end of the spectrum are computers where the motherboard contains only the bus: the processor and memory are on expansion boards. This latter setup appears to make it easier to upgrade the system, but there is a problem in that these processor and memory expansion cards have no common standard, and must therefore be bought from the manufacturer of the motherboard (and usually at a higher price than you would pay otherwise for such components). Another disadvantage is that nonstandard cards usually become unavailable after a few years, just about the time you want to upgrade.

A *video card* (also called a *display adapter* or *graphics card)* is one of the three cards present in all PCs (unless it's integrated with the motherboard). There's a wide variety of video cards available, from standard VGA cards to accelerated high-resolution graphics cards with several megabytes of VRAM (video memory). Changing the video card is often a simple way to significantly improve the performance of a PC.

A local bus video card is practically indispensable if you're using a graphical interface such as Microsoft Windows. Some video cards even include a built-in Windows graphics processor, which serves to free the microprocessor from Windows' graphics-intensive tasks.

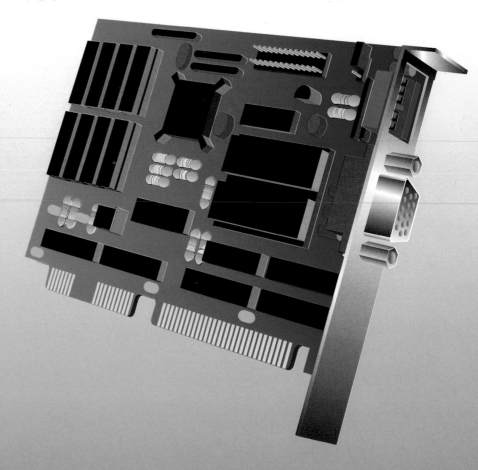

ISA graphics card

VESA graphics card

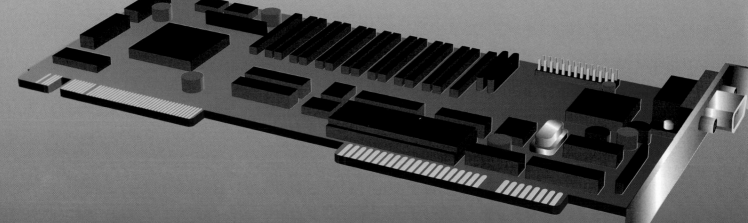

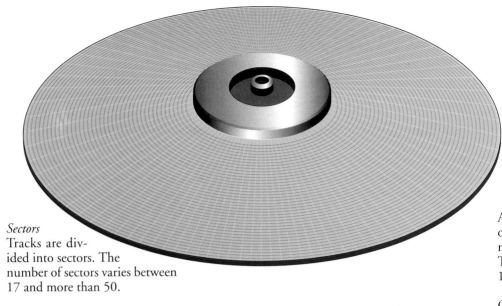

The geometry of a hard disk

A hard disk drive is defined by its geometry, or, in other words, the configuration and number of its heads, cylinders, and sectors. The disk in the preceding illustrations has 14 heads, 723 cylinders, and 51 sectors.

One surface of one platter is often reserved for head-positioning information, and so isn't available for programs and their data. That's why many disks have an odd number of heads. Also, one or more cylinders are often reserved for internal disk functions.

Sectors
Tracks are divided into sectors. The number of sectors varies between 17 and more than 50.

Note that sectors vary in size. Sectors near the center of the platter are smaller than sectors near the outer edge, but each sector contains the same amount of data. Data density is higher nearer the center of the disk.

The storage capacity of a hard disk drive

Just like internal memory, the amount of data a disk can store is measured in bytes (one byte = one character). Measurements are usually given in terms of kilobytes (KB or K), equal to 1,024 bytes, megabytes (MB), equal to 1,024 kilobytes, and gigabytes (GB), equal to 1,024 megabytes. (1,024 is not a random number. It corresponds to 2^{10}, a number easily manipulated by computers, which compute in binary—base 2—numbers.)

A disk's storage capacity depends on its geometry and the sector size. A sector usually contains 512 bytes (0.5 kilobytes). In our example, the disk can hold:

Bytes per sector	x	Sectors per cylinder	x	Number of cylinders	x	Number of heads		
0.5 KB	x	51	x	723	x	14	=	**258,111 KB** or about **252 MB**

Addresses of data on a disk
Addresses are used to find data on a disk. The address of a sector consists of its head number, cylinder number, and sector number.

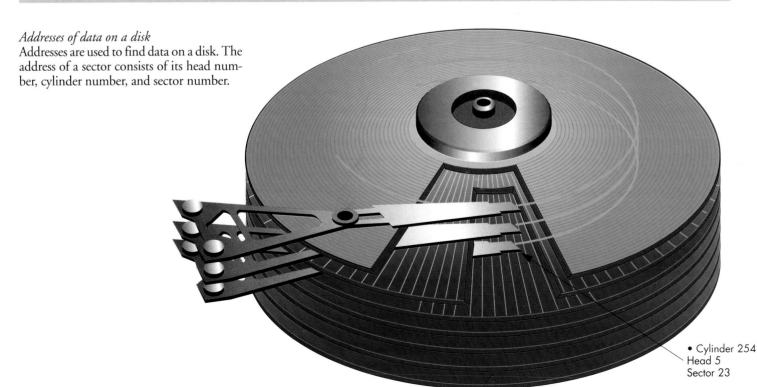

• Cylinder 254
Head 5
Sector 23

The read/write head

The read/write head floats on a cushion of air on the surface of a rotating platter. This air cushion (an aerodynamic phenomenon that occurs between the head and the rotating platter) lifts the head about 0.5 microns away from the surface of the disk. This leads to several potential problems.

The first problem is that no particle of any kind can be allowed to slide into the space between the disk and the read head. The illustration below shows the relative size of common particles and the space between the head and the disk. If any of these particles found its way between the head and the surface of the disk, both the head and the magnetic coating on the disk, if not the disk itself, would be damaged. That's why hard disk drives are protected with an airtight case. To avoid serious damage, never open the case!

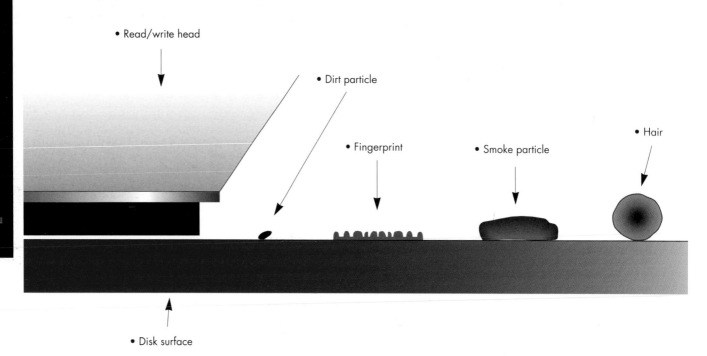

• Read/write head

• Dirt particle

• Fingerprint

• Smoke particle

• Hair

• Disk surface

On some disks, the case has openings blocked with labels. Never remove those labels—it could void the warranty and damage the disk. Also, there's usually a label sealing the case to its cover. It's then impossible to open the case without breaking the label, which voids the warranty.

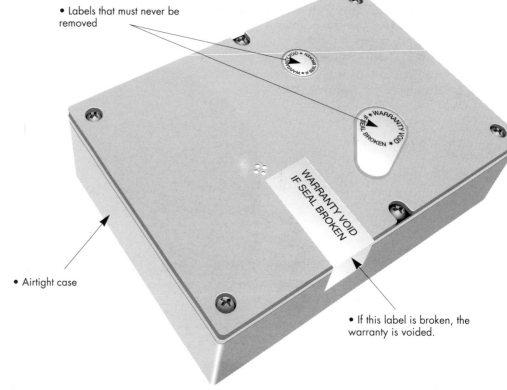

• Labels that must never be removed

WARRANTY VOID IF SEAL BROKEN

• Airtight case

• If this label is broken, the warranty is voided.

Another potential problem occurs when the disk drive is off—because there's no air cushion, the head settles on the magnetic coating. The head rises when the computer is turned on and lands when it's turned off. During takeoff and landing the head rubs against the surface of the disk. If the magnetic coating is damaged, data is lost. To make sure that no area with data gets damaged, one track on each surface is reserved for takeoff and

landing and is called the *landing zone*. If you install a disk yourself, you'll need to provide the landing zone's track number to the BIOS. The BIOS uses this information to park the head over the landing zone before turning the computer off. Most modern disks automatically park the heads when there is a power failure. For those disks that don't, turning off the computer without parking the head can lead to deterioration of

the magnetic coating on the disk and to loss of data.

It's useful to know that since tracks are numbered starting at 0, the number of the track used as the landing zone is usually equal to the total number of tracks on the disk. If a disk has 751 tracks (or 751 cylinders), it means that 751 tracks are available for data. These data tracks are numbered from 0 to 750; the landing zone is on track 751.

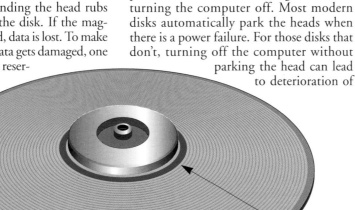

• The landing zone is usually the track nearest the center of the disk (the track with the highest number).

Precautions

With older disks, it was necessary to run a program to park the read/write heads before turning off the power. This isn't necessary anymore, but there is another, related, problem. When a disk is in use, the head remains over the last track that was written or read. As long as the computer is on, any physical shock to the computer can make one or more of the read/write heads touch down on the track, causing data loss. If you leave your computer on unattended for long per-

iods of time, and many people have access to your office (to clean it, for example), your computer might get jolted and the disk damaged while you're away. It's better to turn off your computer if you're going to be away for a long period of time. If, however, you prefer to leave your computer on, use a head-parking program to park the heads before you leave. This is even more important if your computer is located on the floor (which is not recommended!).

• The linear speed is proportional to the distance between the track and the center of the disk. It is highest at the outer edge, usually more than twice as fast as at the interior track.

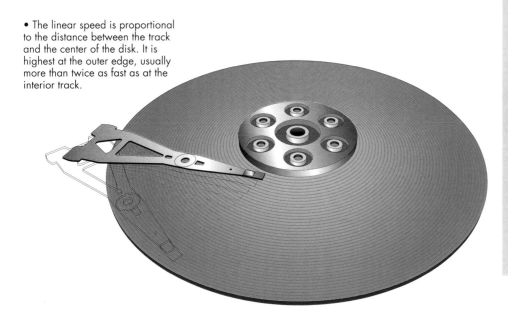

The interior track is used for the landing zone because that's where the relative speed of the disk surface and the read/write head is slowest. Head speed relative to the disk is highest at the outer track of the disk and lowest at the center track. It's impossible to park the head exactly at the center of the disk (the spindle is in the way), but parking as close to the center as possible is the best solution.

Writing data

To write data on a disk, the drive sends a current through the electromagnet in the read/write head. This current creates a local magnetic field that orients magnetic particles in the coating on the surface of the disk.

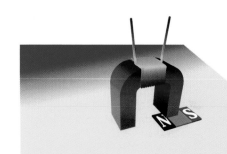

• When the disk is blank, the magnetic particles on the surface of the disk have no particular magnetic orientation.

• Electrical current

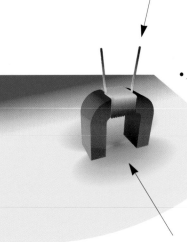

• A pulse of electric current sent through the read/write head creates a magnetic field between the poles of an electromagnet.

• Magnetic field

• The magnetic field magnetizes the surface of the disk, creating a dipole, that is, an area that has a north and south pole, like a magnet.

Reading data

Reading data relies on the opposite phenomenon: variations in the magnetic field near a magnet result in electrical currents being generated in the read head's magnet. Those pulses (identical to the previous write pulses) are then sent back to the computer.

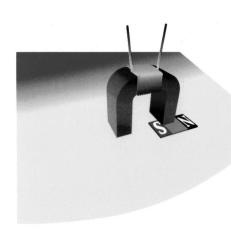

• Movement of the dipoles on the surface of the disk relative to the read head causes an inversion of the magnetic field.

• This magnetic field inversion induces current in the read head.

Data is written to the disk as 1s and 0s. What's the best way to represent these values using electrical pulses? The simplest technique consists of coding a 1 with a pulse and a 0 with the absence of a pulse. However, this has two major disadvantages. First, magnetic pulses are used not only to represent data, but also to synchronize the timing of a read with the rotation of the disk. Under the "1 = pulse, 0 = pulse absence" coding scheme, a very long string of 0s would lead to read desynchronization. The second disadvantage is that a long string of 1s would put successive pulses too close together on the disk. Pulses must be spaced far enough apart on the disk surface to avoid interference between their magnetized areas. (An infinite number of pulse absences can be put on one track of a disk, but the maximum number of pulses is limited by the length of the track.)

To solve the first problem, a coding system can be used that always includes a pulse, whether the data is a 1 or 0. This system is called *frequency modulation* or FM. A 1 is represented by sending two pulses; a 0 is represented by sending a pulse followed by a silence. This way, there are never two consecutive periods of silence.

• A pulse

• Absence of a pulse

This system doesn't solve the second problem, though, so more advanced techniques have been developed. MFM (*modified frequency modulation*) technology allows twice as much information to be stored. RLL (*run length limited*) technology, the most widely used with modern disks, increases disk capacity by another 50 percent. The goal of these techniques is to minimize the number of pulses that have to be written on a disk and, more important, to make sure that pulses are always spaced with silences. Because a pulse magnetizes the surface of a disk, sufficient space is needed between two pulses to prevent the magnetized areas from interfering with one another. In addition, if there are never two successive pulses, data density can be increased. With MFM technology, pulses are always spaced by at least one silence. With RLL technology, at least two periods of silence occur between each pulse.

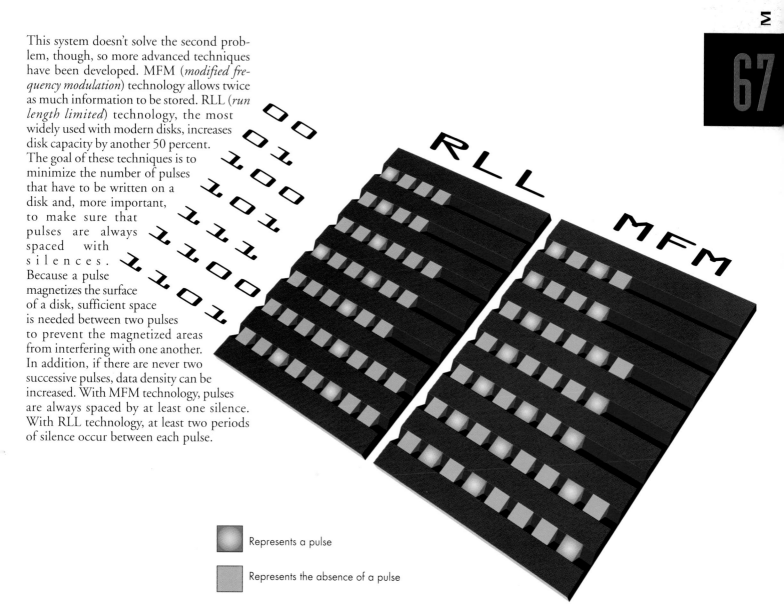

□ Represents a pulse

▢ Represents the absence of a pulse

Reducing the write current

As seen in the previous section, one of the main problems encountered when increasing disk capacity is maintaining the proper separation between magnetized areas. Magnetized areas that overlap interfere with one another, potentially altering the data. This is a *linear density* problem and arises when manufacturers try to increase the amount of data in a given track length.

By looking closely at the layout of data on a disk, you'll immediately see that all tracks aren't the same length. Tracks near the center are much shorter than tracks near the outer edge. Therefore, data is packed more densely on tracks near the center.

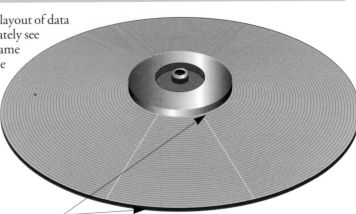

• The outer track is about twice the length of the inner track.

This doesn't create any synchronization problems, because the disk's linear speed is proportionally slower on the inner tracks than on the outer tracks. The amount of data scrolling in front of the read/write heads at a given time is always the same. However, because the size of the magnetized areas controls how densely data can be packed, the area close to the center of the disk can't be used—the magnetized areas would overlap.

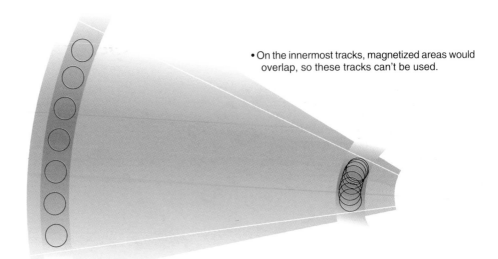

• On the innermost tracks, magnetized areas would overlap, so these tracks can't be used.

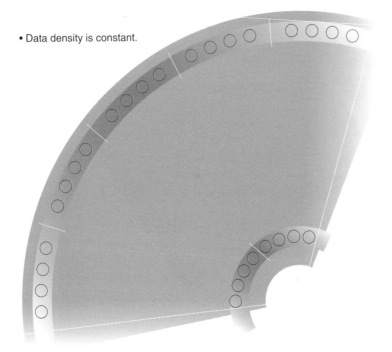

• Data density is constant.

What, then, is the best use of the available disk surface? Two possible solutions exist. The first consists of keeping the same data density throughout the surface of the disk. Outer tracks then contain more data than inner tracks. The main disadvantage of this solution shows up when you consider how read synchronization occurs. Data must be read at a constant rate, so the disk would have to accelerate to read inner tracks and slow down for outer tracks. This would force disk manufacturers to build complex disk drive mechanisms.

The second, much simpler, solution consists of decreasing the size of the magnetized area on the interior tracks. Given the lower linear speed on the inner tracks, this approach is a logical solution. To make the size of the magnetized area smaller, the disk drive electronics reduce the write current when writing data on inner tracks.

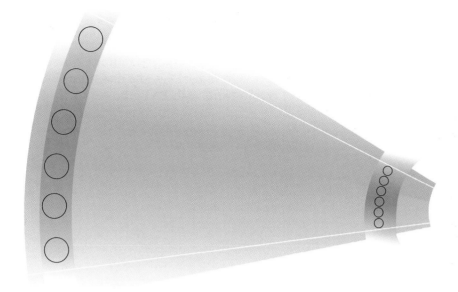

• On the inner tracks, the write current is reduced and the size of the magnetized areas is smaller.

Write precompensation

Increasing disk density creates another problem. The magnetized areas on the surface of the disk act like individual magnets. When they are very close, their poles interact; identical poles repel each other and opposite poles attract each other. This interaction shifts around the magnetized areas, causing problems when the data is read.

To solve this problem, a process called *write precompensation* is used. Data is shifted forward while it's being written to compensate for any shifting that occurs when data is written next to it. When the next data is written, interaction between the poles of the magnetized areas shifts the data back into its proper position.

When this technique is used, it is applied starting from a given track. When you install a disk, you'll need to know the number of this track so you can supply the correct configuration parameters to the BIOS.

• Without precompensation

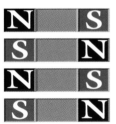

• Data is written this way.

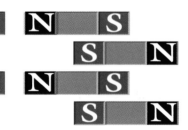

• Interaction between the poles shifts them this way.

• With precompensation

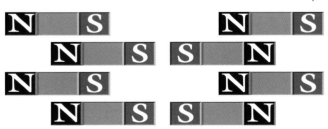

• Data is written this way.

• Interaction between the poles shifts them this way.

The disk controller

The PC's microprocessor doesn't handle disk operations. These tasks are performed by the *disk controller,* a specialized electronic interface. On older PCs, the disk controller was on an interface card that was plugged into the bus. This type of architecture, called ST 506 (short for ST 506/412 !), is no longer used.

Layout of ST 506 disk drives

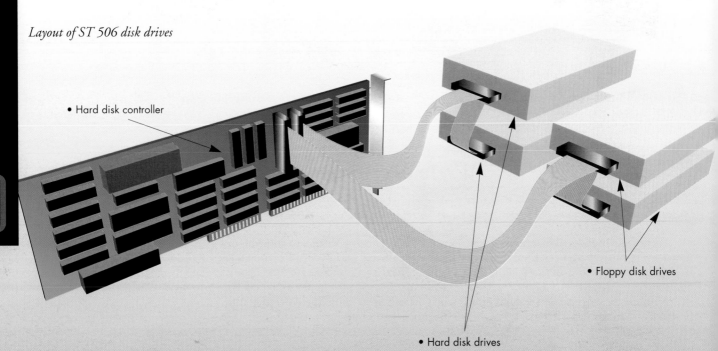

• Hard disk controller

• Floppy disk drives

• Hard disk drives

Nowadays, IDE and SCSI disk drives are the most widely used architectures. IDE disk drives are most popular for capacities up to 540 megabytes. SCSI is generally used for larger drives—300 MB and up. Each drive has its own on-board controller. IDE interface cards simply provide a connection between the bus and the disk controller. Such a card typically also includes a floppy disk drive controller. For SCSI drives, the role of the interface card is more complex, because it allows you to link as many as seven chained peripherals to the computer. A SCSI interface card usually doesn't include a floppy disk controller; a separate card is required to run floppy disk drives.

IDE and SCSI disk controllers contain a small memory cache. If you need better performance, you can use an interface card that has additional cache memory and its own cache memory controller.

Sector relocation

When you install a new disk drive on a PC, you must tell the BIOS the number of cylinders, heads, and sectors on the disk. The PC was designed during an era when it was thought the most hard disk space you'd ever need would be a few dozen megabytes. So BIOS designers set the upper limits for cylinders, heads, and sectors to match those expectations: 1,024 cylinders, 16 heads, and 64 sectors. Disk designers in search of higher capacities later found that it's easier (and cheaper) to increase the number of cylinders on a disk (by using a higher density) than

to increase the number of read/write heads. The current trend, in fact, is to manufacture disks with just one or two platters. To get around the upper limits imposed by the BIOS, a technique called *sector relocation* is used. A disk then has a *logical geometry* different from its *physical geometry*. For example, a disk with 1,429 cylinders and 11 heads is seen as if it had 995 cylinders and 16 heads. The disk controller makes the translation during each disk access.

Layout of IDE disk drives

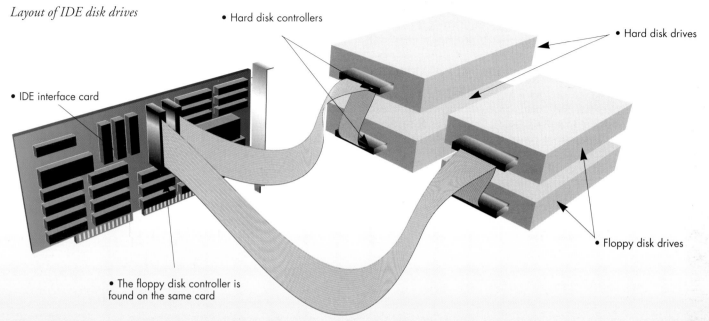

- Hard disk controllers
- Hard disk drives
- IDE interface card
- The floppy disk controller is found on the same card
- Floppy disk drives

Layout of SCSI disk drives

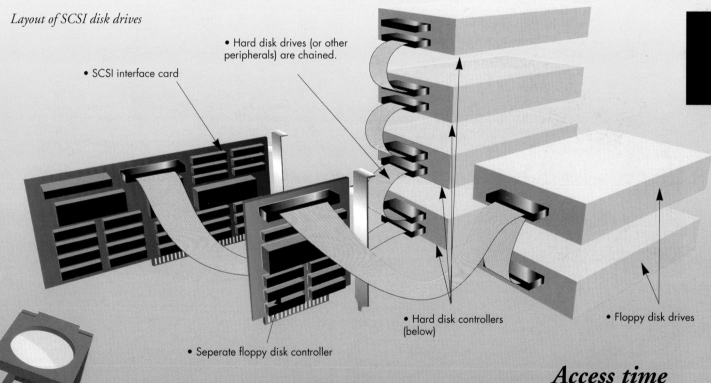

- Hard disk drives (or other peripherals) are chained.
- SCSI interface card
- Hard disk controllers (below)
- Floppy disk drives
- Seperate floppy disk controller

With modern disks, it is possible to configure any logical geometry as long as the BIOS limitations or the actual disk capacity isn't exceeded. However, all logical geometries aren't the same in terms of performance, so when installing a hard disk use the cylinder, head, and sector values suggested by the manufacturer.

Access time

In addition to its capacity, a disk drive is characterized by its access time. Access time is the average delay required to access any one area of the disk. For modern disks, access times are between 8 and 20 milliseconds. When a manufacturer claims a much lower access time (3 milliseconds, for example), it's a claim based on access from cache memory, not from the disk surface. Ignore such claims.

Organization of data on the disk

Low-level formatting

Recall that data is written on a disk in tracks divided into sectors. This division into sectors isn't made at the time the disk is manufactured. In fact, the manufacturing process determines only a maximum number of tracks and sectors, and that number is imposed by the maximum data density allowed by the magnetic coating on the disk. The actual number of tracks and sectors is determined when the disk is *formatted*. Formatting is a multi-level operation. The first level is performed by a program located in the read-only memory of the disk controller and is called *low-level formatting*. Low-level formatting uses magnetic markers to create tracks and sectors. If there are defective sectors, they are marked to ensure that they won't be used to save data. It's normal for the magnetic surface to have defects in some sectors; this is harmless as long as no data is written on those sectors. Because a sector is 512 bytes, the overall capacity isn't greatly diminished if some sectors are defective and unused.

It's important to know that low-level formatting is done by the manufacturer and should not normally be done again by the user.

Partitioning the disk

After low-level formatting, you need to partition the disk. (Today, computers are delivered with a hard drive that is already formatted and partitioned.) Each partition on the hard disk acts as one or more different disk drives (called *logical drives*), and each partition can hold a different operating system. One partition can contain several logical drives. Usually a disk contains only one partition, encompassing the entire capacity of the disk. A disk *must* be partitioned before it can be used.

High-level formatting

High-level formatting consists of organizing sectors so they can be used by the *operating system* (DOS). The operating system doesn't use sectors; it uses *allocation units* or *clusters*. A cluster consists of several sectors. On a floppy disk, a cluster has two sectors—the two sectors opposite one another on either side of the disk. On a hard disk, the number of sectors in a cluster varies from 2 to 16 or even more. This way of arranging sectors into clusters has both advantages and disadvantages. For the operating system, reading all the sectors in a cluster is a single operation. If the disk controller can read all the sectors in a cluster at one pass, access time is considerably shortened. Where clusters have sectors opposite one another on both faces of a floppy disk, reading speed is doubled.

• Low-level formatting consists of laying out tracks and sectors on the disk, and marking defective sectors.

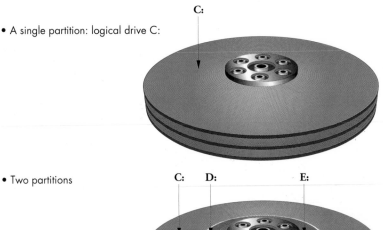

• A single partition: logical drive C:

C:

• Two partitions

C: D: E:

• Partition 1: logical drive C:

• Partition 2: logical drives D: and E:

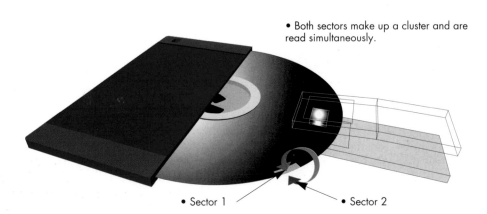

• Both sectors make up a cluster and are read simultaneously.

• Sector 1

• Sector 2

Another advantage occurs because the operating system limits the number of clusters on a disk (just as the BIOS limits the numbers of cylinders, heads, and sectors). The limit on the effective capacity of disks can be increased by increasing the number of sectors per cluster.

The major disadvantage of grouping sectors into allocation units is that a *file* must always be written to disk by cluster rather than by sector. Therefore, when clusters comprise eight sectors, the smallest file will occupy

4,096 bytes of disk space—even if the file contains only one character! A 4,097 character file will occupy 8,192 bytes. You can see that the wasted space (called *slack*) amounts, on average, to about half a cluster per file, or 2,048 bytes. A hard disk drive containing 2,000 files (which is not unusual) then has 4 MB of wasted space!

The *file allocation table* (FAT) and the *root directory* are created during high-level formatting. The root directory contains a list of subdirectories and files with the number

of each file's first cluster, the file size, its date and time of creation, and other information. The FAT contains a list of all the clusters on a disk and shows how they are being used. In the FAT, clusters can be marked as free, in use by a file, or unusable. (For security purposes, there are two copies of the file allocation table.) Unusable clusters are those containing one or more defective sectors. Here we can see another disadvantage of clusters that contain a large number of sectors. If an eight-sector cluster contains one defective sector, seven good sectors are wasted.

• Organization of data on the disk

DIRECTORY	CLUSTER	SIZE
FILE 1	2	32 412

• The directory contains the number (or address) of the first cluster.

FILE ALLOCATION TABLE

0	1	2	3	4	5	6
		3	4	5	6	7
7	8	9	10	11	12	13
	8	27	0	0	0	0	0
14	15	16	17	18	19	20
	0	0	0	0	0	0	0
21	22	23	24	25	26	27
	0	0	0	0	0	0	28
28	29	30	31	32	33	34
	29	end	0	0	0	0	0
35	36	37	38	39	40	41
	0	0	0	0	0	0	0
42	43	44	45	46	47	48
	0	0	0	0	0	0	0

• In the file allocation table, each address corresponding to a cluster contains the address of the file's next cluster. The address of the last cluster contains an "end of file" marker.

Clusters and sectors are numbered sequentially. The operating system (DOS) doesn't use the absolute address of a sector (cylinder, head, and sector) but, rather, its ID number—called the *DOS sector number*.

Deleting data

When a file is deleted, the first character of the file's name in the main directory is replaced by a special character (σ), and the file allocation table entries for clusters occupied by the file are set to 0.

This marks those clusters free for allocation to other files. However, the data in those clusters is not modified or erased. That's why some utility programs are able to undelete previously erased files as long as their sectors haven't been overwritten.

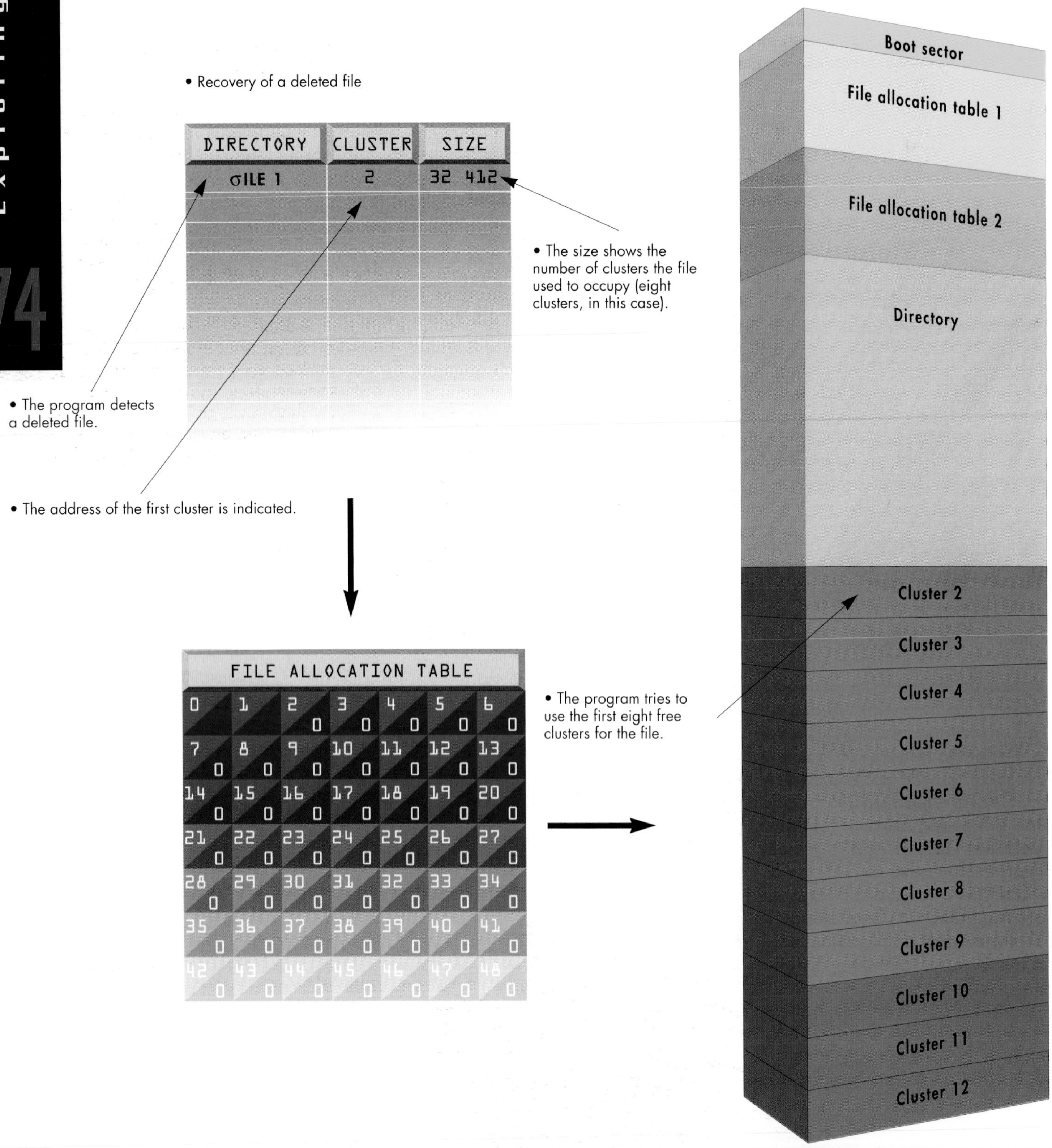

• Recovery of a deleted file

DIRECTORY	CLUSTER	SIZE
σILE 1	2	32 412

• The size shows the number of clusters the file used to occupy (eight clusters, in this case).

• The program detects a deleted file.

• The address of the first cluster is indicated.

FILE ALLOCATION TABLE

0	1	2	3	4	5	6
	0	0	0	0	0	0
7	8	9	10	11	12	13
0	0	0	0	0	0	0
14	15	16	17	18	19	20
0	0	0	0	0	0	0
21	22	23	24	25	26	27
0	0	0	0	0	0	0
28	29	30	31	32	33	34
0	0	0	0	0	0	0
35	36	37	38	39	40	41
0	0	0	0	0	0	0
42	43	44	45	46	47	48
0	0	0	0	0	0	0

• The program tries to use the first eight free clusters for the file.

Boot sector

File allocation table 1

File allocation table 2

Directory

Cluster 2

Cluster 3

Cluster 4

Cluster 5

Cluster 6

Cluster 7

Cluster 8

Cluster 9

Cluster 10

Cluster 11

Cluster 12

File fragmentation

Data is written to the first unoccupied clusters found on the disk. After several iterations of file deletion and creation, files tend to become *fragmented.* File fragmentation increases disk access time and decreases the chances of salvaging a file when there is a problem. Periodically, it makes sense to use a special utility program to *defragment* the disk, that is, move data on the disk so that files are stored in contiguous clusters.

File compression utilities

To increase a disk's effective capacity, you can use a *file compression utility*, sometimes known as a *disk doubler.* A disk doubler program intercepts data sent to the hard disk drive, compresses it, and stores it in a single file that appears to the system as an additional disk drive. This provides three advantages:

• Compressed data usually occupies 1.5 to 2 times less space.

• There's physically only one file on the disk, so the problem of wasting space when sectors are combined into clusters is avoided.

• With a powerful PC, the time required to compress data is balanced by a decrease in the time it takes to write and subsequently read the data. Overall performance doesn't suffer.

However, there's one important disadvantage. When there is a problem, the unusual structure of the files makes recovering data much more difficult. Also, because all files reside within one large, compressed file, if that file gets corrupted *all* your data is at risk.

75

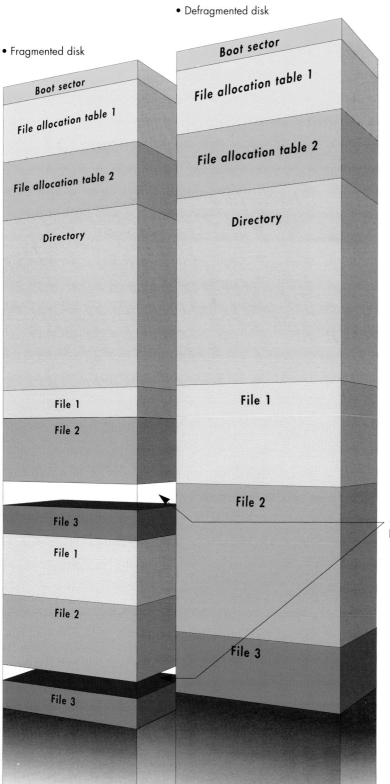

• Defragmented disk

• Fragmented disk

Boot sector

File allocation table 1

File allocation table 2

Directory

File 1

File 2

File 3

File 1

File 2

File 3

Boot sector

File allocation table 1

File allocation table 2

Directory

File 1

File 2

File 3

• These spaces are caused by the deletion of old files.

How the processor accesses a disk

When a program wants to access data on a disk, it has to follow a very specific procedure involving several steps. Following this procedure allows several different programs coexisting in memory to access the disk without getting in each other's way. Programmers are often tempted to bypass some of the intermediate steps to speed up data access. When PCs could load only one program at a time, flouting disk access conventions didn't cause many problems. (The major drawback was that those programs would not work on all PC compatibles.) Nowadays, especially with the arrival of graphical interfaces such as Windows, it's essential that programs follow all the disk access conventions.

• When an application running under Windows wants to load a file from disk into memory, it accesses the data using the Windows environment access conventions.

APPLICATION WINDOWS DOS BIOS DISK CONTROLLER MEMORY

File name

• For any disk access, Windows almost always uses the disk operating system (DOS), transmitting its request using DOS disk access conventions.

APPLICATION WINDOWS DOS BIOS DISK CONTROLLER MEMORY

File name

• DOS builds a structure used for accessing the file (the file descriptor) and asks the BIOS for the sectors corresponding to the clusters occupied by the file, using DOS sector ID numbers. If the file isn't found, an error message is sent to Windows, which then sends an error message on to the application.

APPLICATION WINDOWS DOS BIOS DISK CONTROLLER MEMORY

DOS sector number

• The BIOS transmits the request to the disk controller using the logical addresses (cylinders, heads, sectors) of the requested sectors.

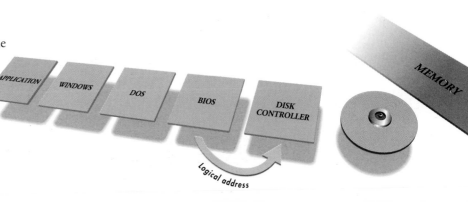

APPLICATION WINDOWS DOS BIOS DISK CONTROLLER MEMORY

Logical address

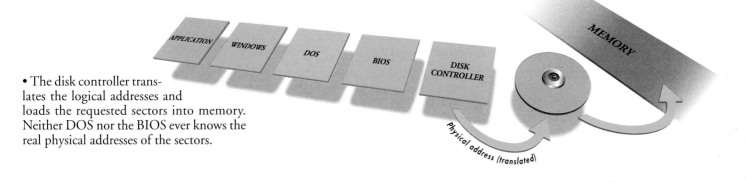

• The disk controller translates the logical addresses and loads the requested sectors into memory. Neither DOS nor the BIOS ever knows the real physical addresses of the sectors.

• If the disk operation succeeds, the controller sends the appropriate message to the BIOS. If the disk operation fails, the controller tries again. If it doesn't succeed after several attempts, the controller sends an error message to the BIOS.

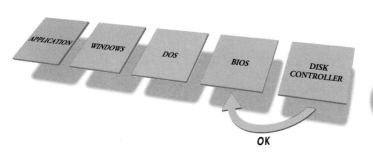

OK

• After the BIOS receives a success message from the disk controller, it in turn sends a message indicating success to DOS. If the BIOS has received an error message from the disk controller, the BIOS tries several more times before sending an error message to DOS.

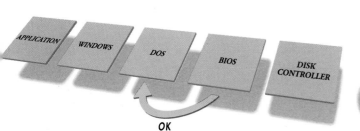

OK

• When DOS receives the message that the disk operation was a success, DOS sends the file's descriptor to Windows, which transmits it to the application. The application can then use the data in memory. If the disk operation fails, an error message is displayed. You can then choose between aborting or retrying the disk access.

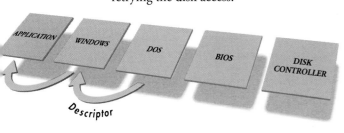

Descriptor

When a disk access error message is displayed, it usually is useless to repeat the operation if the problem hasn't been resolved. (Often, the problem is either that a removable disk or floppy disk isn't inserted properly, or that you tried to save data on a write-protected disk.) Whenever there's a problem, both the BIOS and the disk controller always make several access attempts. So you can be pretty sure that if an error is displayed, it's not just some random error.

Using a disk cache

Cache memory is perfectly suited for speeding disk accesses, especially because disks are so much slower than the processor. Two types of caching exist: setting aside main memory for a cache (called a *software cache*) or installing an independent cache controller (a *hardware cache*).

Software cache

This type of cache doesn't require any cache-specific hardware other than enough memory. A software cache reserves part of main memory (RAM) for use as a disk cache. The cache controller is a program executed by the PC's processor. The controller program is resident in memory and intercepts all disk accesses. A software cache has numerous advantages:

• The cost is low—the only hardware you have to add is memory. However, don't forget that your current computer hardware dic-

tates how easy it is to add memory. If, for example, you have to use an expansion card to add memory and you don't have any free slots, additional memory could be quite costly.

• Upgrading the cache controller is extremely easy—you only have to replace the cache controller program to gain performance benefits.

• Some configuration options are available only with this type of cache. SMARTDRV.EXE, the cache controller program provided with DOS and Windows, allows automatic adjustment of the amount of memory dedicated to the cache depending on whether Windows is in use.

• The controller can work with all types of disk drives, even those with a device-specific interface (a CD-ROM, for example).

The main drawback is that the processor can't do anything else while managing the cache memory. This limits overall processor performance.

Hardware cache

A hardware cache consists of dedicated memory on a disk interface card along with a dedicated processor to control caching operations. The main advantage of a hardware cache is high performance, but there are several drawbacks:

• The cache controller is an added expense.

• Dedicated cache memory can never be used for another purpose.

• Cache memory works only with those disk drives addressed by the interface. (A caching IDE interface can't cache a CD-ROM, for example.)

• The cache control program is in read-only memory on the interface card. Upgrading the program can be expensive, and sometimes impossible. Some disk interface cards with cache memory can't be used with the next generation of the computer.

How a cache works

A disk cache uses the same techniques as an internal memory cache.

• When the BIOS wants to upload a sector, the cache controller looks for it in cache memory.

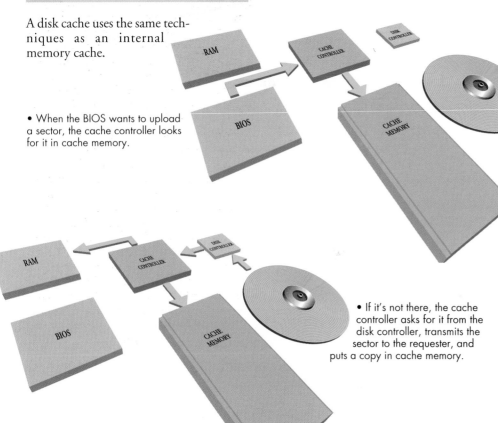

• If it's not there, the cache controller asks for it from the disk controller, transmits the sector to the requester, and puts a copy in cache memory.

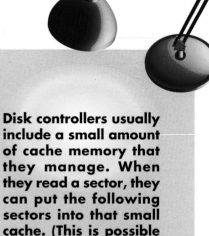

Disk controllers usually include a small amount of cache memory that they manage. When they read a sector, they can put the following sectors into that small cache. (This is possible because modern disk drives can read all the sectors of a track in a single operation. Older disks couldn't read more than two or three sectors at a time.)

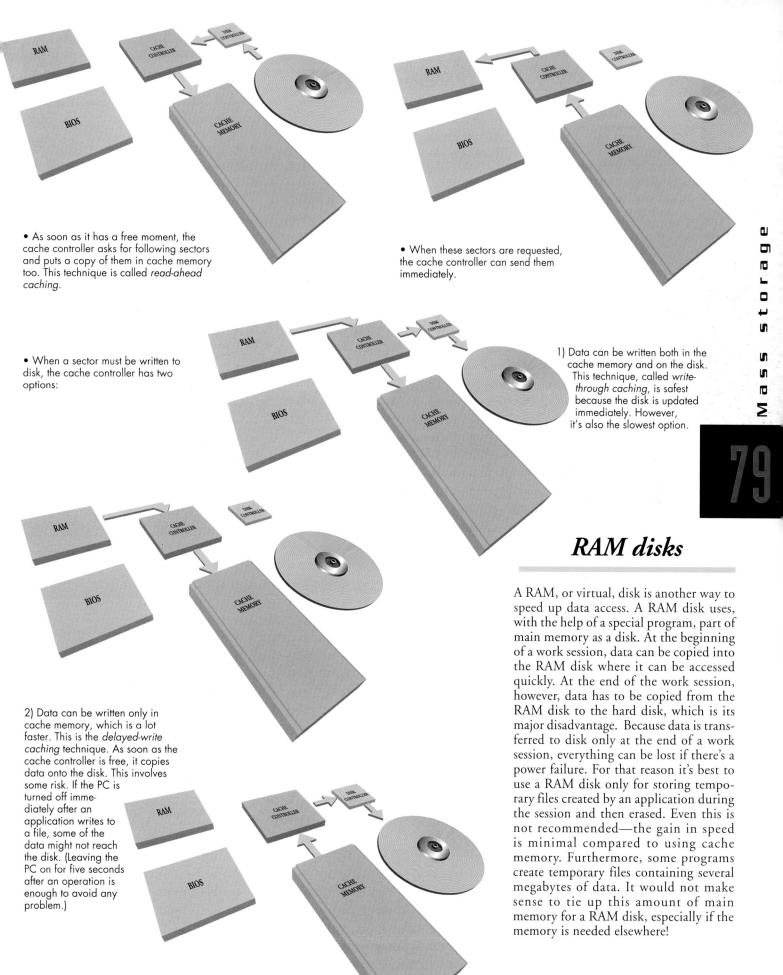

• As soon as it has a free moment, the cache controller asks for following sectors and puts a copy of them in cache memory too. This technique is called *read-ahead caching*.

• When these sectors are requested, the cache controller can send them immediately.

• When a sector must be written to disk, the cache controller has two options:

1) Data can be written both in the cache memory and on the disk. This technique, called *write-through caching*, is safest because the disk is updated immediately. However, it's also the slowest option.

79

2) Data can be written only in cache memory, which is a lot faster. This is the *delayed-write caching* technique. As soon as the cache controller is free, it copies data onto the disk. This involves some risk. If the PC is turned off immediately after an application writes to a file, some of the data might not reach the disk. (Leaving the PC on for five seconds after an operation is enough to avoid any problem.)

RAM disks

A RAM, or virtual, disk is another way to speed up data access. A RAM disk uses, with the help of a special program, part of main memory as a disk. At the beginning of a work session, data can be copied into the RAM disk where it can be accessed quickly. At the end of the work session, however, data has to be copied from the RAM disk to the hard disk, which is its major disadvantage. Because data is transferred to disk only at the end of a work session, everything can be lost if there's a power failure. For that reason it's best to use a RAM disk only for storing temporary files created by an application during the session and then erased. Even this is not recommended—the gain in speed is minimal compared to using cache memory. Furthermore, some programs create temporary files containing several megabytes of data. It would not make sense to tie up this amount of main memory for a RAM disk, especially if the memory is needed elsewhere!

Changing or adding an IDE hard disk drive

You can increase your PC's mass storage capacity in two ways: you can replace a hard disk drive with another drive that has more storage capacity, or you can add another disk drive. The second option usually seems like the best solution, but it's not always available. There are two potential problems. The first is that an IDE interface usually allows for only two disk drives. If your PC already has two hard drives, you must replace one of them to increase storage capacity.

The second problem has to do with compatibility between drives. In theory, all IDE drives can work together. However, in a two-drive system, one of the drives must be configured as the master and the other as the slave. This relationship requires operational compatibility between the two controllers, and this doesn't always exist. Choosing both disks from the same manufacturer usually solves the problem.

When you add or replace a drive, you'll need to take a few precautions while you handle and configure it—disk drives are delicate devices.

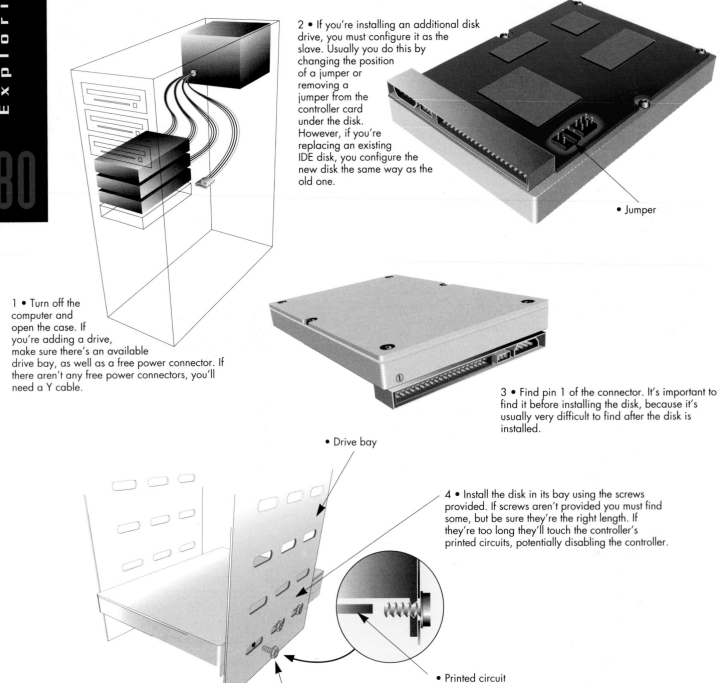

2 • If you're installing an additional disk drive, you must configure it as the slave. Usually you do this by changing the position of a jumper or removing a jumper from the controller card under the disk. However, if you're replacing an existing IDE disk, you configure the new disk the same way as the old one.

• Jumper

1 • Turn off the computer and open the case. If you're adding a drive, make sure there's an available drive bay, as well as a free power connector. If there aren't any free power connectors, you'll need a Y cable.

3 • Find pin 1 of the connector. It's important to find it before installing the disk, because it's usually very difficult to find after the disk is installed.

• Drive bay

4 • Install the disk in its bay using the screws provided. If screws aren't provided you must find some, but be sure they're the right length. If they're too long they'll touch the controller's printed circuits, potentially disabling the controller.

• Printed circuit

• Screws

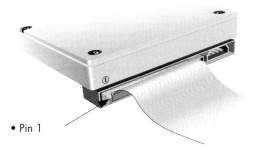

• Pin 1

5 • Connect the data cable to the disk. The data cable is a flat cable with a colored wire on one side to indicate where pin 1 is located. The cable should already be connected to the first disk drive and usually has a second unused connector.

6 • Plug in the power cable (it's a keyed connector so if it's difficult to insert, turn it around) and put the case back on the PC.

7 • Reset your computer's BIOS configuration to include the new disk drive. The exact procedure depends on the type of BIOS in your computer, but you'll need to enter the number of cylinders, heads, and sectors of the new drive, as well as the write precompensation cylinder number and the head-parking cylinder. The values you'll enter are logical values rather than physical values (the controller does the translation). Check your drive's documentation for the correct values to use, although theoretically you can use any values as long as they don't exceed the BIOS limits (1024 cylinders, 16 heads, and 64 sectors) or the drive's capacity. The last step is to partition and format the hard disk drive.

Adding a SCSI disk

With SCSI disk drives, the limit on the number of drives that can be installed is rarely a problem—up to eight peripherals can be installed. However, you still must take the same precautions when handling and configuring the drive. The main difference is that SCSI peripherals are chained. The interface is linked to the first peripheral, which is linked to the second, and so on. The first step is to find the number of a free link in the chain. Peripherals are numbered from 0 to 7. You choose a free number and assign it to the hard disk drive using jumpers.

You must remove the terminator from the last peripheral on the chain and put it on the hard disk drive (assuming you put the hard drive in at the end of the chain).

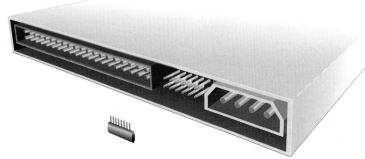

Usually, you'll also have to install a special program called a device driver, because SCSI drives aren't directly controlled and managed by the BIOS. (This, among other things, allows SCSI drives to have a higher storage capacity than the upper limits dictated by the BIOS.)

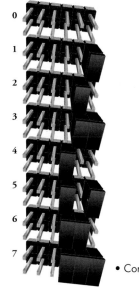

0
1
2
3
4
5
6
7

• Configuration jumpers

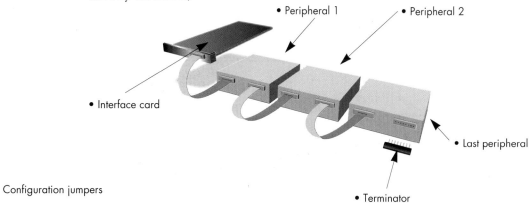

• Peripheral 1   • Peripheral 2

• Interface card

• Last peripheral

• Terminator

Data security

Data security is an important issue that isn't directly linked to the use of computers, but its importance has grown exponentially since computers were invented. When data was kept on paper, security problems were easy to handle (if not to solve). With a piece of paper, it's easy to see how to keep data secure. If you put a piece of paper in a safe, it will always be there, and as long as that is the only copy of that piece of paper, nobody but you will be able to read it. If you crumple it up and throw it in the garbage, you know very well that anyone can find it and read it. If you tear a piece of paper in two pieces, you can still read half of it. With computers, it's all different. You can't (usually) put your computer in a safe. When you put a copy of the computer's data in a safe, you've created a backup in case data is lost (you have achieved data integrity), but the original data is still on the hard disk (you haven't achieved data confidentiality). Deleting the original isn't much more efficient than throwing a piece of paper in the garbage, because it's often possible to retrieve a deleted file. On the other hand, you can sometimes lose access to an entire file if only one character of the file is destroyed! It's important that you not only know, but also take, the steps necessary to keep your data secure.

Backing up data

With computers, always assume that the worst will happen. It's computer technology's version of Murphy's law. If a power failure or disk crash can happen, it will, one day. If you expect to get away with not backing up your data, experience will soon give you reason to change that view.

To avoid potential problems, be sure to follow all of the procedures described in books and manufacturers' documentation. However, even this won't completely prevent problems from happening. One day your hard drive will fail and you won't be able to read its contents. Don't think it can't happen to you. It will—as everybody knows who's had car problems at one time or another. What's important is to make every effort to limit the damage, and for that there's only one solution: backing up your data.

Backing up data is simply making a copy of the data you'll want to be able to retrieve if a problem arises. It can be done on floppy disks, removable disks, magnetic tapes, etc. Backing up data is different from archiving data, although the methods are the same. Different backup strategies offer different levels of security.

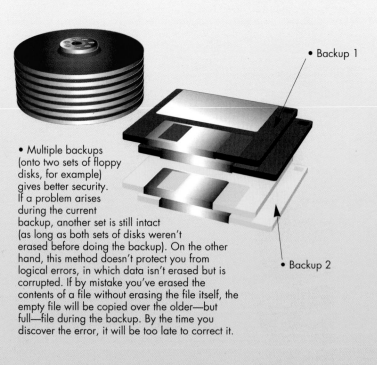

• Backup 1

• Backup 2

• Backing up on only one medium (floppy disks, for example) gives very limited security, because before copying the data over a previous backup, the diskettes' current contents must first be erased. If a problem arises during the latest backup, chances are you'll lose much of your data.

• Multiple backups (onto two sets of floppy disks, for example) gives better security. If a problem arises during the current backup, another set is still intact (as long as both sets of disks weren't erased before doing the backup). On the other hand, this method doesn't protect you from logical errors, in which data isn't erased but is corrupted. If by mistake you've erased the contents of a file without erasing the file itself, the empty file will be copied over the older—but full—file during the backup. By the time you discover the error, it will be too late to correct it.

• Backing up data

Backup techniques

There are lots of backup techniques. If every day you back up all your data, you unnecessarily copy data that has not changed since the last backup. You need only back up data that's been modified or added since your last backup. To do this, you must use a specialized program to manage what's known as *incremental* and *differential* backups. Incremental and differential backup techniques copy only files that have been changed; the other files on your computer are not saved, nor are the corresponding files on your backup disks overwritten. However, these types of backups are not risk-free—so when your disk fails, you might still have a difficult time reconstructing its contents. Furthermore, those techniques don't manage deleted files (or do so poorly). So even though you voluntarily delete a file from the hard disk drive, the backup program doesn't delete it from your backup disks. Another drawback to these techniques is that each backup session will add a number of floppy disks to your backup set.

The best way to eliminate these problems consists of backing up all your data to a medium with enough storage capacity to accommodate the entire backup (to a magnetic tape, for example). If that's not possible, try to decrease the quantity of data on your disk by archiving the files you don't work on every day (save them on disks and then reload them only when you need to use them). You can also separately back up data that doesn't change often or that is easy to retrieve (applications, for example). Don't forget, though, that when a problem arises, it will take a while to restore everything to the hard disk drive. That's when you'll appreciate only having to copy the contents of a single magnetic tape.

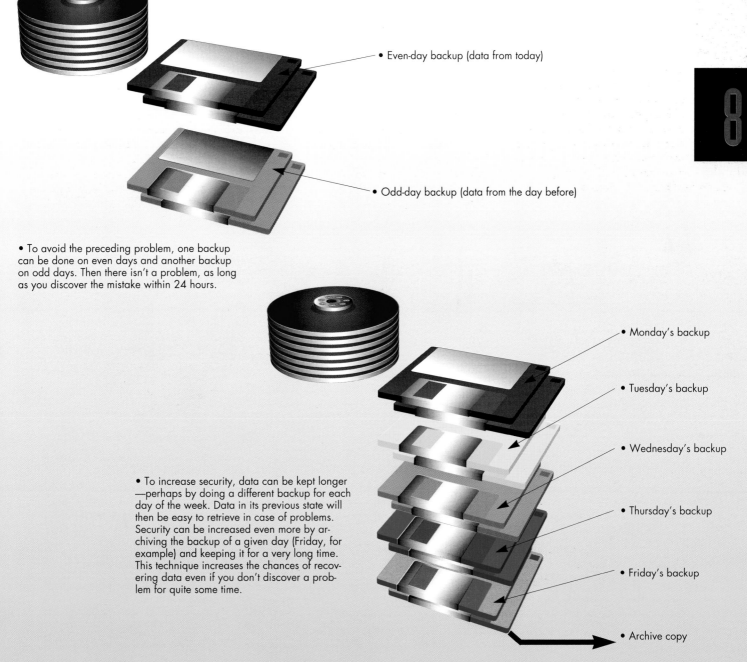

• Even-day backup (data from today)

• Odd-day backup (data from the day before)

• To avoid the preceding problem, one backup can be done on even days and another backup on odd days. Then there isn't a problem, as long as you discover the mistake within 24 hours.

• To increase security, data can be kept longer —perhaps by doing a different backup for each day of the week. Data in its previous state will then be easy to retrieve in case of problems. Security can be increased even more by archiving the backup of a given day (Friday, for example) and keeping it for a very long time. This technique increases the chances of recovering data even if you don't discover a problem for quite some time.

• Monday's backup

• Tuesday's backup

• Wednesday's backup

• Thursday's backup

• Friday's backup

• Archive copy

Common ways of losing data

You can lose data in numerous and varied ways. Hardware problems, or complete hardware failure, are major causes of data loss. However, many incidents that aren't hardware-related also lead to data loss. You can't totally avoid losing data, but you can easily minimize the damage by understanding how things work.

The most common ways of losing data that don't involve hardware failure are accidental file deletion, accidental disk formatting, and corruption of the file allocation table. The first two can be avoided by taking the right precautions.

Checking the name of a file before deleting it and reading confirmation messages carefully before formatting a disk will suffice. Corruption of the file allocation table can be caused by four things: the incorrect use of a utility program that modifies the table, a virus, turning off the computer (intentionally or accidentally) while a file is being written, or changing floppy disks after a write error. In every case, the files can no longer be accessed, because the information in the file allocation table is either wrong or missing.

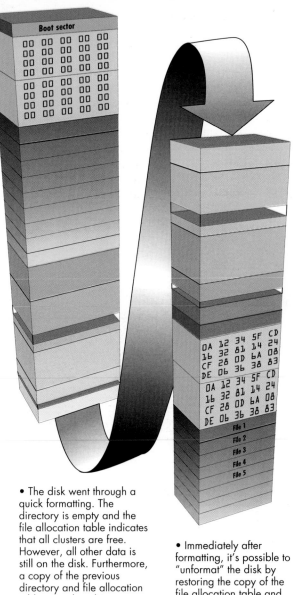

• The disk went through a quick formatting. The directory is empty and the file allocation table indicates that all clusters are free. However, all other data is still on the disk. Furthermore, a copy of the previous directory and file allocation table was placed in a different location on the disk.

• Immediately after formatting, it's possible to "unformat" the disk by restoring the copy of the file allocation table and directory.

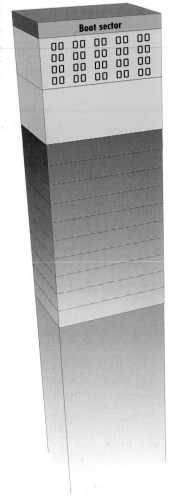

• The disk was just formatted. The file allocation table indicates that all clusters are free. The directory is empty.

• After many work sessions, the disk now contains numerous files. The directory contains file names along with the address of each file's first cluster. The file allocation table contains the list of each file's following clusters.

Page 74 illustrated how it's sometimes possible to retrieve a deleted file. Often, accidental formatting can also be reversed. When you format a disk for the first time, the formatting program lays out pristine tracks and sectors, and the newly formatted disk contains no data at all. On the other hand, if you format a disk that already contains data without specifically requesting its destruction, the formatting process is completely different.

Cross-linked files

Cross-linked files are files that share (through an error in allocation) one or more of the same clusters. Cross-linking of files is a frequent problem, although its causes are sometimes obscure. The DOS disk verification programs CHKDSK and SCANDISK, among others, will show you when files are cross-linked. CHKDSK has a strange way of solving the problem—it truncates the files, which makes them practically unusable. There is, however, an easy way to deal with this problem. If two files are cross-linked, copy each of them under a different name. Chances are that one of the two copies will be intact.

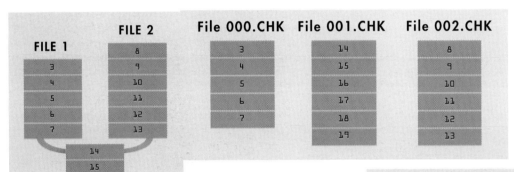

DIRECTORY	CLUSTER	SIZE
FILE 1	2	
FILE 2	8	

FILE ALLOCATION TABLE						
0	1 / 3	2 / 4	3 / 5	4 / 6	5 / 7	6
7 / 14	8 / 9	9 / 10	10 / 11	11 / 12	12 / 13	13 / 14
14 / 15	15 / 16	16 / 17	17 / 18	18 / 19	19 / end	20 / 0
21 / 0	22 / 0	23 / 0	24 / 0	25 / 0	26 / 0	27 / 0
28 / 0	29 / 0	30 / 0	31 / 0	32 / 0	33 / 0	34 / 0
35 / 0	36 / 0	37 / 0	38 / 0	39 / 0	40 / 0	41 / 0
42 / 0	43 / 0	44 / 0	45 / 0	46 / 0	47 / 0	48 / 0

• These two files are cross-linked. The file allocation table indicates that they both use sectors 14 to 19.

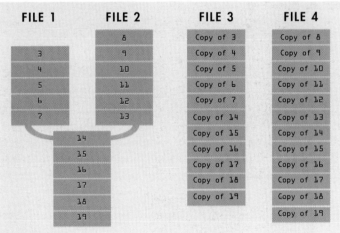

• CHKDSK makes three unusable pieces out of them.

• A simple copy often allows you to retrieve one of the two files. (The original files then have to be erased.)

Data confidentiality

The fact that you can retrieve deleted files and unformat disks can also have negative consequences. If you think you've destroyed confidential data by deleting the files or formatting the disk, you could be in for some surprises. In fact, anyone can copy the data that you "deleted." This problem often happens with floppy disks. When you format a floppy disk to pass files to a friend or coworker, all the "free" space on that disk actually contains the data that was there before formatting. The only way you can truly delete all of the files is to do an *unconditional format*, by adding the /U switch to the end of your FORMAT command. For the same reasons, if you want to make sure that a given file is totally deleted, you must use a special program that replaces all the old data with 0s.

Viruses

Viruses are the most widely known threat to computers and data. They are also among the easiest problems to prevent. The main danger from viruses comes from believing that they happen only to other people. That's why those who already have been victims of computer viruses always take the proper precautions. However, most users who've never had to deal with a virus take practically no precautions. Some even doubt that viruses exist. Protecting your computer against viruses is easy and doesn't require any special software. All you have to do is avoid actions that potentially expose your system to viruses. However, since no one is completely protected from accidents, it's a good idea to use an antivirus program just in case.

What is a virus ?

A *virus* is a program, written by a programmer. Although a virus is a foreign and sometimes destructive entity whose reproduction mode is similar to a human virus, the similarity stops there. When a virus is placed on your hard disk drive, the computer doesn't become "sick." It works absolutely normally. It's just executing a program written by someone who, most often, wants to scare or harm other people by tampering with their data. Sometimes, the goal of the virus is simply to cause as much damage as possible. Although not as common, other virus authors have terrorist goals and demand a ransom for eliminating the effects

of the virus. Most often, viruses are the work of irresponsible programmers who simply want to prove how clever they are. Sometimes, viruses are programs written with an altruistic goal but, because of programming errors, end up causing countless problems. For example, some programmers wrote "virus hunter" programs that used the same techniques as their enemies to distribute themselves. Unfortunately, it turns out that these programs often did more harm than good.

A virus consists of two programs with independent functions. The goal of the first program is to reproduce the virus—it creates as many copies of itself as it can. The second program in the virus executes some action

to either destroy data or simply show its presence and scoff at the user. During the propagation phase (the incubation period), the virus is very discreet. Only the first virus reproduction program is executed. At a certain moment (perhaps a precise date, or when a sufficient number of copies of the virus have been made, or when the user performs a specific action), the second program is executed. It can, for example, format the hard disk drive (all data is lost), damage the drive (by programming the controller to put the read head on a track that doesn't exist), display a political or humorous message, or simply make the display impossible to read (by reversing the text or making the characters dance, for example).

Executable-file viruses

There are two main categories of viruses. The first attacks executable files (programs). The second, and much more harmful virus, attacks an area on the hard drive called the *boot sector*.

All viruses must find a way to get onto your hard disk drive. Viruses that plague pro-

grams most often use the *Trojan Horse method*—a program insidiously placed on a floppy disk or *server* (the computer that runs a network) is named to entice users to execute it. Most often, it appears to be a game or utility program. This type of virus

contains two programs. The second is an actual game or utility program, but the first, executed without your knowledge, is the virus.

• You'll find, on a floppy disk or server, an executable program that seems interesting. You copy it to your hard disk drive. In fact, it's a virus along with a game.

VIRUS

Game

Word processor

Accounting program

Spreadsheet

VIRUS

Game

Word processor

Accounting program

Spreadsheet

• You execute the program. The virus part runs for a few seconds, and then the game starts. Without your knowledge, the virus has put copies of itself into some of your executable files.

Boot sector viruses can use the Trojan Horse technique to get onto your hard disk. Some are even able to contaminate both boot sectors and files. Virus-detection programs are able to identify a certain number of viruses because they know their *signature* (typical characteristics

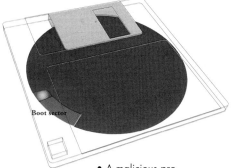

• You erase the game from your hard disk (or you give a copy to a friend!) and forget about it. However, as soon as you execute one of the contaminated programs, it contaminates other programs. It looks for victims on all disks of your system, and it will eventually contaminate a program on a floppy disk. If you loan that floppy disk to someone, the epidemic will spread.

• One fine morning, you turn on your computer and a sardonic message appears on the screen. Your hard disk drive has just been format-ted and contains no more data! Protection against such viruses is very simple. If you never execute questionable programs, you'll never have problems. However, if your disk is already infected, you'll have to use an antivirus program. It should be emphasized that the presence of such viruses is easy to detect, because they increase the size of files. Some viruses even infect files that were already infected. In this case, disk space use continues to increase and the virus eventually brings the system to its knees by filling the hard disk drive.

Boot sector viruses

This type of virus is much more harmful than an executable-file virus. The first sector of a disk or floppy disk always contains a program. If it's a system disk (one that includes a copy of the operating system), the program simply loads the system. If it's not a system disk, this program simply displays a message indicating that it doesn't contain the system. The boot sector program of your hard disk drive is therefore executed each time you turn on your PC. If a floppy disk is in a drive, the program on its boot sector is executed. If you want to test this, format a floppy disk, leave it in the drive, turn off your computer, and turn it back on. You'll see a message indicating that it's not a system disk.

• A malicious pro-grammer placed a virus in the boot sector of this floppy disk.

•f the program). They can also detect when the size of files increases and when boot sectors do not contain the usual program. Unfortunately, some viruses recognize detection programs and are able to send them a correct image of the boot sector. Progress never ceases—even for the bad guys!

• If you turn on your computer with the disk in the drive, the boot sector program is executed. The virus puts a copy of itself on the boot sector of the hard disk.

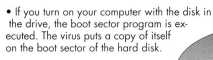

• Virus

• From now on, the virus is executed every time the computer is turned on. The virus then contaminates every disk and floppy disk it comes in contact with. Some of these viruses can even stay in memory until the computer is turned off, increasing their chances of contaminating another file or disk. The way to prevent this type of virus is obvious. Never turn on your computer with a floppy disk from a doubtful source in the drive.

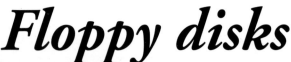
Floppy disks

When PCs first appeared, using hard disk drives was out of the question—they were much too big and expensive. The only medium available to record data was the floppy disk. (In fact, the very first PCs didn't even have a floppy disk drive—they had only a tape recorder interface!) The first PC floppy disks were 5.25-inch disks that were miniature versions of the 8-inch disks used in computers up until then. The first floppy disks could store 160 KB on single-sided disks and 320 KB on double-sided disks. After techniques rapidly increased disk capacity to 360 KB (by formatting 9 sectors rather than 8), several years went by before standards advanced and high-density 1.2 MB floppy disks were introduced. Today, a new format, rigid 3.5-inch floppy disks, is in common use. Their capacity keeps increasing, from 720 KB when they were introduced, to 1.44 MB and now to 2.88 MB. When hard disk drives weren't common, floppy disks were used as a mass storage medium. Today, they are used for archiving data and exchanging data and programs. Even these two uses are losing their importance. Archiving is now often done using magnetic tapes, and the growth of local area networks and modems reduces the need for using floppy disks to exchange data. Software is still mostly sold on floppy disks, but because the size of programs keeps increasing, more and more software publishers are beginning to use compact disks (CD-ROMs) to distribute their products.

Anatomy of a 3.5-inch floppy disk

A floppy disk is a mylar (a form of plastic) disk coated with a magnetic film. The center of a 3.5-inch disk has a metal hub with a square hole for the drive pin.

The disk is enclosed in a rigid plastic case to protect it against shock, dust, and other hazards. This plastic case has an opening at the center that exposes the hub. Another opening gives the read heads access to the magnetic surface. This opening is protected by a moveable metallic cover that itself has an opening. When the floppy disk is inserted in the disk drive, the cover slides sideways so the opening in the cover matches the opening in the plastic case, giving the read heads access to the magnetic surface. When the floppy disk is ejected from the drive, a spring slides the cover back to its original position.

The floppy disk also has one or two square openings on the plastic case opposite the metallic cover. The one on the right (looking from the front) is on every disk and can be blocked with a plastic tab. When the opening is blocked, data can be read and written on the floppy disk. When it's open, the disk can be read but not written to, making the disk *write-protected*.

The opening on the left side of the disk indicates that it's a 1.44 MB high-density floppy disk. Disks with 720 KB do not have that opening.

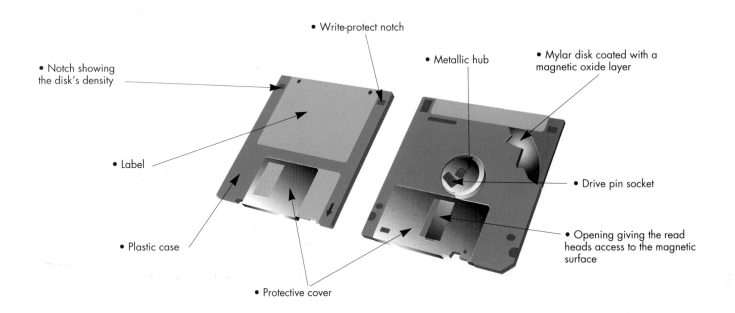

- Write-protect notch
- Metallic hub
- Mylar disk coated with a magnetic oxide layer
- Notch showing the disk's density
- Label
- Plastic case
- Protective cover
- Drive pin socket
- Opening giving the read heads access to the magnetic surface

Floppy disk drives

A floppy disk drive has a front opening (protected by a plastic cover) for inserting the floppy disk. When in position, the floppy disk locks in place automatically. When you insert the disk in the drive, the floppy disk compresses a spring. Pushing the eject button releases the spring and ejects the floppy disk. The faceplate of the drive also has an indicator light that's on when the drive is reading or writing data. When the light is

on, never eject the floppy disk or turn the PC's power off. If you do either, you could lose data and damage the drive.

When a floppy disk is inserted in the drive, its metallic cover is automatically shifted by a mechanism that places

disk's rotation speed is much lower than that of a hard disk drive (300 RPM as compared to 3600 RPM). Also, unlike a hard disk

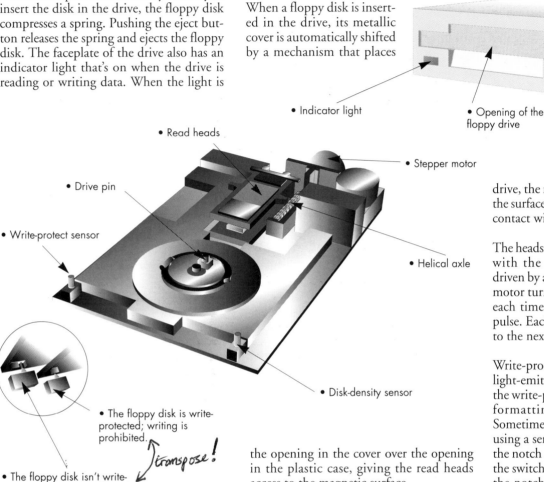

- Indicator light
- Opening of the floppy drive
- Eject button
- Read heads
- Stepper motor
- Drive pin
- Write-protect sensor
- Helical axle
- Disk-density sensor
- The floppy disk is write-protected; writing is prohibited.
- The floppy disk isn't write-protected; writing is allowed.

transpose!

drive, the read/write heads aren't held above the surface of the disk but rather are in direct contact with it.

The heads move from front to back with the help of a helical axle driven by a *stepper motor*. A stepper motor turns through a given angle each time it receives an electrical pulse. Each pulse moves the heads to the next track.

Write-protect status can be detected using a light-emitting diode. If light goes through the write-protect notch, writing, erasing, or formatting the disk is prohibited. Sometimes, write-protect status is detected using a sensor containing a microswitch. If the notch is closed, inserting the disk closes the switch and writing is then permitted. If the notch is open, the arm of the switch extends into the notch, the switch is not closed, and writing is prohibited. The same method is used to determine the density (capacity) of a floppy disk.

the opening in the cover over the opening in the plastic case, giving the read heads access to the magnetic surface.

The disk is driven by an electric motor whose drive pin is inserted in the drive pin socket in the floppy disk's hub. A floppy

Some users punch a hole in the case of 720 KB floppy disks to make high-density disks out of them. This sometimes works, but not always. Floppy disks are *certified,* which means they are guaranteed to be error-free for a given data density. In one manufactured batch, some disks can be significantly over the certified standards while others just achieve them. Using disks for a density higher than the one guaranteed is therefore risky. In any case, never make holes in the disk's case using a drill! Drilling can produce chaff—little plastic shavings that get inside the plastic case and damage the read heads. Although you can buy a special tool to punch holes in disks, if you care about your data, don't take the chance of storing it on substandard media.

CD-ROM (compact disk read-only memory)

The compact disk or CD-ROM is the mass storage medium that's currently gaining most rapid acceptance. Until recently, it was used only by those who could afford, or had good reason to buy, such an expensive device. Nowadays, compact disk drives are much less expensive and readily available. The more users take advantage of compact disks, the more software publishers become interested in using this medium to distribute their software. Unlike floppy disks, CD-ROMs are *pressed* from a *master copy* instead of being recorded one by one. It's expensive to produce just a few copies of a CD-ROM, but as soon as a few thousand are made, the cost drops very quickly. CD-ROMs have other advantages for publishers, the most important being that they are difficult to copy, so the risk of software piracy is much lower. For users, the advantages are even greater. First, the fact that there is less risk of piracy leads to significantly lower prices for the software. Also, installation is much simpler. There is no need to sit in front of a PC for an hour just to install the 24 diskettes necessary for a word processor, for example. The performance of CD-ROM drives never ceases to improve, and some software can even be used directly from the CD-ROM instead of having to be transferred to disk, which makes installation very simple. However, manufacturers must create distribution and upgrade disks with more caution. If many hundreds of thousands of CD disks are manufactured and then errors are found, those disks must be disposed of because they cannot be reused. However, a new technology allows the creation of *multisession* disks, which can be recorded at different times. While it's not possible to change existing data, these disks do allow new data to be added; thus they can be reused until they are full.

How a CD-ROM works

A CD-ROM is a disk made of a layer of reflective aluminum sandwiched between two layers of transparent plastic. Data is represented by tiny *pits* (indentations) and *lands* (flat spaces) in the reflective material. A beam, emitted by a laser, is reflected from the surface and picked up by a photodetector serving as the read head.

When there's a pit in the surface, the beam is scattered instead of reflected—a much smaller portion of the laser's light reaches the photodetector. The electronic circuitry converts these variations in reflected light into data.

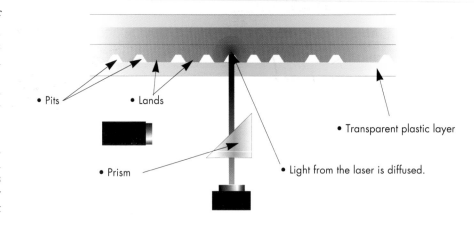

• Pits
• Lands
• Transparent plastic layer
• Prism
• Light from the laser is diffused.

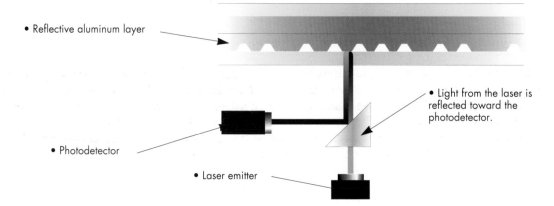

• Reflective aluminum layer
• Light from the laser is reflected toward the photodetector.
• Photodetector
• Laser emitter

The CD-ROM drive

The mechanism of a CD-ROM drive is similar to that of a floppy disk drive. It has one motor for rotating the disk and another for moving the laser head, which is guided by slides. A third motor drives the disk insertion and ejection mechanism. The disk can be placed in a drawer or in a protective case called a *caddy*. A button on the front of the disk drive activates the motorized ejection of the disk. A headphone jack and a volume control knob can also be found on the front of most units. Special software enables almost all CD-ROM drives to play audio disks.

CD-ROM drives transfer data at different rates, depending on whether they are single, double, triple, or quadruple speed. It is very likely that drives that are even faster will soon be available. Nowadays, a double-speed drive is the minimum necessary to be able to fully use the latest multimedia software.

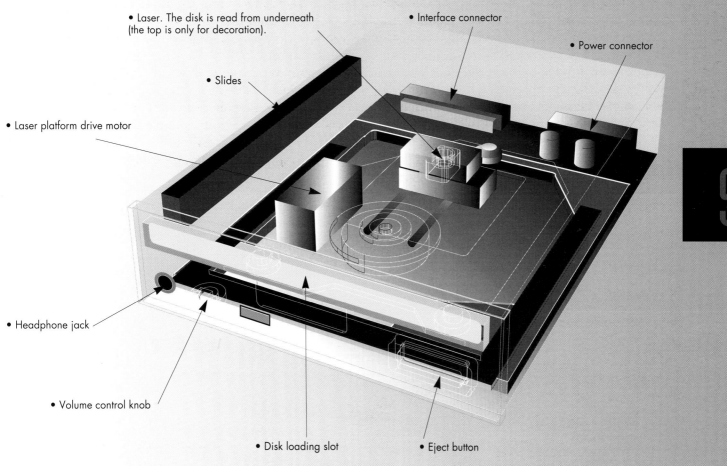

• Laser. The disk is read from underneath (the top is only for decoration).

• Interface connector

• Power connector

• Slides

• Laser platform drive motor

• Headphone jack

• Volume control knob

• Disk loading slot

• Eject button

Unlike floppy disks or hard disk drives, a compact disk isn't divided into cylinders. Data is contained on a single track, which consists of sectors one after the other in a continuous spiral. Sectors are all the same size, so disk rotation speed must be varied continuously as the read head moves from the outside to the center. This makes it possible to read data continuously (which is a basic requirement of an audio CD). On the other hand, accessing data in the middle of the disk can take longer.

Removable disks and magnetic tapes

Data backup and archiving are important issues. Data exists and is maintained on hard disk drives. As with any mechanical component, disk drives are subject to failure. The value of the disk drive itself is minor compared to the work necessary to recreate the data that's lost when there's an accident. It's therefore important to back up data regularly on another medium. Also, the capacity of a hard drive is limited. Even the highest capacity drives will end up being filled if you don't regularly erase data that isn't needed anymore. Still, before erasing data, it's often necessary to archive it in case you need it later. Archiving and backup are operations that both use a removable medium, allowing for unlimited data storage. Floppy disks can be used, but their capacity is too small, compared to modern hard disk drives, to be appropriate for backups. On the other hand, they *can* be used for archiving. It's the cheapest solution, but not necessarily the most convenient.

Removable hard disks

Removable hard disk cartridges have only one platter, enclosed in a rigid plastic protective case. They come in 5.25- and 3.5-inch formats and offer from 40 to 100 MB capacity. The drives are available in internal (linked to the PC's power supply) and external (with their own power supply) versions. They use either a proprietary interface or a SCSI interface. They're very convenient for archiving but much less convenient for backing up, because their capacity is limited. They are also widely used to exchange files.

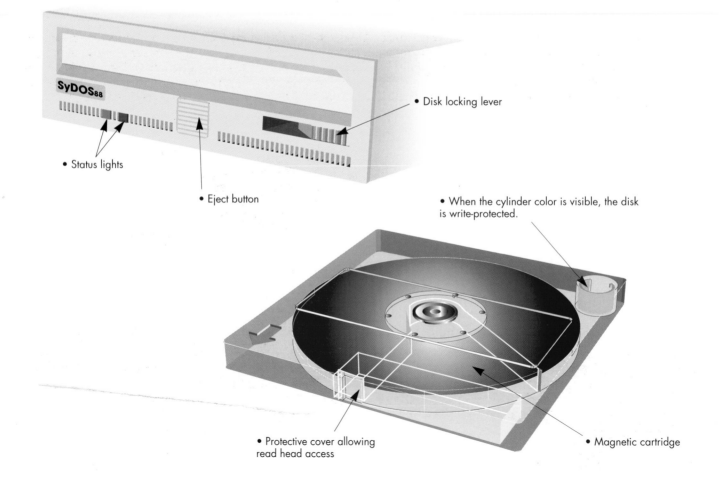

SyDOS88

• Disk locking lever

• Status lights

• Eject button

• When the cylinder color is visible, the disk is write-protected.

• Protective cover allowing read head access

• Magnetic cartridge

Magneto-optical disks

While removable hard disks use the same writing technique as fixed disks, magneto-optical disks operate under a totally different principal. A laser beam heats the surface of a disk covered with crystalline metal until the crystals are released and can be rearranged by a magnetic field. A read/write head, similar to that on a hard disk drive, then writes data by moving the crystals. The advantage is that the magnetized area is limited to the area heated by the laser. It's therefore much smaller than on a hard disk drive, which makes it easy for a 5.25-inch disk to contain up to 300 MB per side. To read the data, a low-intensity laser beam is projected onto the surface of the disk. The orientation of the magnetized crystals reflects the beam to a sensor similar to the one used in CD-ROM drives. Although this kind of disk is expensive, it can be used for archiving as well as backup because of its high capacity. These drives can read only one side at a time, so the disk has to be flipped over to access the other side.

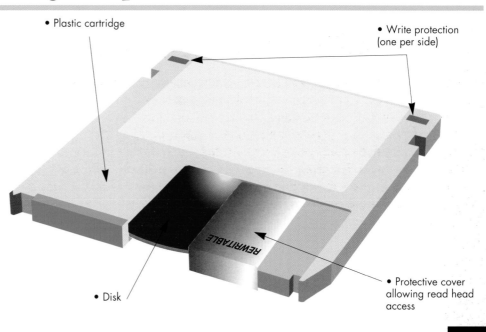

- Plastic cartridge
- Write protection (one per side)
- Protective cover allowing read head access
- Disk

REWRITABLE

Magnetic tapes

The most convenient and economical way to make backups is to use magnetic tape. Magnetic tapes come in different formats, and some have been specially developed for computers. Others are by-products of audio or video technologies. DAT (digital audio tape) or 4 mm magnetic tapes were created to record sound. They can contain up to 4 gigabytes of data. Data is recorded on linear tracks that run the length of the tape. 8 mm tapes are identical to videocamera tapes of the same size. Data is recorded in oblique lines using the same principal as in recording video images, and these tapes can contain up to 16 gigabytes.

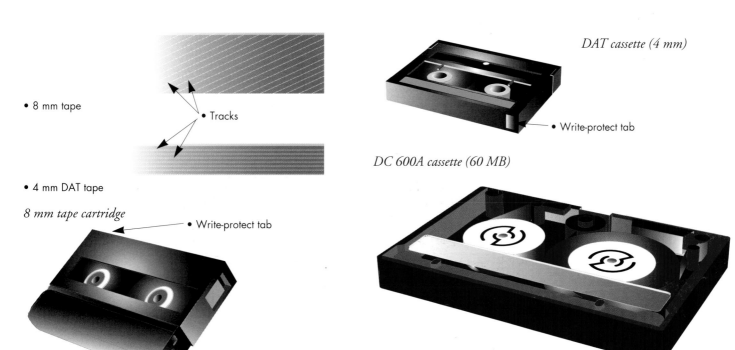

- 8 mm tape
- Tracks
- 4 mm DAT tape

DAT cassette (4 mm)

- Write-protect tab

DC 600A cassette (60 MB)

8 mm tape cartridge
- Write-protect tab

DISPLAYS AND DISPLAY CONTROLLERS

- How a color CRT monitor works.....96
- Display modes 100
- Liquid crystal displays 102
- Video animation 104

How a color CRT monitor works

A monitor is the output device essential to all PCs. It lets the computer communicate with the user. With the arrival of graphical interfaces, performance requirements of monitors have greatly increased. Early PCs had monochrome monitors displaying 25 lines of 80 characters in green on a black background. These monitors were incapable of displaying graphics. The first graphics monitors had a 640 x 200 pixel resolution and could display four colors simultaneously. In fact, this limitation was caused by the *video controller card* rather than the monitor itself. Monitors used today have improved greatly. They offer a much higher resolution and display more colors for a price often lower than that of the first monochrome monitors.

Basic principles

A color monitor has three electron guns emitting beams of electrons that hit a phosphor coating on the rear surface of a cathode ray tube (the screen that you look at), causing the point of impact (called a *pixel*) to glow. The three guns produce red, green, and blue dots respectively. The mix of these three colors creates all shades from black (no color) to white (all three colors at maximum intensity). The intensity of the electron beams determines the intensity of the colors.

The electron guns are aimed toward the center of the screen. To activate all points (pixels) on the screen, the beam has to be deflected. It goes through vertical and horizontal deflections, called *scanning*. Scanning starts in the upper-left corner (the beam is moved by the *deflection coil* to the side and top of the screen) and moves toward the upper-right corner. When a line has been scanned, the beam moves to the beginning of the next line, and so on until it reaches the bottom of the screen. Each pixel of the screen is therefore successively lit. The pixel continues to glow until the next scan because of a phenomenon called *persistence*—the phosphor takes a while to fade. The *vertical frequency* indicates the number of complete images displayed per second. This frequency can be 60 Hz or more. The *horizontal scanning frequency* indicates the number of lines displayed in a second. In theory, it should equal the vertical frequency multiplied by

the number of lines. In reality it's always greater, because the display of the first line doesn't start immediately after the display of the last line is complete. For a 480-line monitor with a vertical frequency of 60 Hz, the horizontal scanning frequency will be, for example, 31.5 KHz. Modern monitors are generally multifrequency to accommodate different resolutions. Obviously, there is no use having a monitor with a high vertical frequency if the horizontal frequency doesn't allow for the desired resolution. However, there is a way of overcoming this deficiency. It consists of displaying only odd lines during one scan of the screen and even lines on the next scan. This technique is called *interlacing*. The major disadvantage is that it takes longer for a pixel to be *refreshed*, which causes an annoying flicker in the image.

To make sure the electron beams light the pixels in their respective colors, they go through a metal plate punched with holes laid in staggered rows. This plate is called a *mask*. The distance between the holes is called the *dot pitch*. It determines the maximum number of displayable points, or the monitor's *resolution*.

• The three primary colors combine to produce all possible colors.

A monitor emits radiation that can be harmful to the user, so safety standards have been created by various organizations. Monitor manufacturers usually follow most of these standards, but not always all of them. It should be noted that American FCC standards are among the least strict. German (VDE and TUV) and European (CEI 950) standards are much more stringent. The MPR II Swedish standard offers the best protection for users.

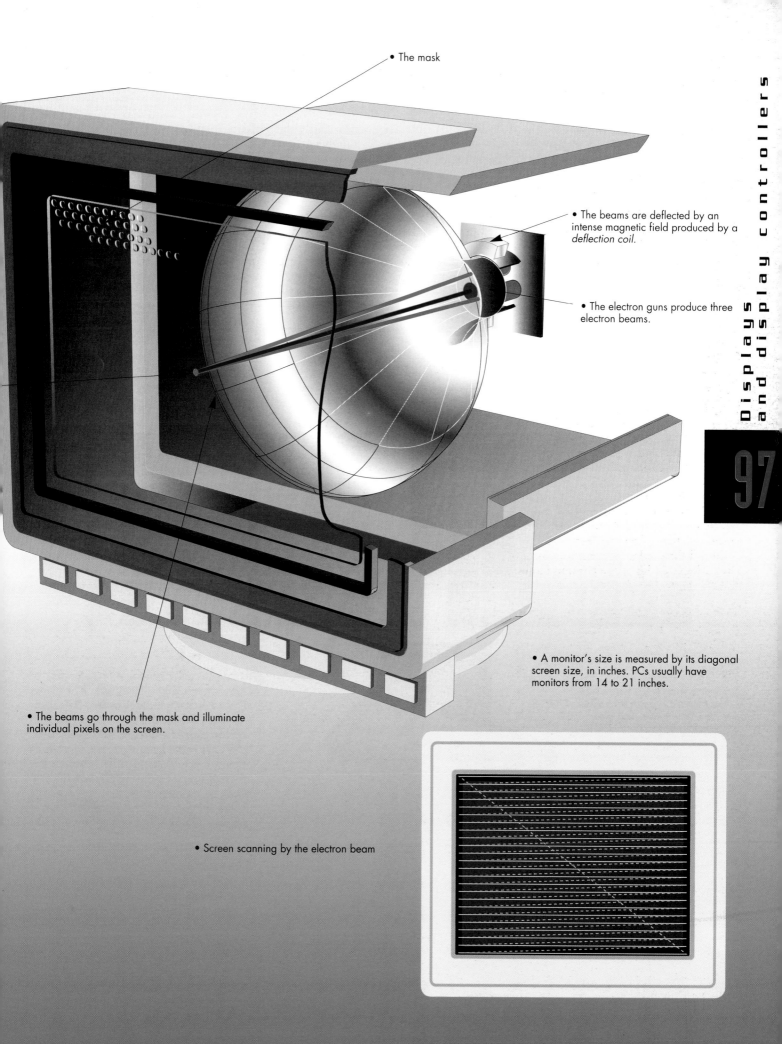

• The mask

• The beams are deflected by an intense magnetic field produced by a *deflection coil.*

• The electron guns produce three electron beams.

• A monitor's size is measured by its diagonal screen size, in inches. PCs usually have monitors from 14 to 21 inches.

• The beams go through the mask and illuminate individual pixels on the screen.

• Screen scanning by the electron beam

Display operations

Monitors are *analog* devices—they use analog electronics to drive the screen, so the intensity of a pixel can vary continuously from zero to maximum intensity. Also, the horizontal or vertical placement of a pixel on the screen can vary anywhere within the boundaries of the screen. However, the computer deals in *digital* data. A *converter* transforms the data from digital form (groups of bits that can have the value 0 or 1) to analog form (variations in the intensity of the scanning electron beam).

Independently of the monitor's size, the computer displays a specific number of horizontal lines. Each line contains a specific number of pixels. The lines and pixels together are called the display *resolution*. The *aspect ratio* (width to height) of a standard monitor is 4:3, and screen resolutions usually follow the same ratio. The standard resolution of a PC is 640 x 480. Other common resolutions are 800 x 600, 1024 x 768, 1280 x 960, and 1600 x 1200. A 1280 x 1024 resolution is sometimes used, but it doesn't follow the usual 4:3 height/width ratio.

In the computer's memory, each pixel on the screen is represented by a specific number of bits. The number of different colors that can be displayed depends on the number of bits per pixel. To show two colors, one bit is sufficient (0=black and 1=white, for example). 4 bits allow 16 colors to be displayed. With 8 bits per pixel, 256 colors can be displayed. To get output of photographic quality, 24 bits per pixel are necessary. To create special effects, such as a transparency, 32 bits are needed. The number of bits per pixel is sometimes called the color *depth*.

Using palettes to represent colors

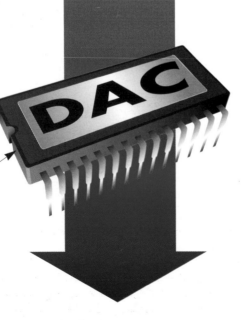

• Palette 1

• Palette 2

• A color palette has been selected. The palette is a table of 16 colors, each with red, blue, and green components.

• A digital-to-analog (DAC) converter transforms digital values into analog signals understood by the analog electronics in the monitor.

To the monitor

In a 24-bit color system, 8 bits are used for each primary color. Therefore, 256 shades of green, red, or blue are possible. The combination of these three colors creates 16.8 million colors that can be represented (256^3). However, you won't see all of them on one screen. A standard PC monitor has a 640 x 480 resolution and displays 307,200 pixels, so it's impossible to simultaneously display more than 307,200 colors. It's also rare that all pixels of an image are of a different color.

4-bit color presents a special problem. One third of the bits can't be attributed to each color, so a *palette* of colors is used. A palette is a group of colors (16, in this case), each of which is identified by its own 4-bit value. It's possible to define several palettes, with different color sets, and then switch palettes depending on the specific image you want to display. For example, you might display a sky with a palette of 16 shades of blue.

Representing colors directly

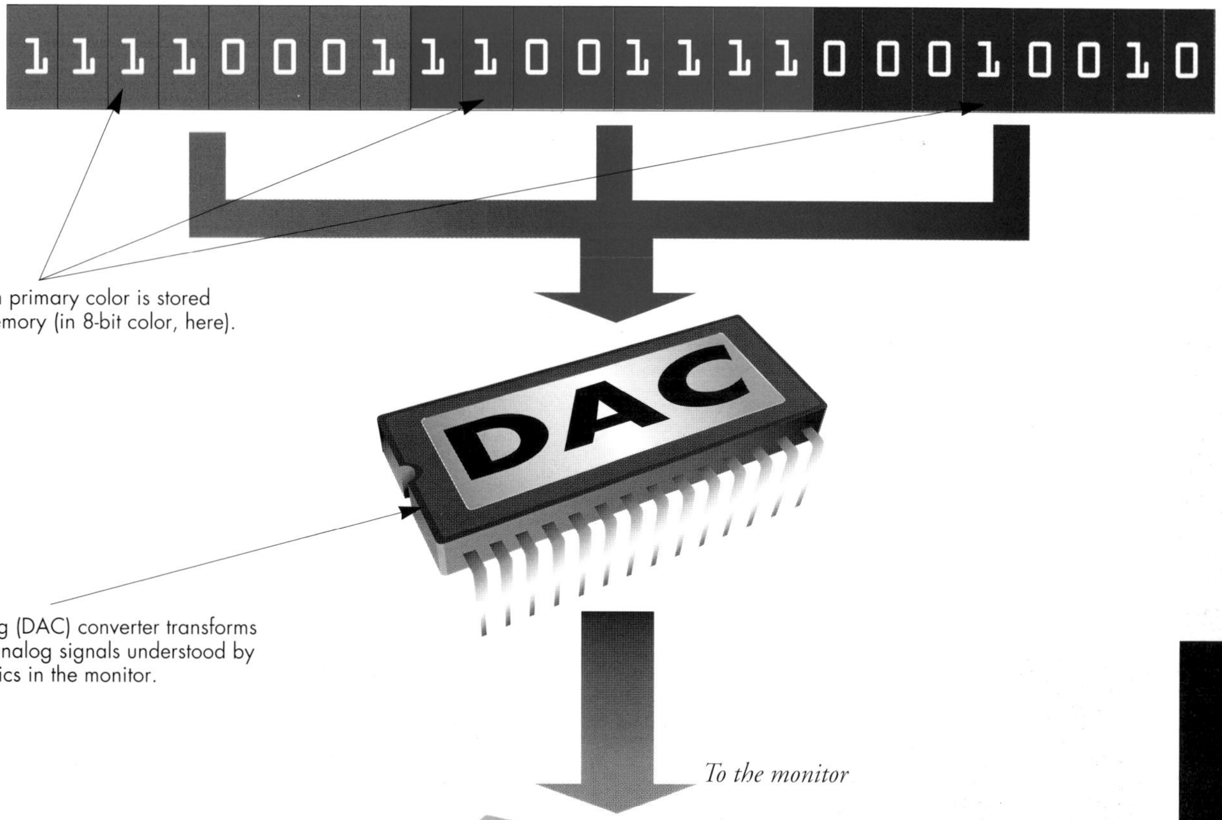

1110001110011110001001 0

• The value of each primary color is stored directly in video memory (in 8-bit color, here).

• A digital-to-analog (DAC) converter transforms digital values into analog signals understood by the analog electronics in the monitor.

To the monitor

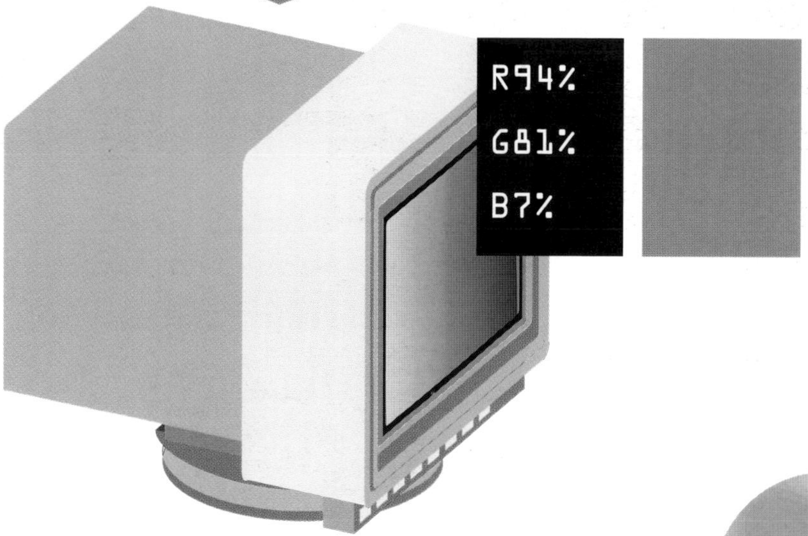

R94%

G81%

B7%

Another technique used to make it easier to generate an image on the screen is to address groups of pixels on the screen, generally four at a time, instead of single pixels. This reduces the resolution (to 320 x 240 instead of 640 x 480), but increases the displayable colors to 65,536 (16^4). This technique is used in many computer games.

Display data is computed by the processor and stored in video memory. A 640 x 480 pixel screen with 16 colors requires 307,200 x 4 bits to represent it, a total of 150 KB of memory. A 512 KB video memory then stores three full screens, called *video pages*. Video memory enables the processor to compute and store in advance up to three screens, then make the transition from one image to another almost instantaneously.

In contrast, 2.25 MB of data are required to display a 1024 x 768 pixel image in 24-bit color. It's easy to see why it takes the processor much longer to prepare each image in this mode.

When you're given a choice between several display modes, consider carefully the number of colors involved. Stepping up from 16 colors (the minimum) to 16.8 million colors (the maximum) multiplies by eight the amount of data to compute. On the other hand, stepping up from 640 x 480 resolution to 1280 x 960 only quadruples the data.

Display modes

PCs can have a variety of different display modes, each with a different resolution and number of colors. The minimum standard today is the VGA display, offering 640 x 480 resolution and 16 colors. A number of manufacturers have tried to impose higher performance standards. In particular, IBM introduced the 8514/A (1024 x 768 interlaced with 256 colors) display card and the XGA standard with an additional mode that could display 65,536 colors at a 640 x 480 resolution. Other new standards, such as VGA+ or Super VGA, appeared, offering higher resolution or more colors. Manufacturers regrouped under the Video Electronics Standards Association (VESA) to define, among other things, the SVGA standard, which offers 1024 x 768 resolution in 256 colors. Display cards conforming to this standard can also display 256 colors in 800 x 600 mode, but with additional memory, this mode can generate as many as 16 million colors.

Which is the best display mode?

The ideal display mode depends on many factors. First, you must consider the size of the monitor and its dot pitch. It's not useful to display a high resolution on a small monitor for the following reasons:

• The higher the resolution, the greater the number of pixels displayed on the screen, and the closer together the pixels will be. Dot pitch controls how close the pixels can be to one another. Dot pitch also indicates the size of the smallest pixel that can be displayed.

(In fact, a "pixel" in this sense is actually a group of three pixels, one each of the three primary colors.) A 14-inch monitor (14-inch diagonal) offers a display area 11-1/8" wide by 8-1/2" high. With a 0.30 dot pitch, 948 pixels can be displayed horizontally and 721 vertically, which is too few for SVGA mode. If you want to use SVGA mode, you'll need at least a 15-inch monitor, or a 14-inch monitor with a 0.28 dot pitch. Otherwise, you'll have to make do with an 800 x 600 screen resolution. You can run the display with a higher resolution, but you'll see a noticeable degradation in image quality.

The performance of the display depends greatly on the number of pixels and colors being displayed. If you want high processor performance, it's theoretically better to choose low resolution and a limited number of colors. That's theory. In fact, manufacturers of display cards provide, along with the card, *display drivers*—programs that manage and run the card. Performance relies heavily on the quality of these programs. Some manufacturers put all their efforts into producing higher resolution on the screen (for marketing purposes), to the detriment of other areas. Because of this, it's not uncommon to see a display card that is faster in a 256-color mode than in a 16-color mode.

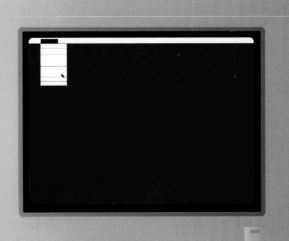

• Even if the monitor's dot pitch allows it, you shouldn't use very high resolution on a small monitor because programs aren't designed for it. Instead of getting a sharper display, you simply get a smaller image with details that are difficult to see.

• A good balance between the monitor's size and display resolution is necessary.

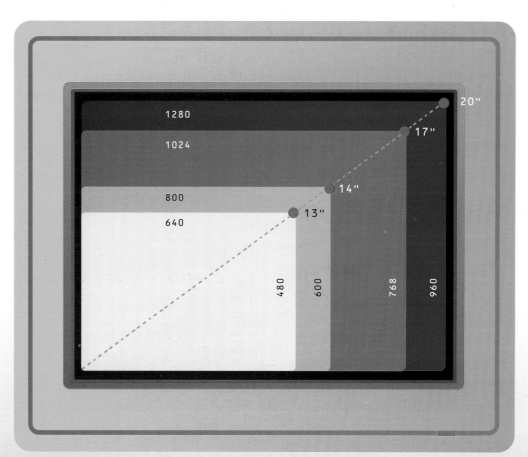

Display cards

To improve performance, some display cards are equipped with special processors. Some are designed specifically to execute instructions from one user interface (Windows). Others are entirely programmable. These cards are called *graphics accelerator* cards. They produce excellent results, especially if they're local bus cards. Their memory can usually be extended if you want to use higher resolutions and more colors.

• Graphics processors take over many computations normally performed by the PC's processor.

• A local bus card improves data transfer speed.

• Video memory can be extended if you want to use higher resolutions and more colors.

Display cards can be used only with the programs for which *device drivers* have been made. Therefore, you'll need to know which drivers are provided with a PC that includes such a card. Most of the popular applications on the market include their own generic device drivers for the common graphics processors (ATI, S3, ET4000, or Western Digital). These drivers are designed for all cards having one type of graphics processor, so they don't usually provide as high performance as those drivers developed for a specific card.

Liquid crystal displays

The first portable computers were equipped with small CRT monitors. These models were not standalone units—they needed power from a 110V wall socket. They were about the same size and weight as a sewing machine. The invention of liquid crystal displays marked the beginning of truly portable computers. Early models had limited resolution and only black-and-white displays. Nowadays, displays with a gray scale having 64 levels or full color are available for portable computers. Two display technologies are on the market: passive matrix and active matrix. The latter offers an exceptionally high-quality display, but its price is very high.

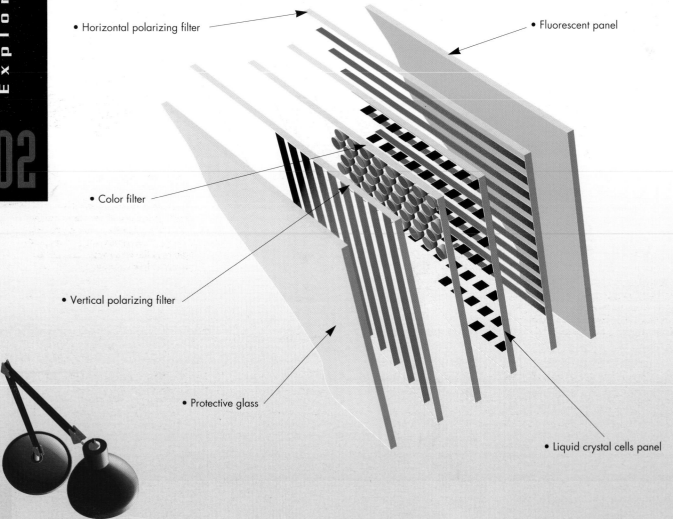

• Horizontal polarizing filter

• Fluorescent panel

• Color filter

• Vertical polarizing filter

• Protective glass

• Liquid crystal cells panel

Active matrix monitors are much more costly to produce, because manufacturing yield is low—more than 75 percent of the units made have defects and have to be destroyed. Yield is even lower with larger monitors. That's why resolution is limited to 640 x 480. Even monitors considered "perfect" can have a few defects. Most manufacturers consider a monitor with three or four defective pixels acceptable. A defective pixel is either permanently on or permanently off. Each pixel of an image is made of a red, green, and blue dot. A defect means that a pixel will be the wrong color.

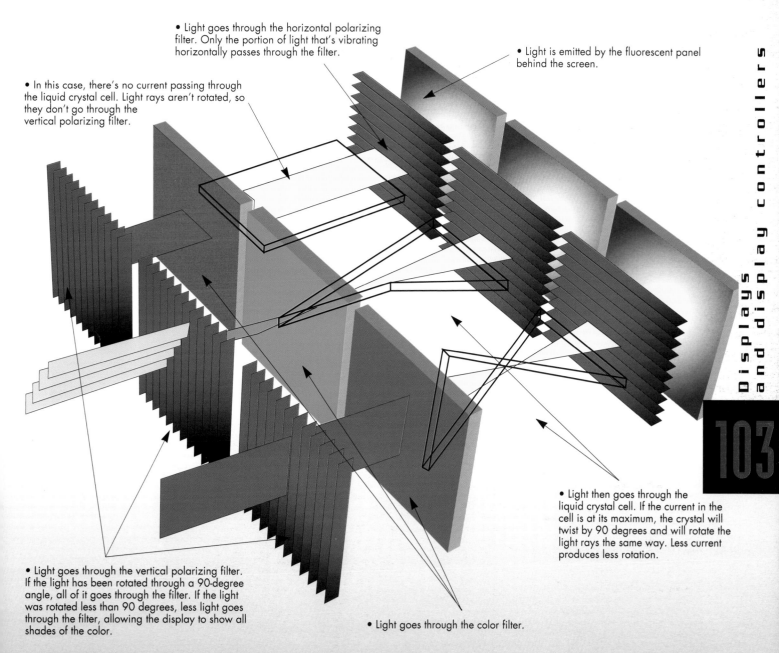

• Light goes through the horizontal polarizing filter. Only the portion of light that's vibrating horizontally passes through the filter.

• Light is emitted by the fluorescent panel behind the screen.

• In this case, there's no current passing through the liquid crystal cell. Light rays aren't rotated, so they don't go through the vertical polarizing filter.

• Light then goes through the liquid crystal cell. If the current in the cell is at its maximum, the crystal will twist by 90 degrees and will rotate the light rays the same way. Less current produces less rotation.

• Light goes through the vertical polarizing filter. If the light has been rotated through a 90-degree angle, all of it goes through the filter. If the light was rotated less than 90 degrees, less light goes through the filter, allowing the display to show all shades of the color.

• Light goes through the color filter.

• In passive matrix monitors, power is applied to the cells first by row and then by column. The first row is energized, then each of its columns is energized, one by one. So the pixels in the first row are lit one after the other. Then the second row is energized, then each of its columns. Pixels are scanned just as they are in CRT scanning. To get a satisfactory image, the cells need to have sufficiently high persistence so that a pixel remains lit until the next scan. The high persistence of passive matrix cells leads to screens that are less luminous and that produce smears when the image moves. In an active matrix screen, all pixels are individually energized. High persistence is unnecessary, smear goes away, and colors are sharper.

• Addressing columns

• Addressing rows

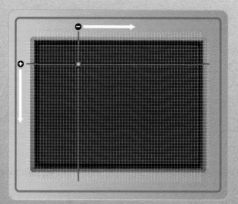

Video animation

Computers have been able to display color images for a long time. However, a still image contains much less information than an animated image, and for good reason. An animated image consists of a group of still images being shown quickly one after the other. In movies, images scroll at a speed of 24 per second. A television displays 50 frames per second. (A frame is made of either the even or the odd lines of an image, because television uses an interlaced display.) The result corresponds to 25 images per second. To display animated images, a computer has to be able to match that rate. Each image has to be computed and transferred to video memory within 1/25 of a second for good-quality animation.

Simple animation

Between two successive images of a movie, some objects don't move. When a car moves in front of scenery, the scenery is often stationary. The computer takes advantage of this to produce simple animation. The scenery's image is calculated only once, and the image of the moving object is superimposed on the scenery. The portion of scenery masked by the object is kept in memory. For the next image, the scenery in the previously masked area is updated from memory, and the superimposed object is shifted over a little to give the impression of movement. Objects manipulated in this way are called *sprites*.

If the object itself is animated, it's represented by several sprites displayed one after the other. For example, a running animal is represented by 10 to 20 different sprites showing the different positions of the body.

• Only the part of the image that was hidden by the object has to be updated.

• Still background

• Moving object

• Still background

• Movement is depicted as a series of still images shown one after the other.

Scrolling

Sometimes, even the background has to be animated. The most common type of animation is continuous *scrolling*. A background image larger than the screen is written into video memory. A *pointer* controls the portion of the image displayed on the screen. The result appears to be scenery scrolling past a window. Animated objects can then be superimposed on each image.

Example of horizontal scrolling

• A *pointer* indicates where the displayed image begins.

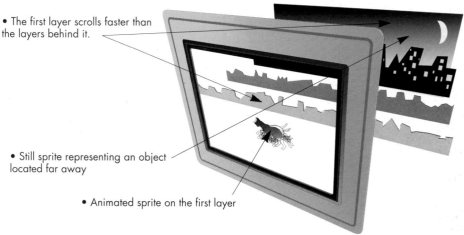

For a more realistic result, a technique called *differential scrolling* is used. It consists of representing the background on several different layers at different speeds to give a 3-D effect.

• The first layer scrolls faster than the layers behind it.

• Still sprite representing an object located far away

• Animated sprite on the first layer

Complete image animation

The techniques just described only approximate true animation. They are the same as the techniques used to create cartoons. These techniques are commonly used in the production of video games, but they're not adequate for more serious applications such as simulators. To obtain more satisfying results, the whole screen needs to be updated for each successive image. Each image can be precomputed. For example, images that have been photographed or scanned and then digitized and stored on a disk can be used. The computer has only to transfer the image into video memory at the appropriate rate. The ideal is to display 24 monitor-sized images every second. However, that's impossible given the amount of data that has to be computed. An image with 640 x 480

resolution and 16 million colors occupies 900 KB. For 24 images-per-second animation, 21 MB of data would have to be transmitted to the screen every second, and that surpasses the capacity of most current PCs. There are several solutions to this problem:

• Decrease the size of the image. If you can use a 320 x 240 window, the quantity of data is reduced by a factor of 4.

• Decrease the number of colors. With 256 colors, you can achieve very reasonable quality, and the data to be computed is reduced by a factor of 3.

• Decrease the number of images per second. At 18 images per second, data is reduced by

a factor of 1.5. However, animation quality suffers.

• Compress the data. If it's acceptable to lose some image quality, you can considerably reduce the amount of data required for each image. However, decompression time increases the time it takes to process an image unless you're using data compression hardware—an expansion card with a processor exclusively dedicated to compressing and decompressing data. It's likely this will become the solution of choice for quality animation on a PC.

105

• At 24 images per second, full-screen mode, and 16 million colors, the PC must compute 21 MB per second.
• At 12 images per second, the amount of data is reduced by a factor of 2.

Computer-generated image animation

It is also possible to create animation by displaying computer-generated images that have been previously calculated, which is similar to the technique just covered. *Real time* computer-generated animation is a whole different problem. In this case, the computer must compute images on the fly as they are being displayed. This is used in most simulation programs. It requires powerful computation capacity and elaborate programming techniques.

• Halving the height and width of the image reduces the amount of data by a factor of 4.
• With only 16 colors, the amount of data is reduced by a factor of 6.

INPUT PERIPHERALS

• The keyboard.................108

• The mouse
and its equivalents..............112

• Joysticks.........................116

• Graphics pads and computers
without keyboards 118

• The scanner 120

• Other input devices.................124

The keyboard

You need a keyboard to communicate with your PC. The keyboard sends commands or data such as text, numbers, or various symbols to the computer. A keyboard comes with almost all PCs. (There are now PCs without keyboards that work through handwritten commands.) Early computers didn't have keyboards. Communication was conducted through *punch cards* whose perforations represented binary data. However, those cards were created on machines equipped with keyboards. People quickly concluded that it was better to equip the computer directly with a keyboard. Despite attempts to modernize it, the PC's keyboard is based on a typewriter keyboard. The layout of characters on the typewriter wasn't meant to make typing easier, but rather to ensure that the arms carrying the characters wouldn't touch each other when people typed quickly. Despite this ergonomic disadvantage, tradition is hard to fight—it is not very likely that any new layout will ever become standard.

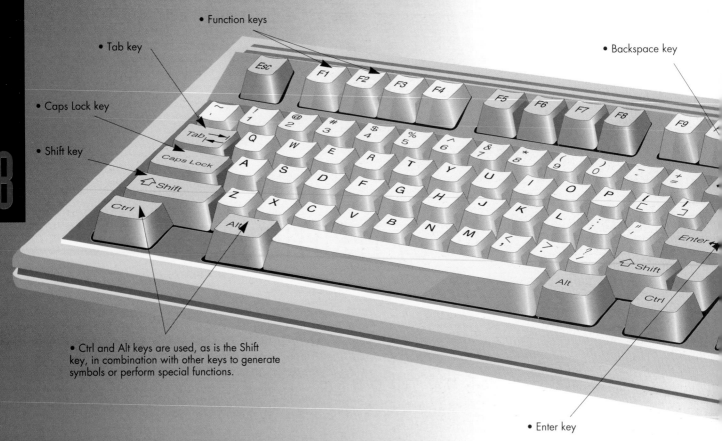

- Function keys
- Tab key
- Backspace key
- Caps Lock key
- Shift key
- Ctrl and Alt keys are used, as is the Shift key, in combination with other keys to generate symbols or perform special functions.
- Enter key

Keyboard layout

A computer keyboard includes all the keys found on a typewriter, plus some additional keys (usually 101 keys total). These additional keys perform special functions: cursor control, insertion, deletion, scroll control, etc. At the right side of the keyboard is the numeric keypad, with numbers and basic math symbols. At the top of the keyboard are the function keys (sometimes these appear on the left side of the keyboard). Their functions are not permanently defined, but depend on the program being run. Each country has its own keyboard layout. American keyboards have the Qwerty layout, so-called because of the layout of the keys on the first row of letters.

Portable computer keyboards are usually different. To save space, there's no numeric key-pad and the cursor-control keys are placed differently.

To maintain compatibility with early PCs, the numeric keypad can also be used for cursor control (moving the cursor around on the screen). This double function is controlled by the NumLock key. The status of the keypad (locked into numeric mode or not) is indicated by the Num Lock light.

How the keys work

There are several sorts of keyboard technologies. Some, called touch-sensitive keyboards, have keys that are sensitive to pressure or electrical conduction. However, most keyboards use motion-sensitive keys. There are several methods used to detect key travel; the most common are switch-based or capacitative.

Capacitative key

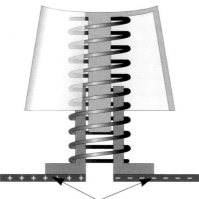

• These two plates form a capacitor.

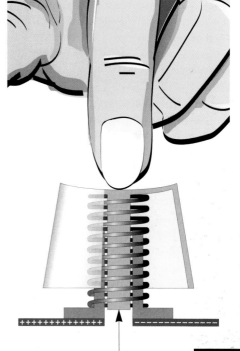

• When a key is pressed, a paddle moves closer to the two plates. The capacity of the capacitor changes, creating a small current. This current indicates that the key was pressed.

• Delete key

• Insert key

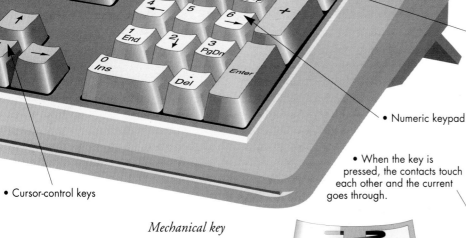

• Num Lock status light

• Num Lock key

• Numeric keypad

• Cursor-control keys

• When the key is pressed, the contacts touch each other and the current goes through.

Mechanical key

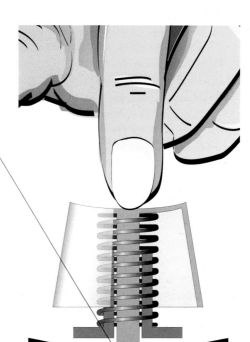

• These two contacts are usually separated by a space.

How the keyboard communicates with the PC

The keyboard contains a processor (not powerful, but enough for what it has to do). When you press a key on a keyboard the processor detects the keypress and sends a number corresponding to that key (called the *scan code*) to the *keyboard controller,* located on the motherboard. The keyboard processor doesn't know which letter or symbol corresponds to the key that

was pressed. The same key can be used for different characters, depending on the keyboard layout (layouts differ from one country to another). The code is transmitted to the microprocessor, which processes it with a program called a *keyboard driver.* The driver translates the codes into their corresponding characters. Different drivers exist for each keyboard layout. If a manufacturer wants to make a keyboard with a non-standard key layout, the manufacturer has

only to write a keyboard driver and put identification labels on the keys to match the new layout. However, these key-translation procedures can have the effect that the symbols shown on the keys aren't necessarily the symbols that show up on the screen. Note that the computer's BIOS has an American keyboard driver. If no special driver is installed, the American keyboard layout is used by default.

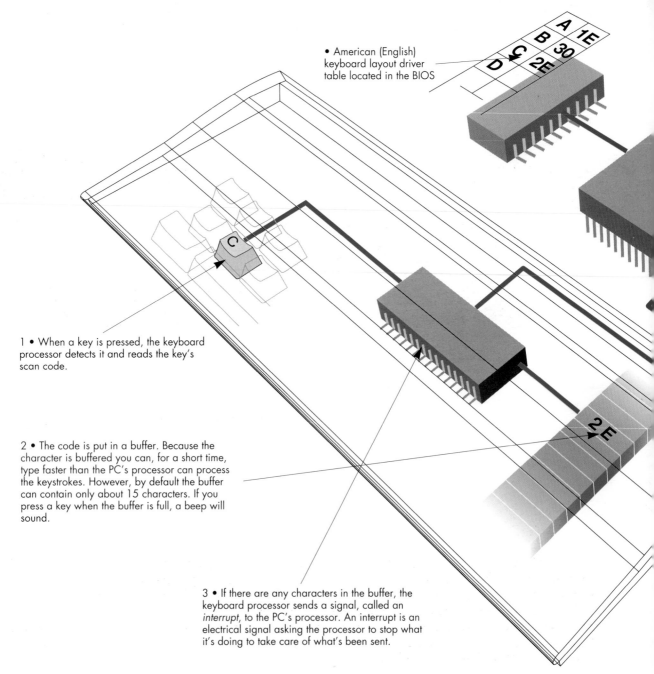

• American (English) keyboard layout driver table located in the BIOS

1 • When a key is pressed, the keyboard processor detects it and reads the key's scan code.

2 • The code is put in a buffer. Because the character is buffered you can, for a short time, type faster than the PC's processor can process the keystrokes. However, by default the buffer can contain only about 15 characters. If you press a key when the buffer is full, a beep will sound.

3 • If there are any characters in the buffer, the keyboard processor sends a signal, called an *interrupt,* to the PC's processor. An interrupt is an electrical signal asking the processor to stop what it's doing to take care of what's been sent.

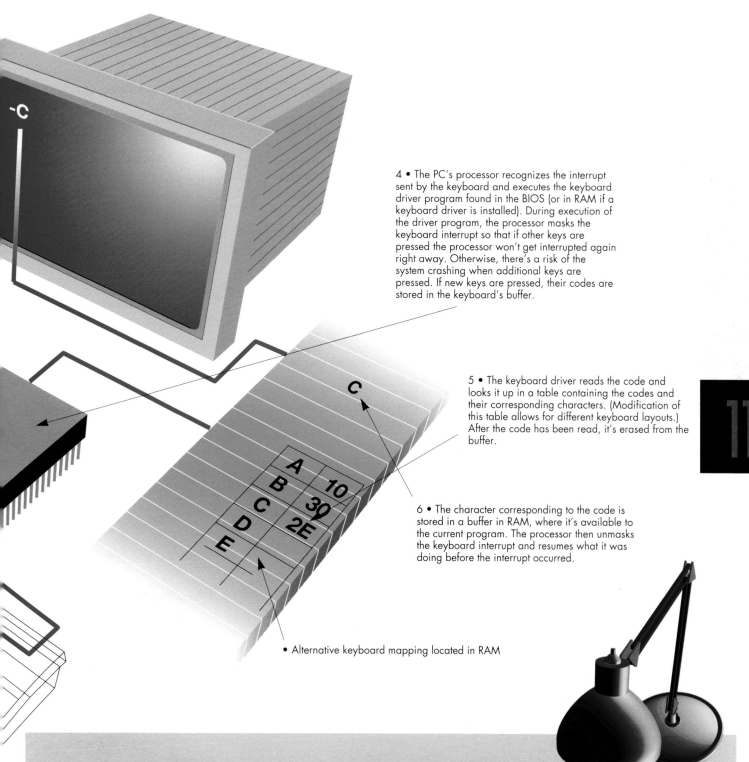

4 • The PC's processor recognizes the interrupt sent by the keyboard and executes the keyboard driver program found in the BIOS (or in RAM if a keyboard driver is installed). During execution of the driver program, the processor masks the keyboard interrupt so that if other keys are pressed the processor won't get interrupted again right away. Otherwise, there's a risk of the system crashing when additional keys are pressed. If new keys are pressed, their codes are stored in the keyboard's buffer.

5 • The keyboard driver reads the code and looks it up in a table containing the codes and their corresponding characters. (Modification of this table allows for different keyboard layouts.) After the code has been read, it's erased from the buffer.

6 • The character corresponding to the code is stored in a buffer in RAM, where it's available to the current program. The processor then unmasks the keyboard interrupt and resumes what it was doing before the interrupt occurred.

A	10
B	30
C	2E
D	
E	

• Alternative keyboard mapping located in RAM

Keys don't necessarily correspond to characters, numbers, or symbols. Some, like the Shift key, are used in combination with others to modify their meaning. When a key is pressed while the Shift key is pressed, its scan code isn't modified. When the keyboard driver detects the Shift key's code, it looks up the next code in another table. (In fact, keys have two codes, one for the press and one for the release. It's then possible for the program to detect if a key remains pressed.) Note that all keys have different codes. The processor can, for example, see the difference between the left and right Shift keys.

The mouse and its equivalents

Just a few years ago, PCs were controlled only through the keyboard. Commands were typed out on the screen and triggered by pressing the Enter (or Return) key. The advent of graphical interfaces has changed this. PCs can now be controlled using *point-and-click* tools: you choose a command from a list of commands called a *menu* and "click" a button to select it. You can also point to an object and manipulate it in various ways. The most common point-and-click tool is the *mouse*. One type of mouse uses a rolling ball; others use optical sensing techniques. They are linked to the PC by a cable or by using infrared light (or even radio waves). They may have several buttons. Mice, while well adapted to regular office PCs, aren't that practical for use with portable computers. Other pointing tools have been designed specifically for portable computers. The most common is the trackball, but the mini-joystick is also in use.

The mouse, which was first used in a commercial product by Xerox, was made popular on PCs by Microsoft as its Windows graphical interface became dominant. A PC mouse has two buttons, sometimes three. The third button is usually reserved for specific applications. It's also sometimes possible to choose, among the three buttons, which two will be used, or to assign independent functions to all three.

Some mice are linked to the computer via infrared or radio transmissions, but most require a cable. This cable is connected to an *interface*, either serial or parallel. A serial mouse can use the same interface as a serial printer. (If you are using a serial printer, you'll need an interface with two serial ports.) A mouse with a parallel interface is called a *bus mouse*. It can't use the interface used by parallel printers but instead needs its own interface card. This type of mouse interface can be used as long as a slot is available for its interface card. (An 8-bit slot would be fine.) Some mice can be connected to either a serial port or a parallel interface card, because they include their own conversion electronics.

Some PCs include an IBM PS/2 custom mouse port. Such setups require a special mouse connector. But because the port is usually built directly into the motherboard, the mouse doesn't use up a serial port or require a separate interface card.

Serial mouse

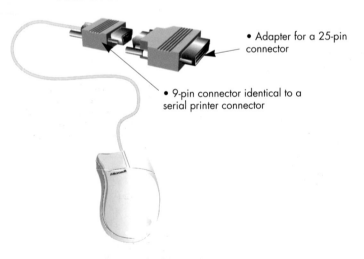

• Adapter for a 25-pin connector

• 9-pin connector identical to a serial printer connector

Parallel or bus mouse

• Interface card

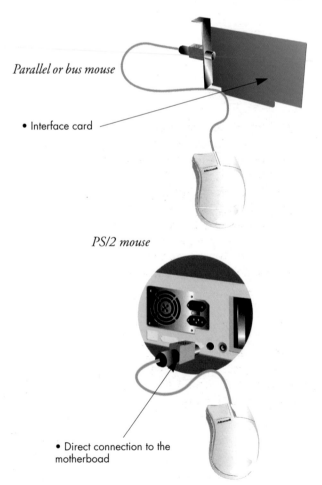

PS/2 mouse

Parallel mouse with a serial adapter

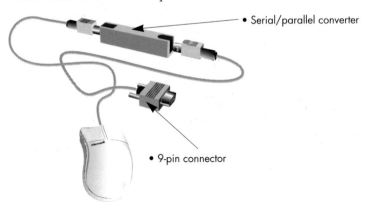

• Serial/parallel converter

• 9-pin connector

• Direct connection to the motherboad

• Signals from the mouse are processed by a program called the *mouse driver*. On screen, up and down movement causes vertical movement of the mouse pointer. Left and right movement causes horizontal movement. What the mouse buttons do depends on the application that's running.

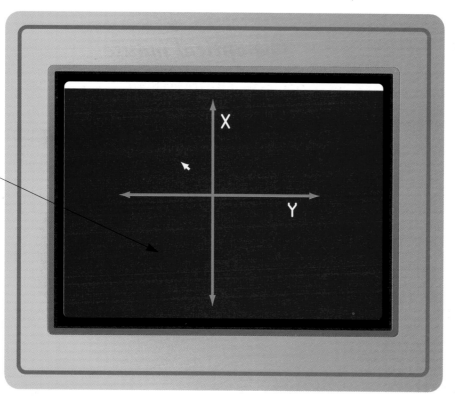

X

Y

113

• Rotation around this axis represents up and down movement.

• Button contacts

• A rubber-covered ball turns when the mouse is moved and rotates the axis in the direction of the movement.

• The coding wheels transform rotation around the axis into electrical signals.

• Rotation around this axis represents left and right movement.

• The signals are converted by internal electronics that match the interface in use. (In this case, it's a serial mouse. Parallel mice have much simpler electronics, because the interface card processes the movement signals.)

Mouse prices vary widely (the most expensive can be ten times more expensive than the least expensive). Working with a bad mouse can be seriously distracting (it has even been known to cause nervous breakdowns!). Having used all sorts, we can assure you that it's better to skimp on anything other than a mouse. Whether or not to use a mouse pad, however, is a matter of personal preference; a good mouse doesn't need one.

• Friction brushes

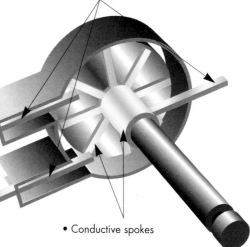

• The coding wheels are disks with conductive radial spokes. Two brushes make contact with these spokes, sending electronic pulses from the mouse. The sequence in which the friction pads make contact indicates the direction, distance, and speed of rotation and therefore displacement. The number of pulses indicates the distance covered by the mouse, and their frequency indicates its speed.

• Conductive spokes

The optical mouse

In an optical mouse, two light sources with photodetectors replace the ball and coding wheels. The light sources emit two rays aimed downward. Because the mouse is on a reflective surface, the rays are reflected back up through two small, transparent plastic lenses. The focused beams are directed by a mirror to the back of the mouse where they reach the photodetectors, which are perpendicular to one another.

In order to work, the mouse must be used on a reflective plate the size of a mouse pad. This plate has tiny horizontal and vertical grid lines. When the mouse moves, the light rays are absorbed by the grid lines, and the photodetectors detect the variations in light intensity. The mouse's electronics transform these pulses into signals for the computer.

Optical mice have a few drawbacks. They have to be handled more gently than regular ball mice. They function only on the reflective plate. And because the mouse's motion is confined to the pad, you have to lift your hand more often.

• Reflective plate with grid lines

Other pointing tools

The mouse is practical where there is space to move it. If you use a laptop computer, however, there may be no space to move a mouse; you need a *trackball* instead. A trackball is essentially an inverted mouse. The ball is on top, and you move it with your fingers. There are many types of trackballs. Some are mounted on the side of a portable computer. Others are integrated into the keyboard itself. There are even some models that can be installed on a desk.

• Trackball adapted for use with a portable computer

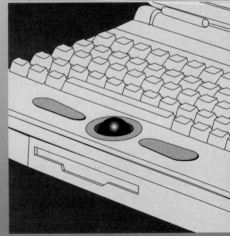

• Trackball integrated into the keyboard

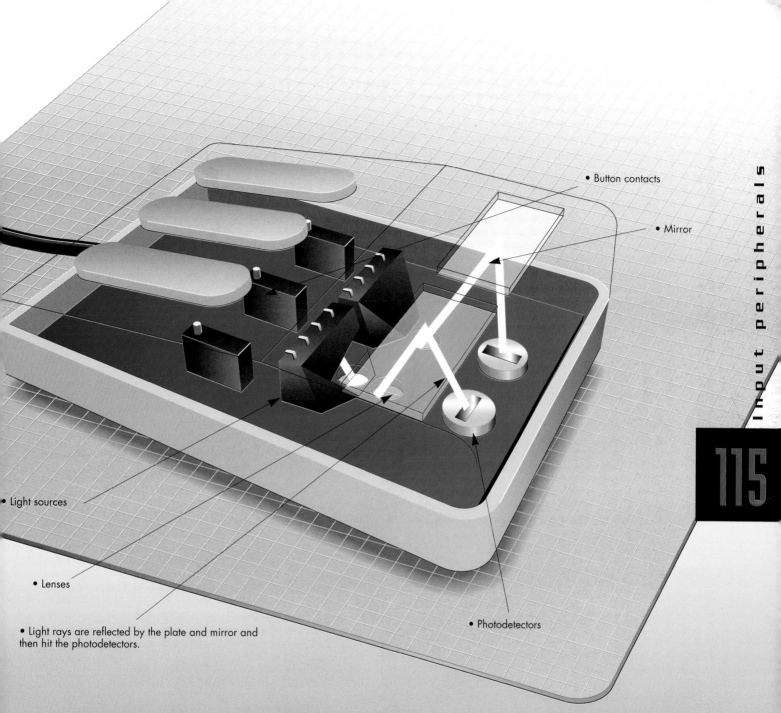

• Button contacts

• Mirror

• Light sources

• Lenses

• Light rays are reflected by the plate and mirror and then hit the photodetectors.

• Photodetectors

Some portables use a small rubber button, resembling a pencil eraser, located in the middle of the keyboard. This button is sensitive to pressure. As you push the button in a given direction, the pointer moves in that direction on the screen. This requires a little getting used to, but it's quite practical.

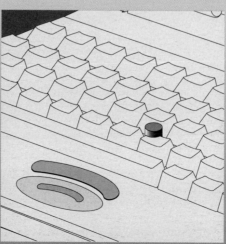

• Some portables are equipped with a pressure-sensitive button.

There are many other pointing systems. Some are even controlled by one's foot. Others, still at the experimental level, are controlled by movement of the user's eyes. A camera tracks the user's eye movements.

Finally, some computers without keyboards use a lightpen and a light-sensitive screen. To access objects or areas on the screen, you point at them with the lightpen. Then, there's no need for a separate pointing system. In some cases (*touch-sensitive screens*), you can even point directly at objects with your finger.

Joysticks

Joysticks, like mice, are input devices that translate physical movement into data a computer can understand. There are two types of joysticks: analog and digital. Analog joysticks have proportional control, which means that a small joystick movement will cause something on the screen to move a small distance. This type of joystick is used mainly in flight simulators. Digital joysticks give a different type of control called *all or nothing*. The amount of movement isn't detected—only its direction is taken into account. This type of joystick is used for arcade games.

Analog joystick

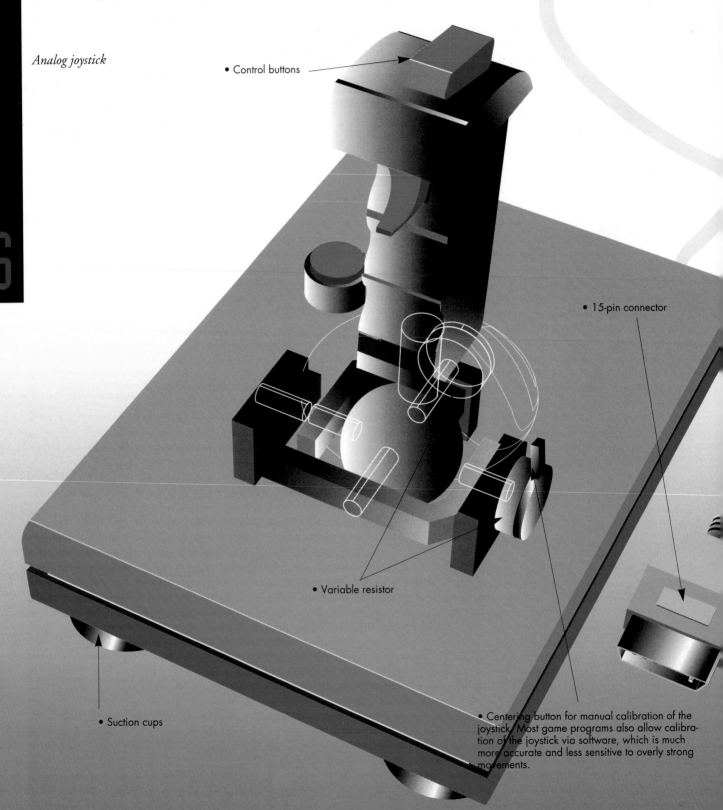

• Control buttons

• 15-pin connector

• Variable resistor

• Suction cups

• Centering button for manual calibration of the joystick. Most game programs also allow calibration of the joystick via software, which is much more accurate and less sensitive to overly strong movements.

An analog joystick is made of two variable resistors adjusted by movement of the handle in two directions. Movements to the front and back adjust one resistor, and sideways movements control the other. There is no zero point. The resistance varies continuously from the minimum value to the maximum, with the average value corresponding to the neutral position of the handle. Most simulation programs expect positive or negative movements from a median position. For example, in simulated car driving, the neutral joystick position corresponds to driving in a straight line. The joystick must be calibrated so that the program will know which value of the resistance corresponds to this neutral point.

A joystick also has at least two buttons used by programs for their commands. Sometimes, a switch allows you to set these buttons in *continuous fire* mode. In this mode a single press of the button is automatically repeated, allowing you to kill as many extra-terrestrial villains as you wish without tiring out your thumb.

The joystick is linked to an interface, usually through a 15-pin connector located either on a multifunction input/output card (including both serial and parallel ports) or on a sound card. You can plug two joysticks into the computer using this connector with the help of a Y cable. Some joysticks use this capability to offer two additional buttons

on a single joystick. To use these extra buttons, a game program must be adapted to use this feature, and you then won't be able to use a second joystick.

Digital joysticks use the same interface as analog joysticks. They simply signal a maximum and minimum value for a movement to one side or the other, and a median value for the central position, without ever sending any intermediate values.

There are all kinds of joysticks. Some look like guns, others like steering wheels or airplane yokes. Video game console fans can even get pads so they can play their games exactly the way they are used to.

This control pad is specially designed for video game console fans.

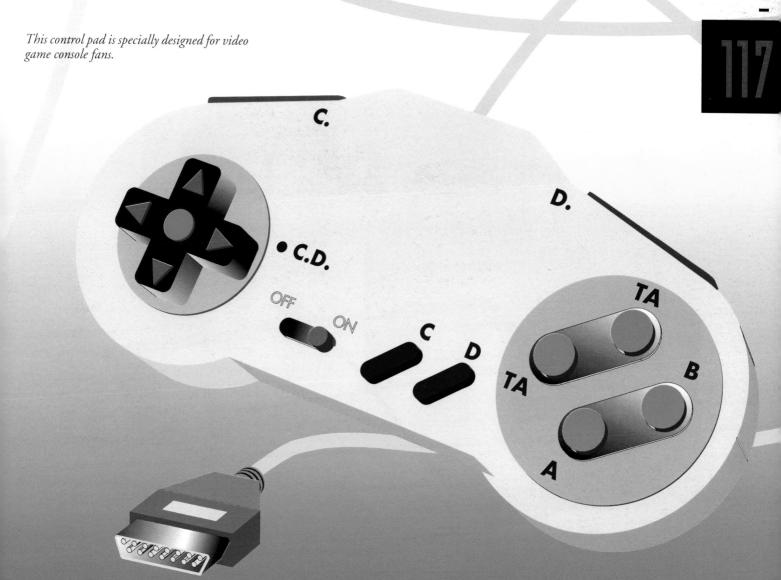

Graphics pads and computers without keyboards

Graphic artists and architects need pointing tools that are more precise than a mouse. The graphics pad (sometimes called a graphics tablet) was created with that in mind. It uses a simple principle. The pad represents the whole screen or just part of it. With a lightpen linked to an interface, you draw on the pad and the drawing is reproduced on the screen. For applications requiring even more precision, the lightpen is replaced by a sort of mouse with a lens and cross-hairs mounted on it. On computers without keyboards, the same principle is used. The lightpen is then powered by a battery, and the surface of the screen acts as a graphics pad. In some cases, the lightpen can be replaced by the user's finger. This type of screen is called a *touch-sensitive screen*.

The graphics pad is linked to an interface card plugged into one of the PC's expansion slots. The pad has a grid of electric wires embedded in the plastic. The wires carry a small electric current, provided by the pad's interface. The lightpen, linked to the pad, contains a magnet in its tip. When the lightpen gets near the surface of the pad, its magnetic field affects the current in the embedded wires. The intersection of the wires with maximum disturbance then shows the position of the lightpen.

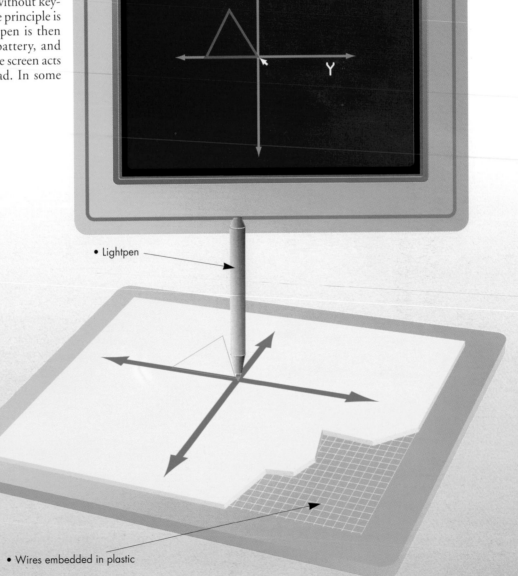

Graphics pad

• Lightpen

• Wires embedded in plastic

The lightpen's tip is usually equipped with a switch. When the lightpen is pressed against the pad, a signal similar to the one triggered by a mouse button is generated. A drawing program can then tell the difference between movement with and without plotting (whether or not you're pressing the lightpen on the pad).

In some lightpens, the switch is replaced by a variable resistor. It's then possible to measure the amount of pressure applied and, for example, have the thickness of the line vary in proportion to that pressure.

If the lightpen has to be used as a mouse to control a graphics interface, a second button can be added.

The same technology is used for computers without keyboards. Conductive wires run under the surface of the liquid crystal screen, and the lightpen is powered by battery. Computers without keyboards need a specially designed operating system. Instead of clicking with a mouse to execute commands, you use the lightpen. To erase a word from existing text, for example, you cross out the word. To allow input of text or data, the computer has to understand handwriting. Existing handwriting recognition programs are still not very good. For best results, you need to train the computer to recognize your own handwriting. Special programs have been designed for this. The teaching process consists of writing characters and correcting the computer when it doesn't identify them correctly. Despite this process, recognition is still far from perfect, which is the main obstacle to wide acceptance of computers without keyboards.

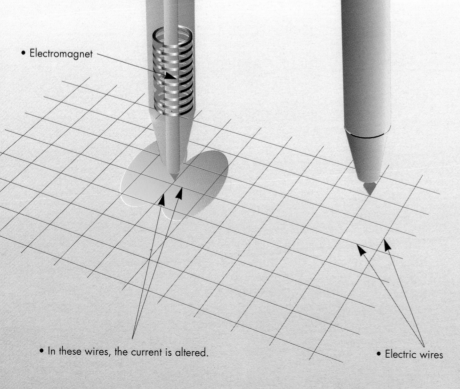

• Variable resistance induced by pressing the tip of the lightpen

• Electromagnet

• Magnetic field disturbing the current

• In these wires, the current is altered.

• Electric wires

The scanner

A scanner allows images to be read into computer memory. Images are digitized, i.e., converted into sequences of ones and zeros. They can then be displayed on the screen, printed, or modified using graphics software. They can also be inserted into a text document when you use word processing or desktop publishing programs. You can thus build up databases of photographs. However, you're not limited to treating the scanned image only as graphics. If you have an image of a page of text, it can be "read" by a special program that converts it into text. This is called *optical character recognition*. The text can then be modified with a word processor or stored in a database. Also, you can use a scanner and modem together to send faxes that can be received on a regular fax machine.

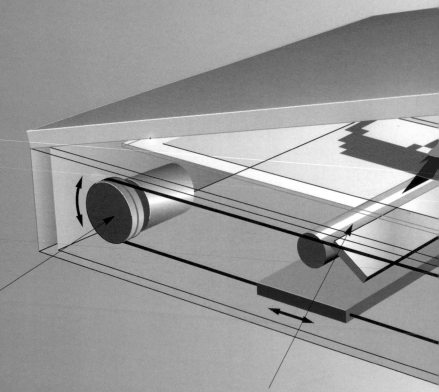

• A stepper motor moves the mirror platform forward an amount equal to the scanning resolution (1/400 of an inch, for example) to input the next row of dots. Color scanners usually work the same way, but the image is scanned three times. On each pass the light is filtered by either a red, green, or blue filter. Therefore, we get three values for each dot. If there are 256 shades of each color, we get an image that's coded in 24-bit color.

• A light source (fluorescent tube) on a moving platform illuminates the image.

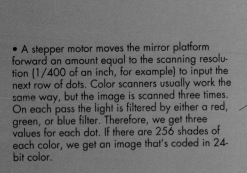

Some scanners get double the resolution of the CCD bank by going over the image twice. The second time it goes over the image, the bank of detectors is shifted sideways the width of half a cell. This technique shouldn't be confused with interpolation. Interpolation is carried out by software that places an additional dot between each two dots, giving it the average value of the neighboring dots. Interpolation, also called *smoothing*, doesn't add detail to the digitized image, but the resolution seems higher because there are more dots.

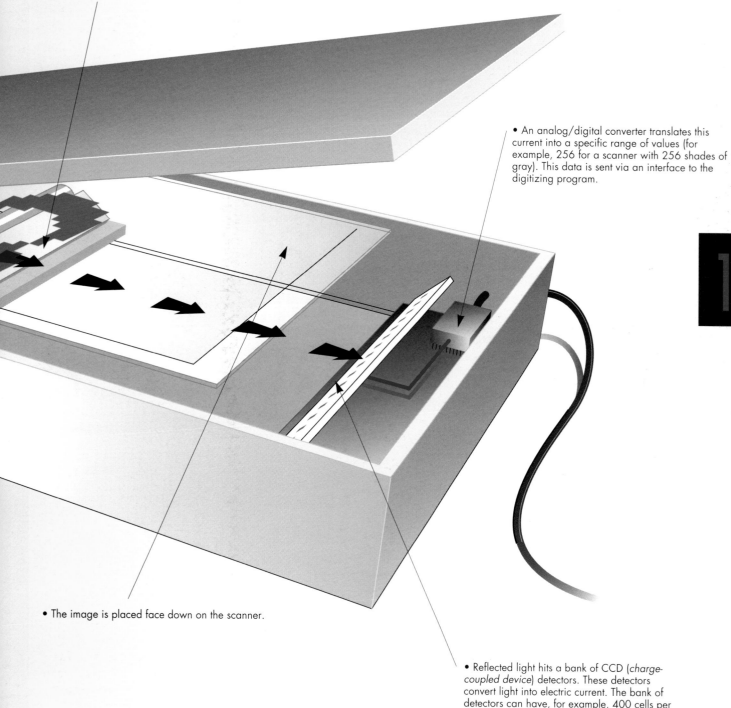

• Light is reflected from the image and then through a system of moving mirrors. Dark areas reflect little light, while bright areas reflect much more light.

• An analog/digital converter translates this current into a specific range of values (for example, 256 for a scanner with 256 shades of gray). This data is sent via an interface to the digitizing program.

• The image is placed face down on the scanner.

• Reflected light hits a bank of CCD (*charge-coupled device*) detectors. These detectors convert light into electric current. The bank of detectors can have, for example, 400 cells per inch, which equals about 3500 cells for an A4 format scanner. Strongly illuminated cells generate high current, while weakly illuminated cells produce a weak current.

Optical character recognition

One application of scanners is to digitize pages of text in order to recreate text files. Recreating text requires a program that recognizes images of digitized characters. The first step is to scan the text page to get a photo-like image of it in black and white dots. Then the program needs to determine which areas of the page contain text—so it won't have to process empty spaces, pho-

tos, or illustrations. Low-end programs need the user's help to eliminate nontext areas. Sophisticated programs can find areas of text automatically. The third step consists of isolating individual characters. With normally spaced characters and a document of good print quality, this step isn't a problem. However, isolating characters is very difficult with fonts that have connected characters, and it's nearly impossible with handwriting. (At the moment, programs

able to process handwriting recognize only unconnected characters.) Once characters are isolated, the most complex phase begins: character recognition. Three techniques can be used.

Matrix analysis

This is the oldest and simplest technique. The program superimposes the matrix of dots that make up a character over a reference matrix and counts the points that correspond. The character is recognized if the number of points that correspond exceeds a specific value. If several matches are found, the program chooses the one with the highest number of matching points. This technique has several disadvantages, the principal one being that the program can recognize only one font, and only one size of that font. Of course, the program can include many sets of font recognition matrices, but the user must indicate which set is to be used. (The program can usually determine font size, because size is a function of character spacing.) This type

of program can easily get a 100 percent recognition rate if the number of matching points required to trigger "recognition" is low enough. However, this pushes up the error rate.

Recognition rate is the percentage of identified characters. Error rate is the percentage of erroneously identified characters. Non recognized characters are flagged by the program, but errors, obviously, are not. It's often preferable to lower the recognition rate to minimize the error rate.

Matrix analysis

• The digitized character is superimposed on different matrices in memory.

• The character with the most corresponding points is chosen.

Morphological analysis

Morphological analysis (the analysis of shape) offers several improvements over the previous method. The digitized character is again compared with a matrix in memory, but the character is first converted into mathematical curves that describe its shape. The advantage of this method (sometimes referred to as ICR, *intelligent character recognition*) is that it works with many fonts, regardless of the size of the characters. Its main disadvantage is that it requires a lot of calculation, so the recognition process is slow.

Morphological analysis

• The character is converted into "features" of lines and loops.

• The program breaks down the character into mathematical curves.

• The curves obtained are compared with the models in memory. Unlike matrix models, the character shapes described by mathematical curves can be made larger or smaller to adapt to the size of the digitized character.

Neural networks

The neural network is the most recent character recognition technique. With this system, characters are not compared with complete models. A digitized character is broken into elements represented by simple curves. The neural network contains *entry neurons,* the group of fundamental curves that make up characters. Each of these neurons has a weight which corresponds to how well that shape uniquely identifies a character. A curve that allows unambiguous iden-

tification of a specific character gets a high weight, while a curve that's found in many characters gets a low weight.

For each curve in a digitized character, the corresponding neuron is activated and given a coefficient of 1. Neurons that don't correspond to any curves in the character get a 0 coefficient.

The neural network also has *exit neurons,* which are models of all the characters. For

each exit neuron (each possible character), the system sums the weight of entry neurons with nonzero coefficients. The system "recognizes" the character by choosing the exit neuron with the highest result. This system gets the best results, but it's also the slowest because of the many calculations required.

Neural network

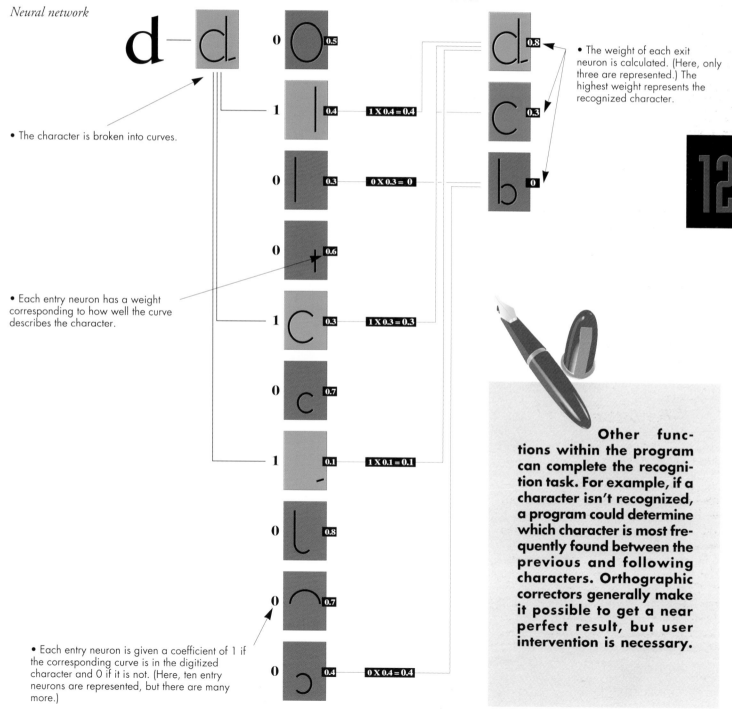

• The character is broken into curves.

• Each entry neuron has a weight corresponding to how well the curve describes the character.

• Each entry neuron is given a coefficient of 1 if the corresponding curve is in the digitized character and 0 if it is not. (Here, ten entry neurons are represented, but there are many more.)

• The weight of each exit neuron is calculated. (Here, only three are represented.) The highest weight represents the recognized character.

Other functions within the program can complete the recognition task. For example, if a character isn't recognized, a program could determine which character is most frequently found between the previous and following characters. Orthographic correctors generally make it possible to get a near perfect result, but user intervention is necessary.

Other input devices

There are many other input devices. Removable disks and magnetic tapes are input devices, because they can be used to input data into the computer. Most applications are delivered on floppy disks or CD-ROM. You can also input data via a network or a modem connected to phone lines. It's then possible to download programs, images, text, or numeric data. Different accessories can also be used to read particular types of data. Thus, identification codes can be read with a bar code reader, sound can be input with a microphone connected to an interface card, and images can be input with a digital photo device or camera.

Bar code readers

A bar code reader is a pen linked by a wire to an interface card. The tip of the pen contains a red light source. Light reflected by the surface of the paper is sensed by a photodetector. Bar codes consist of a sequence of black and white lines of different widths. When the pen is passed over a code, the black lines absorb the light while the white lines reflect it, producing a varying electric current in the photodetector. The duration and number of interruptions in the light ray are translated into a sequence of numbers by the interface. The code is usually also printed in text, either within or above the bar code. Bar codes have been standardized by an international organization to make them compatible all over the world. (There are different types of codes for different applications.)

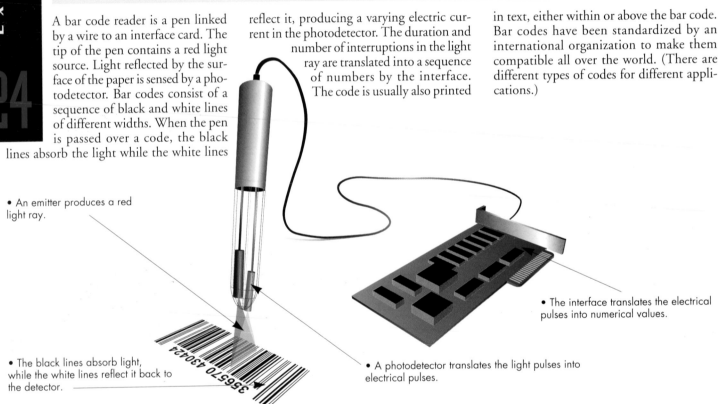

- An emitter produces a red light ray.

- The black lines absorb light, while the white lines reflect it back to the detector.

- A photodetector translates the light pulses into electrical pulses.

- The interface translates the electrical pulses into numerical values.

Microphone and soundcard

With a microphone and a soundcard, you can input sounds into the memory of your PC. The microphone translates the vibrations in the air (sounds) into an electrical current and sends it to the sound card. The electrical signal is then *sampled,* which means that the electronics measures the signal at a specific frequency. The number of samples per second corresponds to the *sampling frequency.* For a 10 KHz frequency, the number of samples is 10,000 per second. The higher the frequency, the better the sound quality. (An audio compact disk works with a sampling frequency of 44.1 KHz. A digital cassette uses a 48 KHz frequency.) The number of bits used to define each sample is also important. Generally, sound cards allow 8- or 16-bit sampling. With 16-bit sampling, the sound will be captured with significantly greater accuracy.

Recorded sounds can be stored for later reproduction (in the form of voice annotation in documents, for example). They can also be analyzed by a program to see what they mean. This is called *voice recognition,* and it actually allows you to use your voice to run a PC. However, voice recognition technology is still in its infancy and has not yet been perfected for microcomputers.

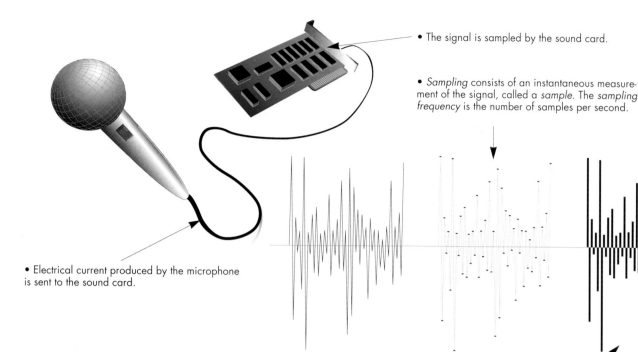

• The signal is sampled by the sound card.

• *Sampling* consists of an instantaneous measurement of the signal, called a *sample*. The *sampling frequency* is the number of samples per second.

• Electrical current produced by the microphone is sent to the sound card.

• Each sample is then represented by an 8- or 16-bit numeric value.

Digital cameras

A digital camera allows you to take digitized pictures without using either photographic film or a scanner. Behind the camera's lens is a bank of CCD cells (similar to the ones used in scanners). Each cell corresponds to a point on the image. It receives a certain amount of light and produces a current of a corresponding value. An analog/digital converter translates this current into a numeric value. To obtain a color image, three sets of CCD detectors are used—one for each primary color.

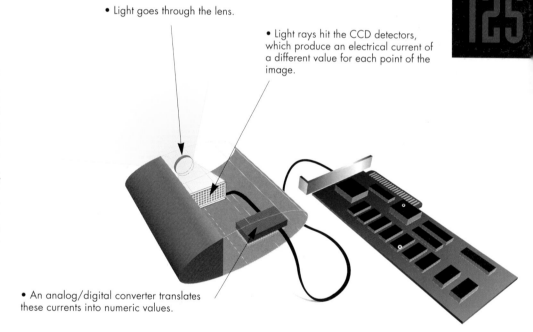

• Light goes through the lens.

• Light rays hit the CCD detectors, which produce an electrical current of a different value for each point of the image.

• An analog/digital converter translates these currents into numeric values.

Frame grabbers

No video cameras are entirely digital at this point—there's too much data to store. In a video camera, data is stored as magnetic fields representing variations in current coming from the CCD detector. To input these images into a computer, they have to be processed. A frame grabber video card is used for this. There are many techniques for digitizing animated images. You can decrease resolution, the number of images per second, or the number of colors to obtain an acceptable volume of data. You can also use real-time data compression so that image data never has to be stored in its original state. This requires a specialized processor (on the frame grabber video card), because the PC's processor isn't powerful enough for that. Another way consists of globally sampling the electrical signal instead of interpreting each point of the image. That's the principle used for the videodisk.

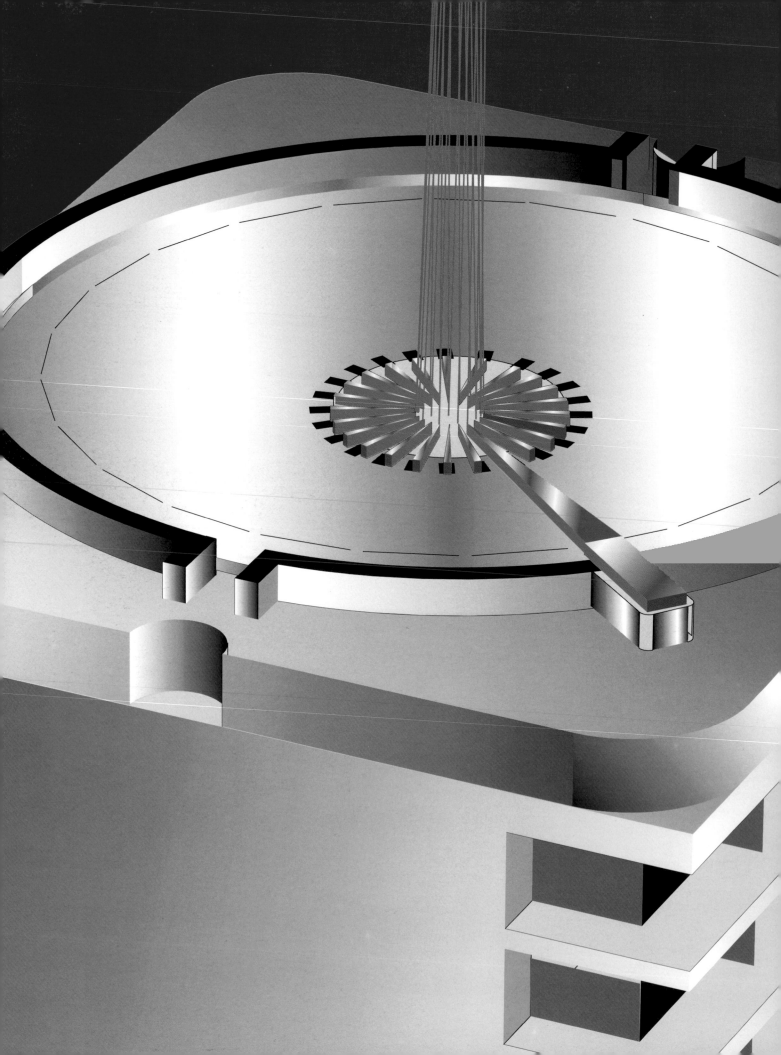

PRINTED OUTPUT

- Dot-matrix printers 128
- Laser printers 130
- Inkjet printers 132
- Color printers 134
- Imagesetters and film recorders 136
- Rendering grayscale and color 138

Dot-matrix printers

The first PCs used two types of printers: daisywheel printers and dot-matrix printers. Daisywheel printers were very slow and noisy. They offered a decent print quality in many different fonts but involved tiresome handling requirements. You had to change the wheel carrying the characters (called a *daisywheel*) every time you wanted to use a different font. Usually, changing fonts meant using italics. Those printers were able to simulate bold characters by hitting the same character twice with a slight horizontal shift. Dot-matrix printers were also noisy and offered mediocre print quality. However, they were much faster and much cheaper. Since then, daisywheel printers have completely disappeared. One would have thought the same would have happened with dot-matrix printers, but they still have a good share of the market because they are so inexpensive.

Dot-matrix printer

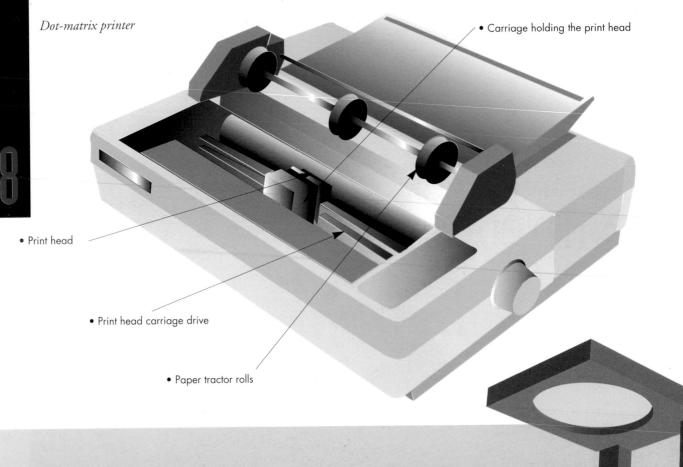

• Carriage holding the print head

• Print head

• Print head carriage drive

• Paper tractor rolls

The best dot-matrix printers give a resolution of up to 360 dots per inch (dpi), which is superior to the resolution of standard laser printers. However, you need to be careful of the advertised figures—such a printer will have output quality much inferior to laser printer output. The number of dots per inch doesn't say it all. The quality of the dot itself is also important (its shape and consistency of size), as well as how precisely the dots are placed. The dot of a dot-matrix printer produced by a print head in horizontal motion is much less precise than a dot from a laser printer. Vertical positioning of the dots printed on a given pass over a line is very precise. However, from one pass to another, positioning of the dots depends on the precision of the paper-feed mechanism, which is very uncertain.

A dot-matrix printer produces an image on a piece of paper using a group of metal rods (pins) that hit a piece of paper. A ribbon is placed between the pins and the sheet, and the impact from the pins causes ink to transfer from ribbon to paper. Characters are therefore created by the impact of the pins. The number of points that make up a character determines the resolution and quality of the printed output. The number of pins in the head also partly determines the print speed. A printer with a 9-pin head can, in theory, produce the same output quality as a 24-pin head printer, but it will have to go over the same line three or four times to do so. To obtain high vertical resolution, print heads on modern printers are equipped with pins laid out in several columns. This way, overlapping dots can be obtained in only one pass over the line.

Horizontal resolution varies according to the pins' repeat-hit rate and the speed at which the print head moves. Low-end printers use slow print heads. To obtain dots that horizontally overlap, the head must be slowed considerably. For this reason, low-end printers use a technique that consists of printing even dots on the first pass and odd dots in a second pass over the line.

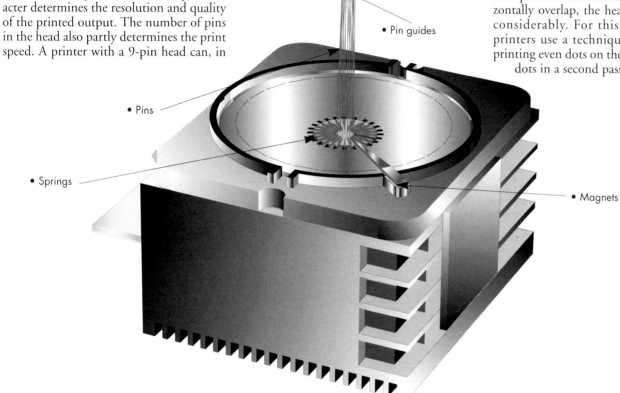

• Pin guides

• Pins

• Springs

• Magnets

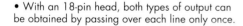

• With an 18-pin head, both types of output can be obtained by passing over each line only once.

• On a 9-pin head with the pins in a single column, the dots obtained are noncontiguous. To get overlapping dots, you have to print twice on the same line, the second time shifting the head over by half a dot. Noncontiguous dots are used for printing in *draft* mode; overlapping dots are used to get better quality (*letter-quality* mode), but the speed of printing is halved.

• With a slow print head, even dots are printed on the first pass and odd dots are printed when it goes over the line the second time.

• With a fast print head, it is possible to print overlapping dots in only one pass over the line.

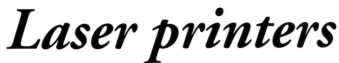

Laser printers

Dot-matrix printers print characters on lines. A dot-matrix printer's speed is measured in characters per second (cps) or lines per second (lps). Although a dot-matrix printer is fine for printing text, graphics pose more problems. They usually print very slowly and with questionable quality, because graphics are created from a sequence of horizontal lines that can never be perfectly aligned. The arrival of graphical interfaces brought with it the use of multiple character fonts in all sizes, as well as mixtures of text and graphics, which required higher performance printers. Laser printers arrived at an opportune moment, providing users with a printing quality that matched the quality of the graphics on their screens.

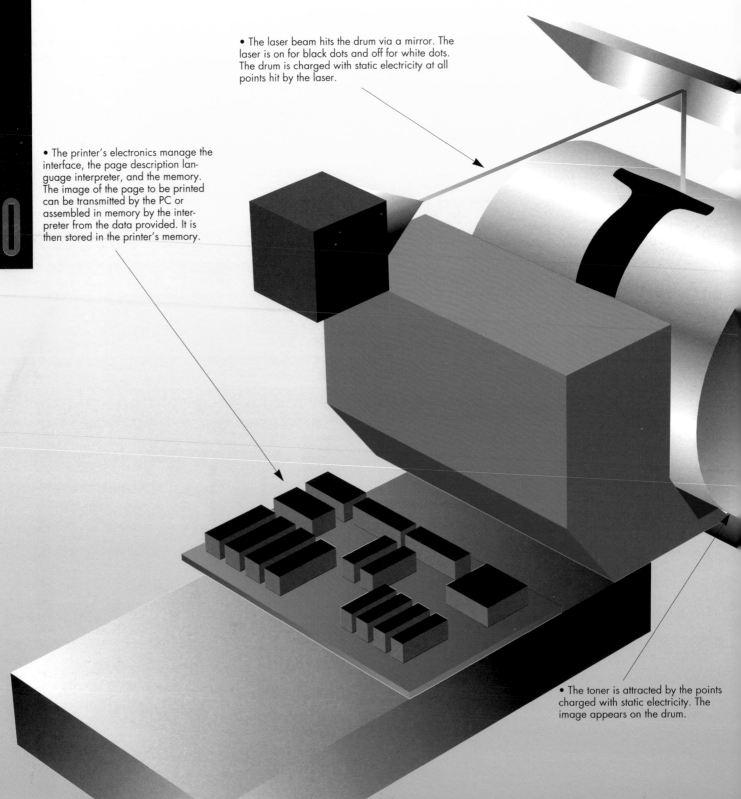

• The laser beam hits the drum via a mirror. The laser is on for black dots and off for white dots. The drum is charged with static electricity at all points hit by the laser.

• The printer's electronics manage the interface, the page description language interpreter, and the memory. The image of the page to be printed can be transmitted by the PC or assembled in memory by the interpreter from the data provided. It is then stored in the printer's memory.

• The toner is attracted by the points charged with static electricity. The image appears on the drum.

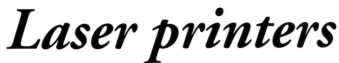

In a laser printer, the image is created using an electrostatic process. A laser ray hits the surface of a drum via a mirror. This surface is treated in such a way that the points hit by the laser develop an electrostatic charge. In this way an image of the page is written on the drum. Each point hit by the laser corresponds to a black dot. For white dots, the laser is off and the surface of the drum doesn't develop any charge.

A solid powder ink, called *toner*, is deposited on the cylinder. Points with electrostatic charge hold the powder. Toner on the drum is transferred to a piece of paper, which then goes through two heating rolls that apply high pressure. The heat makes the powder melt, and the pressure presses it onto the paper.

A laser printer prints much faster and gives much better quality output than a dot-matrix printer. A laser printer's speed is measured in pages per minute (ppm). However, the speed of the *print engine* has to be distinguished from the real speed achieved. Laser printers are often used to print complex pages containing graphics, text, and even photos. Usually the PC simply sends printing commands, such as "trace a straight line from a given point to another given point." The printer contains a program that's able to calculate the position of the dots that will make the line. Such programs (like PostScript or PCL) are called *page description languages*. Calculating where the dots are to be printed can take much longer than to actually print the page. Therefore, a complex document can take many minutes to print each page, even if the printer can print eight pages per minute. In fact, the printer is able to print eight *identical* pages per minute. It may take, for example, several minutes to create an image of a page, but then an unlimited number of copies of the page can be printed by having the drum rotate many times. The laser charges the drum on each rotation from the page image that's kept in the printer's memory.

Less expensive laser printers don't have a page description language. In this case, the PC must calculate the position of the dots on the page, considerably slowing down other programs that are running.

• The paper goes through two heating rolls under high pressure. The toner melts and the image is pressed onto the paper.

• The image is transferred onto the paper. At this point, the toner is still in powder form.

131

Using fonts

Laser printers usually have a specific number of fonts in memory. The characters are described by mathematical curves (*vector* fonts) and, therefore, can be used in all sizes. However, the program producing the document to be printed must know the characteristics of the printer fonts and, in particular, the size of each character to calculate the length of the lines and the height of the pages. (For example, an *m* takes much more space than an *i*.)

Another solution is to use downloadable fonts that are located on the PC's disk drive and sent to the printer by the program that prints or by some utility program. In such cases, you have to use fonts specific to the printer being used: PostScript fonts for a PostScript printer, Hewlett-Packard fonts for an HP Laserjet printer, etc. Alone, those fonts are totally incompatible with each other. But some HP printers also include PostScript, and a program (such as Adobe Type Manager) can be used to print PostScript fonts to almost any printer.

TrueType fonts provide a more elegant solution. These fonts are also defined by mathematical curves, but they are independent of the printer used. If the printer can use vector fonts, the PC's system translates TrueType fonts into a format understood by the printer. If the printer can't use vector fonts, the system calculates by itself the dots corresponding to each character in the size needed and sends the results to the printer. It is then possible to use those same fonts with all printers. The Adobe Type Manager mentioned previously makes PostScript work like TrueType.

Inkjet printers

Laser printers are attractive because of their speed and high print quality, and they are also ergonomically appealing because they are so quiet. However, their relatively high purchase price limits their use. Manufacturers have worked to develop a technology that can give equal quality at a lower price. The inkjet printer seems to meet these objectives—it's almost as quiet, less bulky, and much less expensive. (Because of their light weight, many inkjet printers are designed to be used with your portable computer while you are traveling.) However, while an inkjet printer's output quality is satisfactory, its speed is significantly less than that of a laser printer. Like dot-matrix printers, inkjet printers print line by line using a movable print head.

The print head of an inkjet printer is mounted on a moving carriage, as in a dot-matrix printer. The head has a number of holes, or *nozzles*, behind which there is a cavity called the *ink chamber*. Ink is carried to the chamber by a series of channels. Behind the ink chamber is a resistor that heats the chamber. When the resistor heats the chamber, ink in the chamber boils, forming a gas bubble. When the pressure is high enough, the ink located over the bubble is ejected by the nozzle, producing a tiny black dot on the paper.

Theoretically, inkjet printers work with regular paper, as do laser printers. However, output quality relies a lot on the quality of the paper used. Because the ink is ejected as a liquid, an absorbent paper produces a blotting-paper effect, downgrading the clarity of the dot. It's therefore better to use specially treated paper to get the best possible output. Unfortunately, this type of paper is more expensive.

Also, some printers use a piezoelectric system to eject the ink instead of a heating resistor. An electric current produces vibrations in a piece of quartz, ejecting the ink.

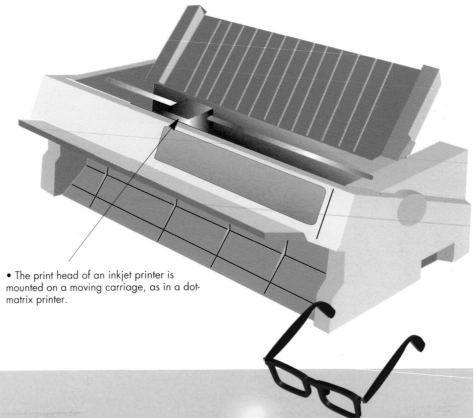

• The print head of an inkjet printer is mounted on a moving carriage, as in a dot-matrix printer.

While an inkjet printer is much less expensive than a laser printer, the cost per page of the ink cartridge is much higher. It can reach up to ten times the cost per page of a laser printer toner cartridge. To compare true costs per printed page, consider the number of pages you'll be printing each month. If you print only a few pages per month, the inkjet printer can be a good choice. If you need to print several dozen pages per day, a laser printer will be less expensive in the long run. Also, laser printers are faster. And don't forget to take into account that an inkjet printer's mechanism isn't made for heavy-duty use, unlike the parts built into a laser printer. Under conditions of high use, an inkjet printer is more likely to fail than a laser printer.

Print head of an inkjet printer

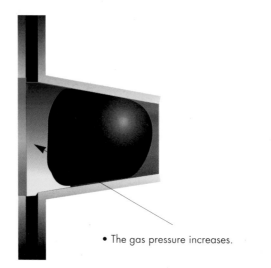

• The gas pressure increases.

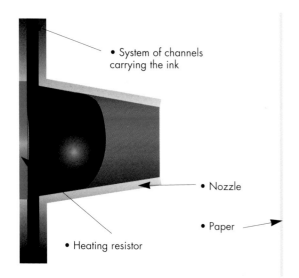

• System of channels carrying the ink

• Nozzle

• Paper

• Heating resistor

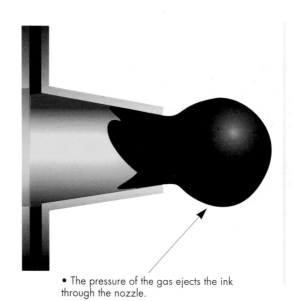

• The pressure of the gas ejects the ink through the nozzle.

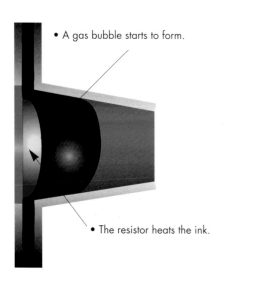

• A gas bubble starts to form.

• The resistor heats the ink.

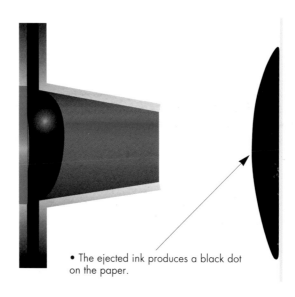

• The ejected ink produces a black dot on the paper.

Color printers

Most computers now have color monitors, but color printers are still quite rare. Yet it's very frustrating to create graphics with nice colors and finally be able to print them only in black and white. With the new technologies available, color printers should quickly multiply and eventually become standard equipment on all PCs. There are many color printing systems and all are based on the same optical principle, subtractive synthesis (as opposed to monitors, which use additive synthesis). Implementation, however, varies considerably. There are solid inkjet, liquid inkjet, thermal transfer, or sublimation color printers.

Printing technique

Color printing isn't fundamentally different from black and white printing. The two principal differences come from the fact that the paper must be printed once for each primary color. However, research into simulating photographic quality has lead to print technologies not used in black and white printing. A solid inkjet printer uses wax-like inks. When heated, the ink liquefies and the system then operates

as a regular inkjet printer. The result is better quality, because the ink doesn't dry by evaporation, but instead solidifies during cooling. Furthermore, the images created by

solid inks don't suffer from the "blotting paper" effect.

Sublimation printers use a different technique. Sublimation is the transition of a substance from a solid state to a gaseous state without any intervening liquid phase. Powerful and sudden heating (to about 500 degrees for these inks) produces gaseous ink.

Subtractive synthesis

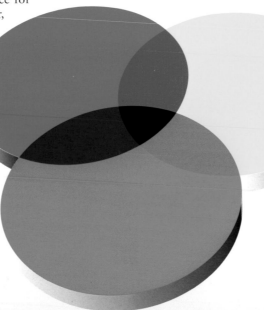

Subtractive synthesis

The process used to display colors on a monitor is called *additive synthesis* because adding the fundamental colors creates the final color. White light is made of red, green, and blue. By mixing equal proportions of the three source colors red, green, and blue, you obtain white. By varying the proportion of the three components, you can obtain all possible shades of all colors.

This technique can't be used to print color, because printed paper doesn't produce light. It simply reflects surrounding light, which is usually white. *Subtractive synthesis* consists of taking away some components from the reflected white light. Red ink absorbs yellow and blue and reflects red. Blue ink absorbs yellow and red. Black ink absorbs all colors and doesn't reflect anything. We can therefore obtain all colors on paper by

using three primary colors: cyan (blue), magenta (red), and yellow. A combination of these three colors produces black.

Actually, this is not completely true, because inks aren't perfect. Combining the three colors produces a dark greenish gray. That's why this process, called a *three-color process*, is not used much. The *four-color process* is preferred. Black ink is used to reinforce dark shades and to get perfect blacks.

Four-color printing with a laser printer

• The laser beam traces the image on the drum.

• The blue image goes through the rolls to melt the toner and embed it in the paper.

• Blue toner is deposited on the drum.

• The paper goes through the print mechanism once for each color.

Imagesetters and film recorders

Desktop printers don't produce documents of sufficient quality for professional publication. To get perfect documents, two types of machines are used: imagesetters and film recorders. An imagesetter produces a document by printing photographic film with a laser. Documents can only be in black and white. In contrast, film recorders produce color documents on film identical to that used in cameras. Imagesetters and film recorders are very expensive; most individuals and small companies can't justify their cost. However, you can use *service bureaus* that specialize in high-quality output to produce this kind of material.

An imagesetter contains a laser whose light hits a photographic film via a revolving polygonal mirror. The photographic film used is different from the film used in cameras. It's a black and white film that's sensitive to the specific frequency (color) of the laser light used. (Lasers emitting lights of different colors can be used.) The main feature of this film is that it doesn't produce shades of gray. All the points (dots) hit by the light are black. All other areas are white. The precision of the laser allows the printing of dots only a few microns in diameter. The resolution of some imagesetters is over 3000 dots per inch.

To obtain high-quality color output, a four-color process can be used to produce one film for each primary color (see the following two pages). A film recorder can also be used. This device generates a color image on a small cathode tube, an image similar to the one you can get on your monitor. This image is reproduced on regular color film, and the result is a color slide. The diffusion of the light creates an image that is not composed of dots but rather continuous shades, like a photograph.

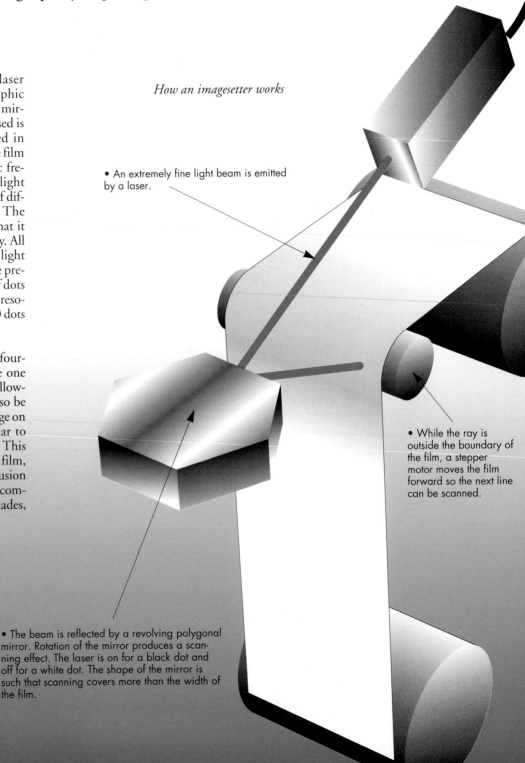

How an imagesetter works

• An extremely fine light beam is emitted by a laser.

• While the ray is outside the boundary of the film, a stepper motor moves the film forward so the next line can be scanned.

• The beam is reflected by a revolving polygonal mirror. Rotation of the mirror produces a scanning effect. The laser is on for a black dot and off for a white dot. The shape of the mirror is such that scanning covers more than the width of the film.

How a film recorder works

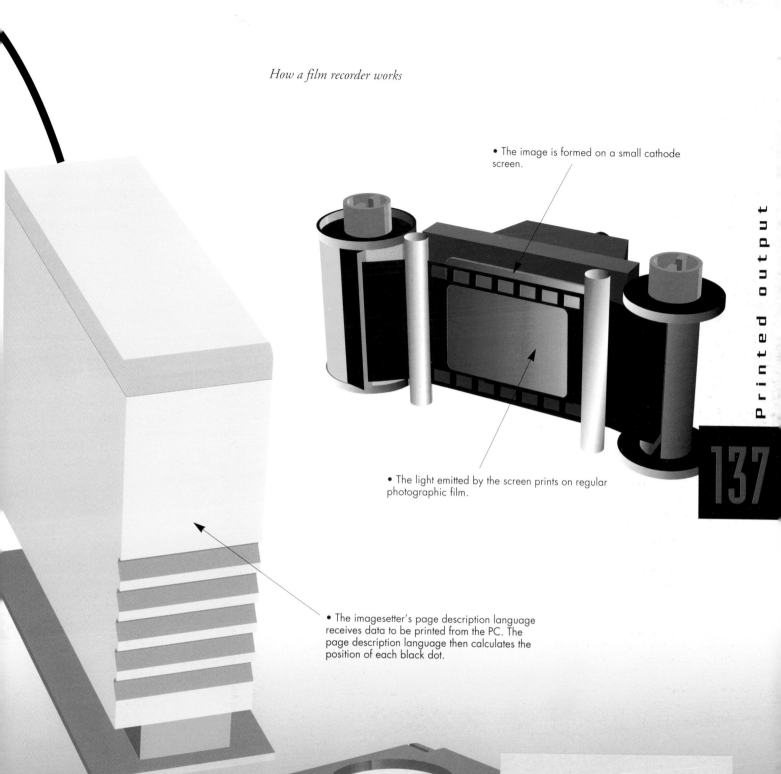

• The image is formed on a small cathode screen.

• The light emitted by the screen prints on regular photographic film.

• The imagesetter's page description language receives data to be printed from the PC. The page description language then calculates the position of each black dot.

Neither imagesetters nor film recorders can produce final documents. As is the case with a photograph, the films must be developed in a special machine. The process is therefore more complex than using a dot-matrix or laser printer.

Rendering grayscale and color

Black and white printers are unable to produce levels of gray (called *grayscale*). They must therefore use a special technique, called *screening,* to simulate intermediate shades. Color printers are also unable to produce shades of color, except for those using thermal transfer or sublimation methods. Screening is also used to simulate shades of color. Some printers let the user choose the screening parameters, which can sometimes result in significantly improved ouput.

Black screens

Simulating average gray with black and white dots seems quite simple. The area to be printed gray must contain half black dots and half white. The only difficulty is choosing which dots have to be black. The most common technique consists of grouping printer dots into *dot screens.* For each dot screen, a given percentage of the dots will be black. The dot lines that constitute the screen are generally positioned according to a *screen angle.* Usually, a 45-degree angle is chosen. The screen resolution is measured in *lines per inch* and is called *linear density.*

The higher the linear density, the better the output quality will be. However, for a given resolution, the number of gray shades that can be obtained is inversely proportional to the linear density. Thus, with a 300 dot-per-inch laser printer, 37 shades of gray can be obtained with a linear density of 50 lines per inch. With 75 lines per inch, the number of shades of gray that can be obtained is only 17. (A horizontal screen is assumed here. With an oblique screen, the results can be slightly different.)

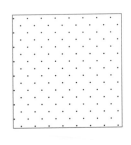

• Gray shades are simulated with a dot screen of a continuous tone and variably sized dots. This is called an *amplitude modulation screen.*

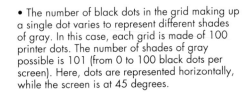

• The number of black dots in the grid making up a single dot varies to represent different shades of gray. In this case, each grid is made of 100 printer dots. The number of shades of gray possible is 101 (from 0 to 100 black dots per screen). Here, dots are represented horizontally, while the screen is at 45 degrees.

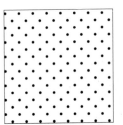
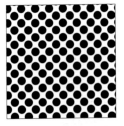
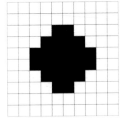
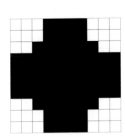

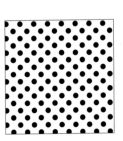

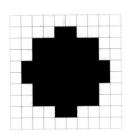

Color screening

To show color shades, screens of the four basic colors (using the subtractive synthesis described on page 134) are superimposed. To avoid moiré effects, each screen must have a specific and unique angle.

• The black screen is oriented at 45 degrees.

• The magenta screen is oriented at 75 degrees.

• The yellow screen is oriented at 90 degrees.

• The cyan screen is oriented at 105 degrees.

Frequency modulation screening

To improve image quality and reduce moiré effects, another screening technique, called *frequency modulation screening*, is used. With this system, shades aren't represented by dots of smaller or larger sizes but rather by dots that are the same size but vary in distance from each other.

The frequency modulation screen

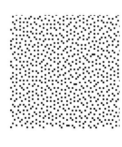

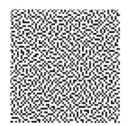

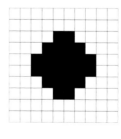

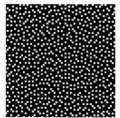

• All dots are the same size. There are more of them in dark areas.

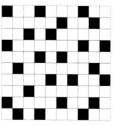

• In an amplitude modulation screen, the gray dot is represented this way.

• In a frequency modulation screen, the same shade of gray is obtained this way. You can see that the result will be much better, especially in low resolution.

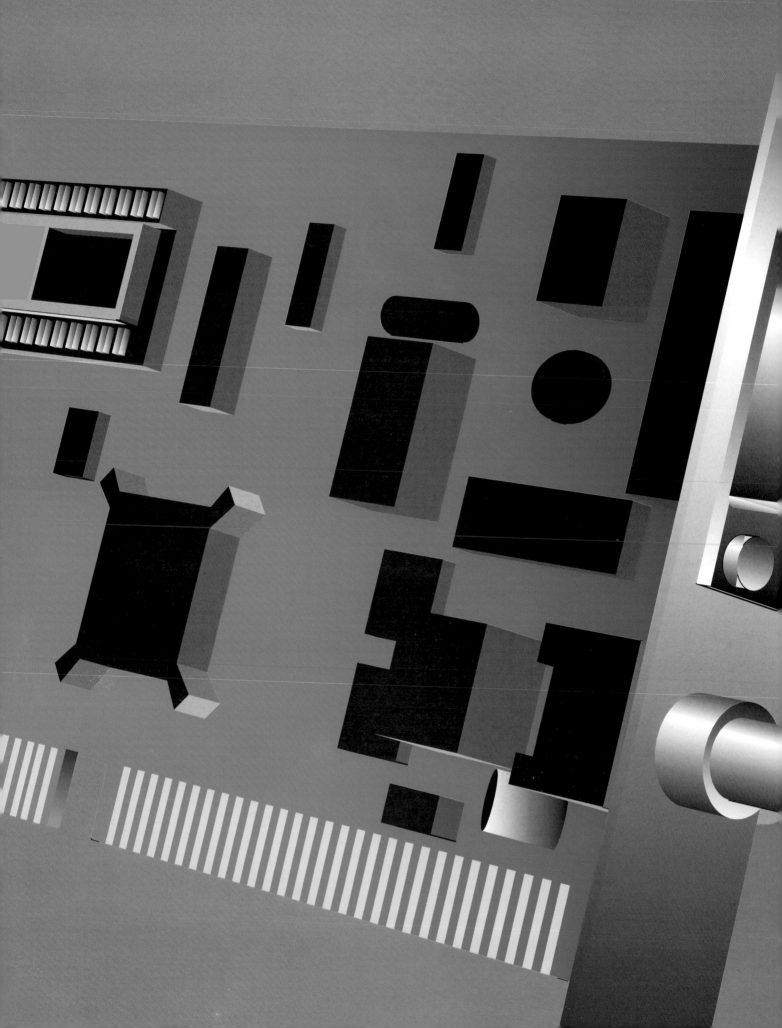

6

TELECOMMUNICATIONS AND NETWORKS

• Local area networks 142

• Modems and digital
telephone networks 148

• Wide area networks 152

• Using a network 154

Local area networks

Until recently, owning a PC was enough to be on the cutting edge of progress and efficiency. Nowadays, an isolated PC seems almost old-fashioned. To be efficient, you've got to be connected! In most companies the PCs are linked into networks. Even geographically isolated users can be connected to a company's network via remote access nodes. For modern PCs, the latest trend is *communication*. Linking PCs starts with a local area network (LAN), which allows information to be shared between PCs in the same building. Many technologies can be used.

Bus networks

A *bus* network has open ends. Each PC is connected to the network via a *network card*. Some peripherals, such as printers, can also be added to the network. Each connected computer or peripheral is called a node. Each end of the network is closed by a terminating resistor, which prevents signal interference. The most common example of this type of network is the *Ethernet* network. The disadvantages of this system are that collision detection is required, and transmission slows down when collisions occur. Each node is authorized to transmit data until a collision occurs. Once a collision has been detected, no other node is allowed to transmit data until the node that detected the collision completes sending its message. This type of network can crash suddenly, and the effect is brutal.

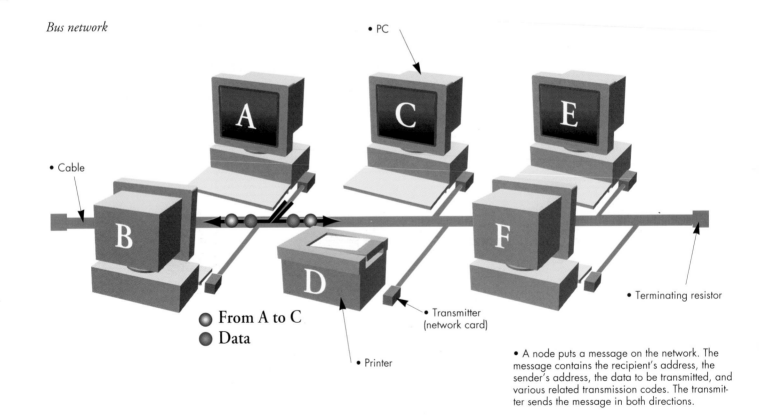

Bus network

• PC

• Cable

• From A to C
• Data

• Printer

• Transmitter (network card)

• Terminating resistor

• A node puts a message on the network. The message contains the recipient's address, the sender's address, the data to be transmitted, and various related transmission codes. The transmitter sends the message in both directions.

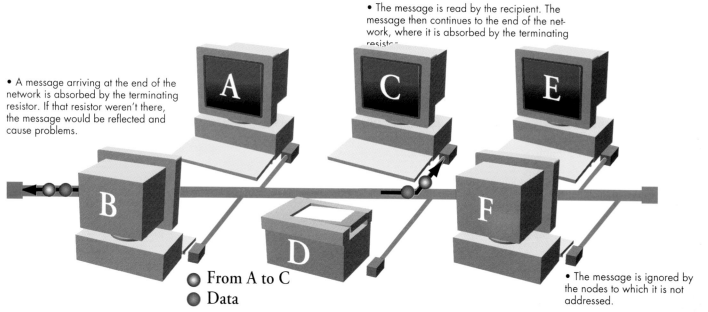

• The message is read by the recipient. The message then continues to the end of the network, where it is absorbed by the terminating resistor.

• A message arriving at the end of the network is absorbed by the terminating resistor. If that resistor weren't there, the message would be reflected and cause problems.

• The message is ignored by the nodes to which it is not addressed.

○ From A to C
○ Data

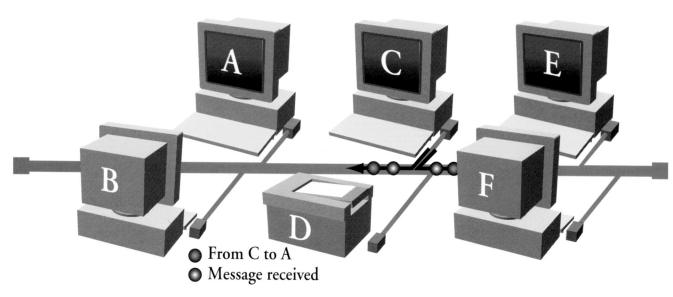

• The recipient sends an *acknowledgment* to inform the sender that it received the message.

○ From C to A
○ Message received

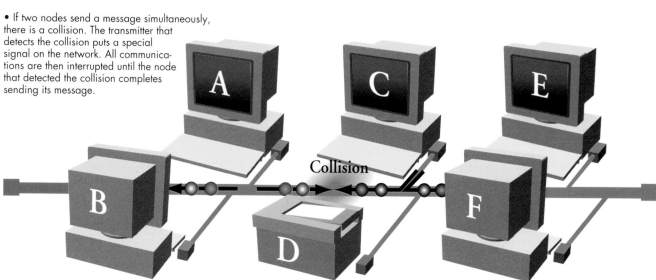

• If two nodes send a message simultaneously, there is a collision. The transmitter that detects the collision puts a special signal on the network. All communications are then interrupted until the node that detected the collision completes sending its message.

Collision

Token ring networks

A *token ring* network has two characteristics that are supposed to solve the problems of a bus network: It's a closed network, in which only one message (the *token*) can circulate at any given time, which makes it impossible to have collisions. To transmit, a node must wait until it intercepts a free token. Each node connected to the network must read the token when it arrives and retransmit it if it hasn't reached its destination. The node that's the destination of a token must send an acknowledgment. This doesn't have to be sent to a specific address, because only the node that sent the message is waiting for an acknowledgment. Other nodes simply retransmit it. This technology seems to solve the problems simply and efficiently. There is, however, a downside to it: Nothing prevents one node from tying up the entire network, because all the other nodes are waiting for the message sender to free the token.

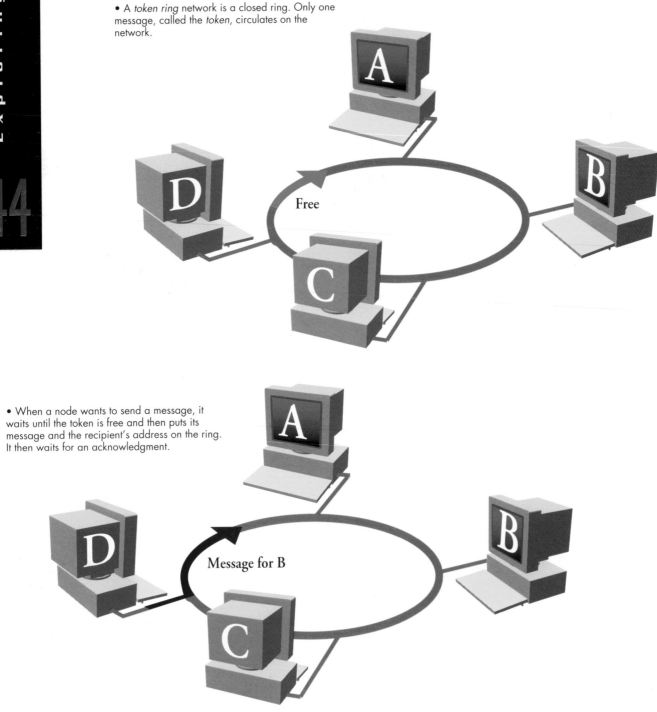

• A *token ring* network is a closed ring. Only one message, called the *token*, circulates on the network.

Free

• When a node wants to send a message, it waits until the token is free and then puts its message and the recipient's address on the ring. It then waits for an acknowledgment.

Message for B

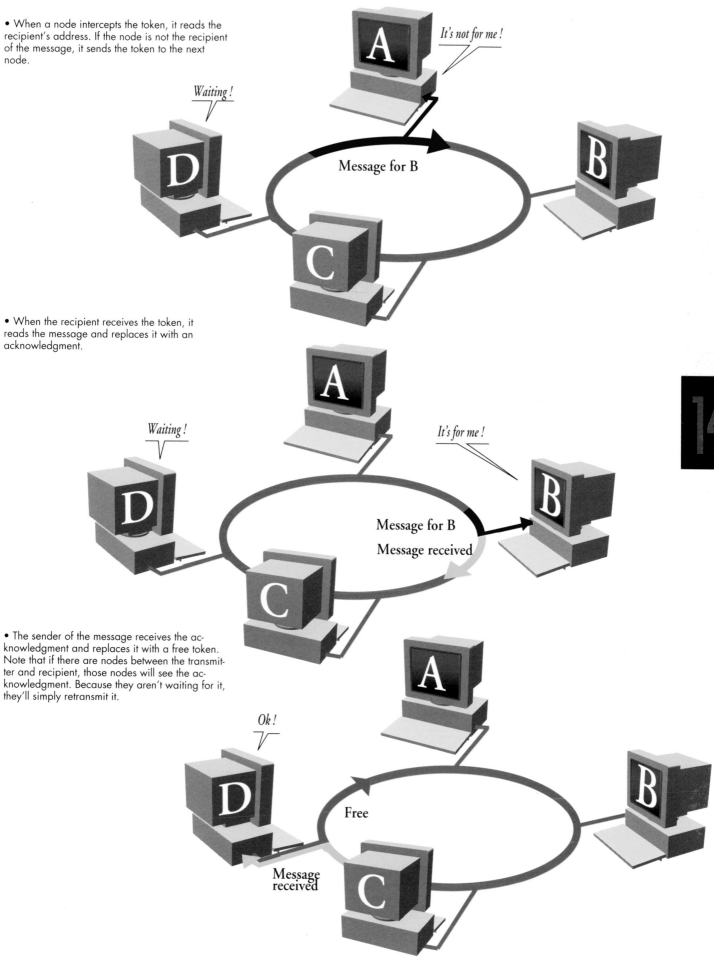

• When a node intercepts the token, it reads the recipient's address. If the node is not the recipient of the message, it sends the token to the next node.

It's not for me !

Waiting !

Message for B

• When the recipient receives the token, it reads the message and replaces it with an acknowledgment.

Waiting !

It's for me !

Message for B
Message received

• The sender of the message receives the acknowledgment and replaces it with a free token. Note that if there are nodes between the transmitter and recipient, those nodes will see the acknowledgment. Because they aren't waiting for it, they'll simply retransmit it.

Ok !

Free

Message received

Star networks

A *star network* has characteristics that make it more efficient than bus or token ring networks. Data exchanges are better organized and more efficient, because they are supervised by a controller.

Furthermore, because each node is linked to the controller by a different cable, there's no risk of collision. However, this type of architecture is more expensive: it requires extra cables and a controller. To optimize the function of a network without incurring exhorbitant costs, several network architectures can be used at the same time. Then the various networks can be linked by an inter-network link.

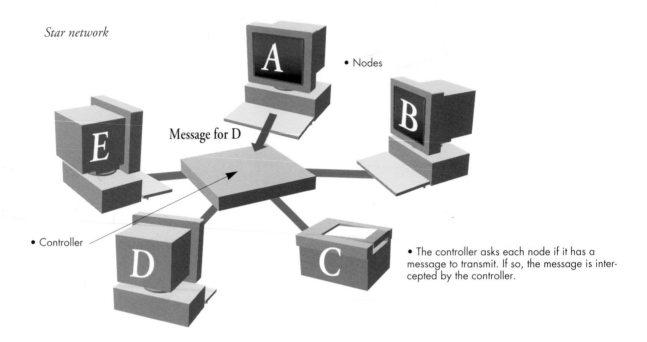

Star network

• Nodes

Message for D

• Controller

• The controller asks each node if it has a message to transmit. If so, the message is intercepted by the controller.

• The controller manages message transmission by breaking it into smaller elements. Between each element, it continues to ask the other nodes if they have messages to send and handles their messages.

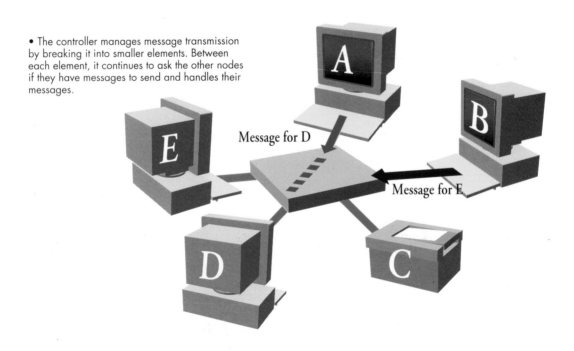

Message for D

Message for E

• Many message exchanges can be performed simultaneously. This way, the network can't be tied up by a single node.

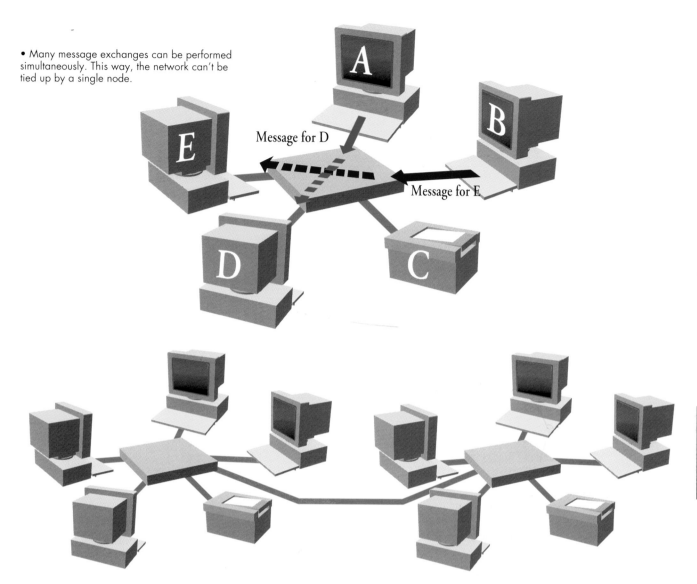

Message for D

Message for E

• To avoid network overflow, the network can be divided into several subnetworks, all linked together.

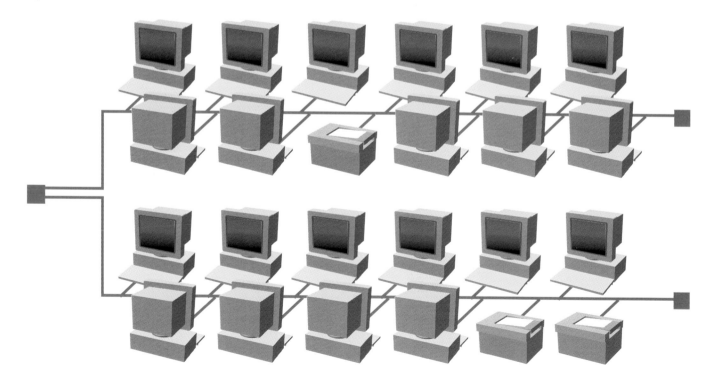

Modems and digital telephone networks

While local area networks allow communication between different computers in the same building, it is often necessary to be able to transmit messages to computers in remote locations. To do that, you can use a combination of telephone lines and a *modem*. Telephone networks were created to carry current, variations of which represent the sounds in your voice. Because computers communicate by exchanging 1s and 0s (bits), those values have to be transformed into sound signals to be transmitted over the telephone. To do that, one frequency is used for a 1 and another for a 0. This conversion is executed by the modem, short for *modulator-demodulator*. The modem is able to convert both bits to sound and sound to bits.

Two computers equipped with modems can exchange messages, but a few conditions have to be met. First, each computer must use a communication program that's compatible with the way its modem operates. Both modems also must operate at the same speed. Transmission speed is measured in *bits per second (bps)*. (Often the term *baud* is incorrectly used as the term for transmission speed. In fact, *baud rate* refers to transmission state changes, each of which may represent more than one bit.) Modem transmission speeds range from 75 bps to over 28,800 bps. The most common high-speed

modems operate at 14,400 bps, and, more recently, 28,800 bps.

Both computers must use the same transmission *protocol*. A certain amount of data must be exchanged in addition to the message being transmitted. Computers must identify themselves, and the recipient must indicate that it's either ready to receive a message or that the transmission must be postponed momentarily until it can process the data already received. The sender must also be able to indicate when data transmission is complete.

To optimize data transmission, many protocols have been standardized. Each transmission is usually preceded by a dialog (called *handshaking*) in which the sender and

receiver decide upon the transmission characteristics: the size of the data blocks to be transmitted, the speed of transmission, the verification protocol, whether compression will be used, and so forth.

Data is usually transmitted in blocks ending with *error checking* codes—these codes allow the receiver to recognize transmission errors. The larger the block size, the faster the transmission. However, if the block contains an error, the entire block must be retransmitted. When using phone lines of questionable quality, smaller blocks usually give better results. Modern communication programs are able to automatically vary the size of the block. If a large block has an error, it is broken into smaller blocks before it is retransmitted.

Communication between two PCs via modems

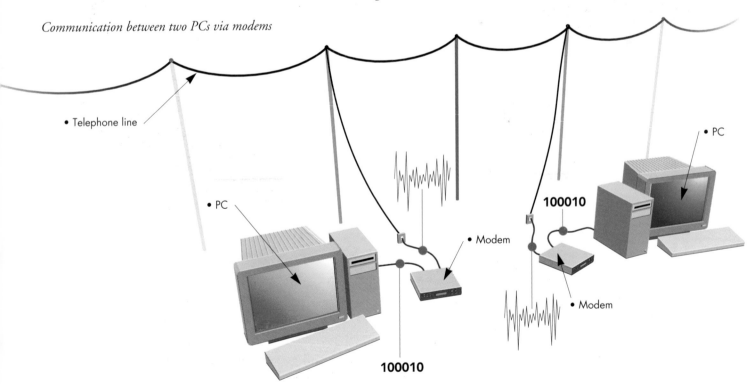

• Telephone line

• PC

• Modem

100010

100010

• PC

• Modem

Different types of modems

Of the different types of modems, the most simple is an *acoustic modem.* Acoustic modems are rarely used anymore—their maximum speed is usually only 300 baud. However, they do have one advantage: they can be used on any type of telephone, even those in phone booths. An acoustic modem has a speaker and a microphone that must be placed over the phone handset.

The other types of modems are plugged directly into telephone jacks. They interface directly with the telephone line and all have internal dialing—the computer dials the number. You don't need to have a telephone.

Acoustic modem

• To the PC's serial port

There are internal and external modems. Internal modems are less expensive and are built on an expansion card that plugs into one of the computer's expansion slots. A cable links it to the telephone jack in the wall. External modems take more space and

are more expensive. Furthermore, they use one of the PC's serial ports, which means that port can't be used for a printer or a mouse. Because PCs rarely have more than two serial ports, this can be a problem. External modems offer several advantages, however: they can easily be switched to another computer, they have their own power supply (so they don't drain the PC's power and they don't generate heat within the computer's case), and they have status lights (or message displays) that allow you to monitor the state of transmission.

Internal modem

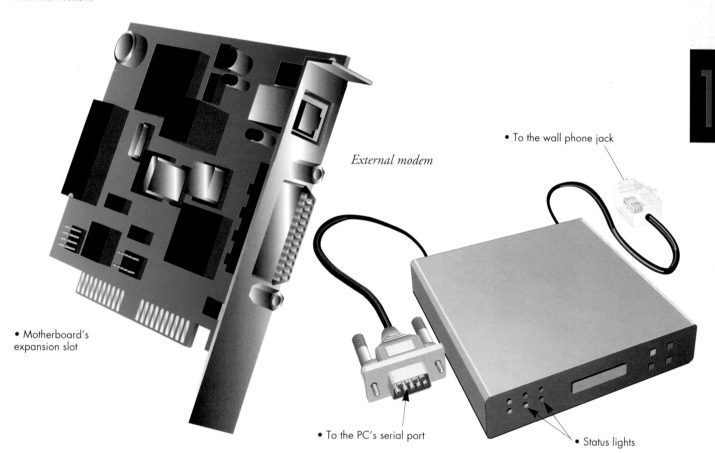

• Motherboard's expansion slot

• To the wall phone jack

External modem

• To the PC's serial port

• Status lights

Using a digital telephone network

The classic telephone network is gradually being replaced by a more modern type of network, called the *digital telephone network* or *ISDN* (Integrated Services Digital Network). If you are linked to such a network, you don't need a modem anymore; a

special interface will suffice. With ISDN, the process is reversed. Your voice is digitized into 1s and 0s before it is transmitted on the network. Computers can therefore communicate without having to convert digital bits to analog pulses and then back

again. This type of communication is much faster and can reach 64,000 bits per second on a single channel. By using as many as three channels in parallel, even higher speeds can be attained.

Fax modems

A PC equipped with a fax modem and fax software can replace a fax machine. To send a fax, you type text using a word processor and then print it. The fax software intercepts the print command and sends the output destined for the printer to the fax modem (after asking the recipient's fax number). To receive a fax, a PC must be turned on with the fax program running. Any fax received is stored on the PC's disk. You can later open the file and read it on the screen. Note that the file is stored as an image, not as a text file. An optical character recognition program can later convert it into a text file.

Any document created from any application can be sent. The recipient's fax acts as your printer. However, if you want to fax a paper document, you'll need a scanner to input the document. Also, if you want to put an incoming fax on paper, you'll need to print the file you receive.

If you want to send a document created by an application to a fax modem on a computer that runs the same application, you can send the recipient a copy of the file instead of a printed image of the file. Also, it's easy to send a file to the recipient along with the fax.

Sending a fax via a fax modem and fax software

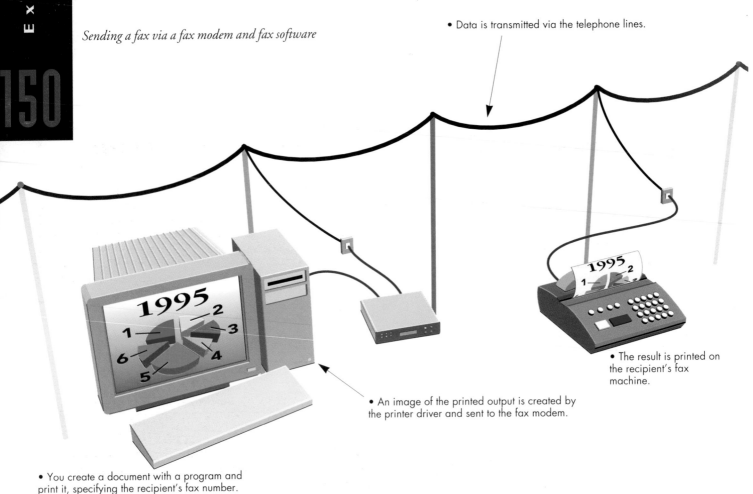

• Data is transmitted via the telephone lines.

• The result is printed on the recipient's fax machine.

• An image of the printed output is created by the printer driver and sent to the fax modem.

• You create a document with a program and print it, specifying the recipient's fax number.

Receiving a fax via a fax modem and fax software

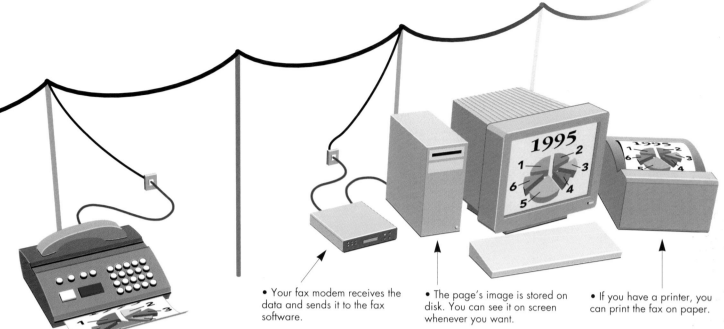

• Your correspondent sends you a fax.

• Your fax modem receives the data and sends it to the fax software.

• The page's image is stored on disk. You can see it on screen whenever you want.

• If you have a printer, you can print the fax on paper.

On-line services

A modem also allows you to log on to many on-line information services. Thanks to the many on-line databases that services maintain (or allow access to), you can have immediate access to all sorts of data, including stock market quotes, train and airline schedules, and supplier pricing. You can also download a lot of free programs (*freeware*) and programs that you can try out before you buy (*shareware*). You can send and receive E-mail (electronic mail) using your own on-line mailbox, and many on-line services offer access to international networks such as the Internet.

Obviously, you have to pay to use on-line services. Typically you have to pay either a subscription fee or connect charges (an amount proportional to the amount of time you're connected to the service), sometimes both. Where it's possible to log on at different transmission speeds, prices usually increase with higher speeds. However, for some operations, such as downloading, a higher transmission speed can significantly reduce your connect time, which will save you money in spite of the increased connect rates.

Remote access to a local area network

With a modem, you can also dial in from a remote site to a local area network. For example, if you are a sales rep on the road and have a laptop with a modem, you can transmit your purchase orders to the office every day. If an important report has to be completed, you can work on it at home. Even if you finish in the middle of the night, you can log on to the office's network and send the file, so it's available first thing in the morning.

Remote access is not only for isolated users. It's also possible, with a modem, to link two local area networks in two different buildings that are across the street from one another or even thousands of miles apart. Companies with many buildings use this type of network, called a *wide area network*.

Everything that can be done with a modem can also be done using a line on a digital network. However, both sides must have the same network access equipment. Because of this, digital links are usually reserved for inter-network connections and for on-line services specifically equipped for digital links (which is still pretty rare). For faxing, or remote access to a local area network from a laptop computer, it's best to use a modem.

Wide area networks

A local area network is one in which the nodes are close enough to one another to be connected on the same cable. Usually, the nodes in a local area network are computers within the same building. However, it's often necessary to have computers in different buildings, cities, or even countries communicating with each other. Then a *wide area network* is required. Originally, this term was used to designate computers linked only by telecommunication lines. Nowadays, a wide area network almost always consists of local area networks connected to one another by digital telephone networks or dedicated phone lines. Some wide area networks are private, providing access only to computers within the organization. Others are commercial; with these you have to pay to become a member. There are also public networks, which anyone with a PC can access for the price of the phone call.

The main problem of wide area networks is transmission speed. On a local Ethernet network, data is transmitted at 10 Mbps (10 megabits per second). However, today's medium-fast modems run at about 10 Kbps, which is 1000 times slower. The problem doesn't lie only in the delays due to slower speed. At about one-tenth of one percent of the capacity of the 10 Mbps network, a 10 Kbps network quickly fills with pending commands and unprocessed data, leading to additional slowdowns or system lockups.

Results can be improved by using specially conditioned dedicated lines to transfer data, or by accessing a digital telephone network. Organizations that rent dedicated lines have exclusive use of them 24 hours a day. Rental cost is proportional to the maximum data transfer rate. Lines exist that can transfer data at 45 Mbps. Due to their cost, they are used mainly by large corporations and institutions.

A digital telephone network is a relatively inexpensive way to build a wide area network. Its maximum speed is 64 Kbps per channel. However, it is possible to achieve faster effective transmission rates by using parallel transmissions on different channels. Cost is usually a function of the duration of the communication and the amount of data exchanged.

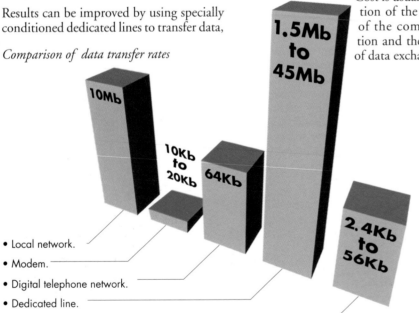

Comparison of data transfer rates

10Mb

10Kb to 20Kb

64Kb

1.5Mb to 45Mb

2.4Kb to 56Kb

• Local network.

• Modem.

• Digital telephone network.

• Dedicated line.

• X.25.

• To link two points, one line is required.

• For three points, three lines are required.

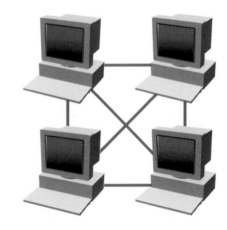

The disadvantage of the two previous solutions appears when more than two local area networks need to be connected. To link two networks, one line is required. To link three, three lines are required. To link four networks, six lines are required.

• For four points, six lines are required.

One common solution is to use a packet-switching network. In this case, users simply have to access a router (via a modem). A router is a point where different lines come together. The topology of this type of network is similar to a local area network. However, the lines are not dedicated and are therefore available to many users. In addition, data is grouped into *packets*, which are sent to the address indicated using the lines available at the time the communication is requested. The packets can follow different paths to get to their destination. Each router receives and sends the packets according to their destination and the available lines. This way, line use is optimized, leading to lower cost and higher transfer speed.

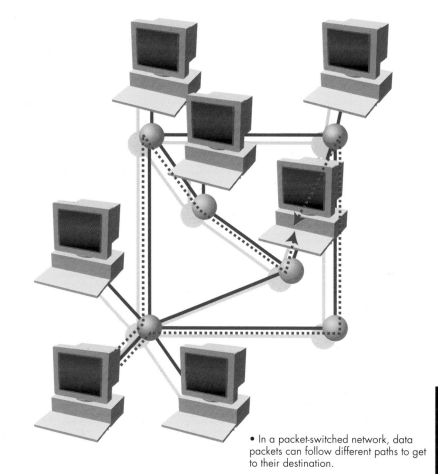

• In a packet-switched network, data packets can follow different paths to get to their destination.

Internet: a wide area network

The largest wide area network is called the Internet. Having originated in the United States as a Department of Defense and defense contractor's network, it now covers the entire world. Its skeleton consists of the NSFnet (National Science Foundation) network, which links 16 data processing centers via dedicated lines working at 1.5 Mbps and 45 Mbps. A multitude of secondary connections give it a high level of redundancy, making it almost impossible to crash the network. In addition, it's linked to other networks throughout the world. The Internet was conceived to provide for information exchange between research centers and universities, but it is accessible to everyone. For individual users, there are many private services providing access to the Internet, as well as on-line services such as CompuServe and America Online.

The Internet network

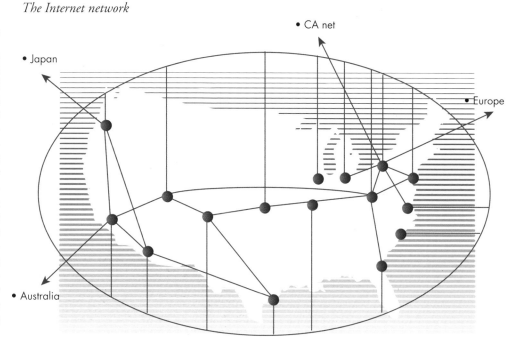

Using a network

As you've seen, a network facilitates the exchange of data. However, a floppy disk given to the person standing by your desk, or sent by mail if the recipient is farther away, achieves the same results. Only the data transfer speed is different. But speed brings something else besides a shorter transmission delay. Faster data transfer makes it possible to create new applications. In fact, the nature of exchanges becomes completely different once they are fast enough to be perceived by the users as occurring in "real time." As an example, let's compare a phone conversation with an exchange of letters by regular mail. The same information can be exchanged in both cases, but the phone is so fast that new applications are available. First, you can show your presence while the other person talks by uttering an occasional monosyllable. The person talking therefore always knows that he or she is being listened to. However, if you send mail, you know only much later whether it reached its destination. If you don't clearly understand something during a phone conversation, you can interrupt the person talking and ask him or her to repeat or clarify what they said. You can also adapt what you say according to the person's reactions. Telephones made possible the development of a new function, conversation at a distance, that mail didn't allow. It is the same with networks.

Resource sharing

A network allows many people working on the same project to do so more efficiently. All files can be kept on a single computer, called a *file server*. The file server can be used to ensure that there is only one version of a file at any one time, which helps prevent errors and slows the proliferation of multiple versions of the same file, conserving disk space. A server can also contain applications. Some programs are available with a *site license*. Say, for example, that three users are authorized to use a word processing program. If your company has a network with five PCs and you are sure there will never be more than three people needing the word processor at the same time, you could put that application on the network. Without a network, either the word

processing application would have to be installed at each workstation, which would be more expensive, or people would have to switch computers according to the application they need to use.

A network equipped with a file server makes backing up data much easier. Because all the data is on the server, all data can be backed up each day by the network administrator without the users having to worry about it.

A print server allows you to share one or more printers. Without a network, each user must either have his own printer or copy the files he wants to print to a floppy disk and then find a free PC with a printer. The first solution is expensive; the second is impractical. With a print server, one printer can

support three or four PCs. If those PC users still don't get their printed output fast enough, a second print server can be installed so that everyone can print without problems. Furthermore, print servers save files on disk before printing them on paper, so your computer can keep on working while the server is printing.

In the same way, many other resources can be shared on a network: a modem or fax modem, a scanner, a CD-ROM drive, a removable disk drive, and so forth.

Servers can also be PCs dedicated to a single application *(dedicated servers)*, or they can be users' PCs set up so that some of their processing resources and hard disk space act as servers for other users on the network *(shared servers)*.

Electronic mail (e-mail)

E-mail lets users send messages and files from one workstation to another. E-mail is generally managed by a specialized program permanently running on a server. This way you can send a message to a user even if that user's PC is turned off. As soon as that user's PC is turned on, the pending message will be sent and the computer will alert the user. On your end, you can find out at any time

whether your message has been read. You can also send a message to several users selected according to certain criteria, such as being members of a particular workgroup.

If your local network is linked to a wide area network, such as Internet, you can send messages and files to any user in the world who also has access to the network.

Teleconferencing

A network allows you to exchange messages in real time, as if you were having a discussion on the phone. You can propose a meeting by consulting the public area of your co worker's agendas. They reply to your proposal by accepting or refusing the meeting. You don't need to remember when the meeting is—the computer will remind you. You can then discuss a project by typing your questions and answers to other meeting participants on the keyboard. This is called *teleconferencing*. Each participant will see your message displayed on his or her screen, and you'll see the same messages the other participants see. You can also send a private message that others won't be able to see. Of course, maybe you'd prefer to get together in a conference room to have the discussion. But remember that in this way you can organize a teleconference with people from all over the world.

Telecommuting

A network also lets you use the resources of your company from a remote site such as your home, if you like working on weekends. A portable modem and computer will suffice to give you access to all your files along with all the resources available on the network. While on the road, you can send to your office all the documents you want: reports, mail, images digitized by a hand scanner, or pictures taken using a digital camera.

The future of networks

There is no doubt that in the future nearly all PCs will be linked to a wide area network, either individually or through a local area network. All information available on most databases in the world will then be accessible to everybody. To achieve this, the data transfer rates on existing networks must be increased considerably, starting at the local area network level. For convenient and efficient access to shared data, latency times ideally should be lower than the delay we now experience when using local networks. Otherwise, users can be tempted to copy remote data to a local computer, where access is quicker. This is risky, because if you copy a file from a server to a local disk, modify it, and copy it back to its original position, you won't know if another user made changes to it while you were updating it. By putting your modified version on the server, you overwrite the work done by your coworkers. Also, if you're the first to place your copy on the server, your local work will be lost as soon as another user does the same.

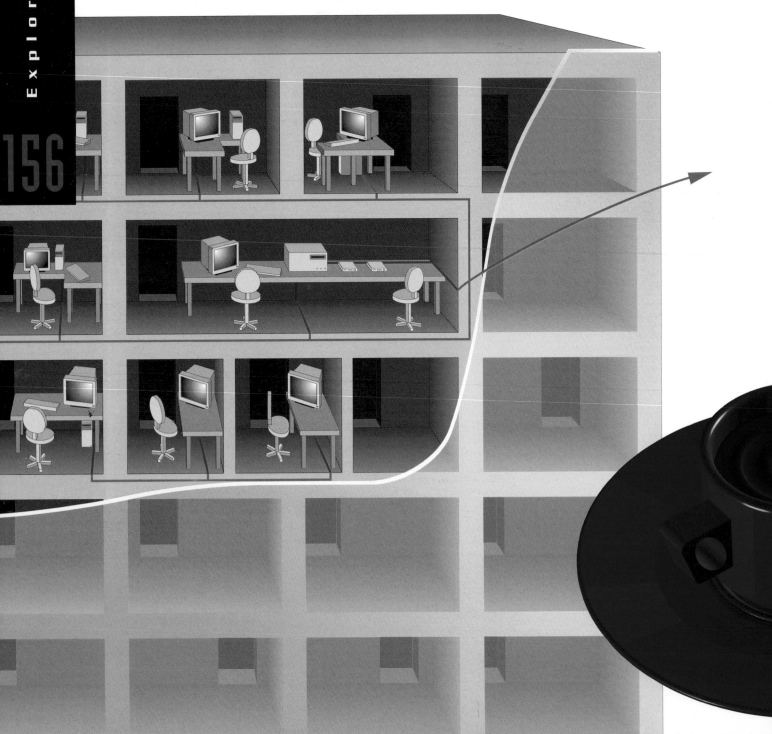

High-speed networks: fiber optics

Fiber-optic networks can be used to obtain high transmission speeds. Fiber-optic cable transmits light rather than electrical signals. Light is reflected by the sides of the fiber. The transmission speed of the signals is equal to the speed of light in the material used for the cable, which is not a huge speed improvement over transmitting electrical signals. However, the advantage is that fiber-optic signals are not sensitive to electromagnetic fields. You can therefore achieve maximum transmission speeds using a conductive fiber that is nothing more than a simple, uninsulated piece of plastic. Moreover, it's easy to make multifiber cables, because there is no interference between one fiber optic conductor and another. The data transfer speed on such networks can reach 150 Mbps, which is 15 times the speed of today's standard networks. At these speeds it's possible to transmit sound and even animated images in real time.

How fiber optics work

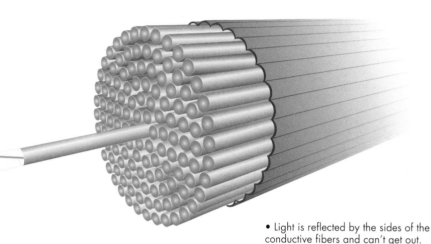

• Light is reflected by the sides of the conductive fibers and can't get out.

• Many conductive fibers can be grouped together without requiring sophisticated insulation techniques.

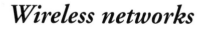

Wireless networks

Another solution currently being developed is wireless networks. Many possibilities open up with wireless networks. The most common is to build a network in which there is no constraint on the location of the various PCs. There's no wiring to install and no wiring to change when moving a workstation. A network that uses radio waves is the easiest to implement. In fact, simply placing two PCs near each other is enough to establish communications.

This type of network connection can be a great help in linking to PCs in a nearby building (on the other side of the street, for example). Installing a transceiver linked to the regular local area network in each building can end up being much less expensive than renting a dedicated line.

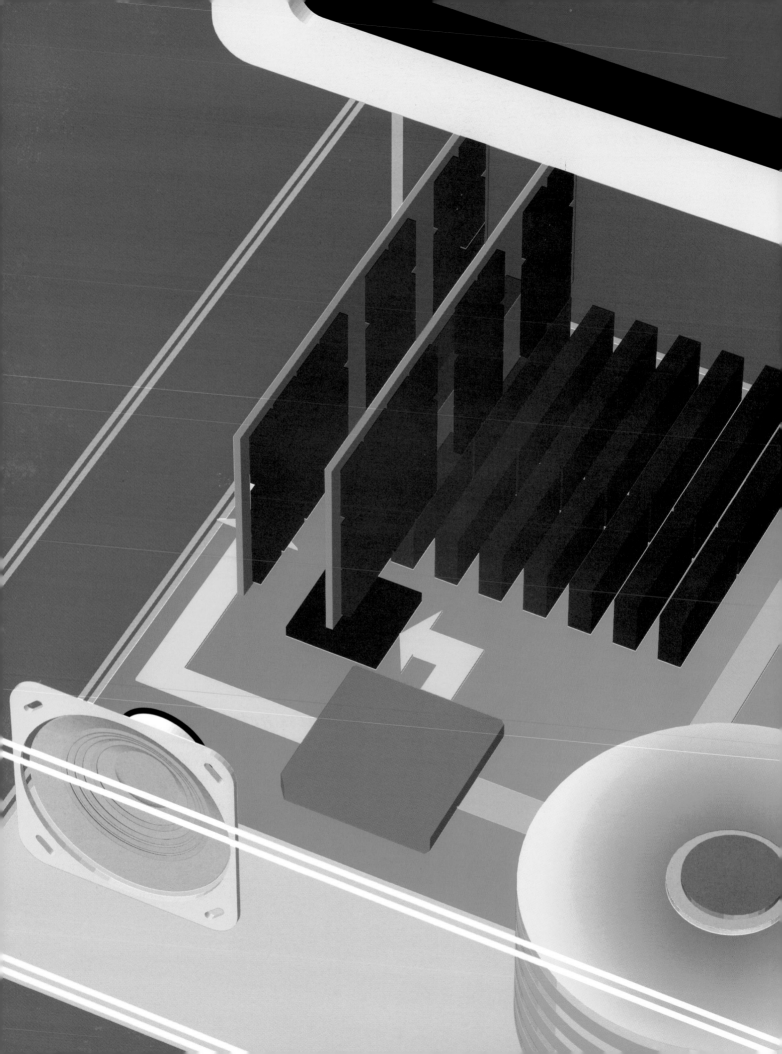

SOFTWARE

- Organization of a PC's software ... 160
- Starting up a PC ... 162
- Applications ... 166

Organization of a PC's software

A computer can't work without software. In fact, two computers with completely different hardware architectures can seem identical to the user if both computers are running the same software. This is true for computers running, for example, the UNIX system software. Thus, two computers manufactured by different companies with neither the same architecture nor the same processor will look the same to the user. On the other hand, two identical PCs using different software can appear to have nothing in common to the person using them. The software described in this section is found on the majority of PCs, but not all. Part of this software, called the BIOS, is located in the read-only memory on the motherboard. The BIOS is easy to find, and the *compatibility* of the system depends on it.

BIOS

The *BIOS* (basic input output system, pronounced *by-ose,* rhymes with *gross*) is the basic software of a PC. It is encoded in the read-only memory on the motherboard. When IBM introduced its first PC, it made public the source code of this software but didn't allow people to copy it. To make computers compatible with IBM's computers, other manufacturers therefore had to write functionally identical programs without falling into plagiarism. Because there aren't many ways to write such programs while keeping them small, the task became increasingly difficult as each manufacturer produced its own version. Some corporations therefore specialized in providing compatible BIOS implementations for PC manufacturers. Two major companies doing so now are Phoenix and AMI. If you have a PC clone, chances are that its BIOS comes from one of these companies.

The BIOS manages the system's input and output or, in other words, serves as an interface between the programs and the hardware. Every time a program wants to display something or read the keys being typed, it must go through the BIOS. Note that programs can access the keyboard or screen directly if the programmer chooses to do so. However, such a program risks not working on all PCs, because not all PCs have identical hardware. Using the BIOS reduces the programming workload and ensures compatibility.

DOS

The first PCs had neither a floppy drive nor a hard disk drive. For reading and writing data they had to rely on an interface to a cassette tape. When floppy disk drives appeared, a file system had to be developed. Reading and writing data on a disk include many repetitive tasks. All of those tasks are handled by *DOS* (the disk operating system, rhymes with *boss*). The term *OS* (operating system, pronounced *o-ess*, does *not* rhyme with *DOS*) is sometimes used instead of DOS. There are many versions of DOS: PC-DOS for IBM computers, MS-DOS for computers supplied by most of the other manufacturers, and Novell DOS, used on a small percentage of PCs. The most common of all, MS-DOS, is on tens of millions of PCs the world over and is now up to version 6.

DOS takes charge of accessing not only the disk but also all the other common peripherals such as the keyboard, the monitor, and the serial and parallel interfaces. In fact, it mediates between the BIOS and the applications to handle the most routine tasks, simplifying the work of the application programmer.

For the user, DOS can present a daunting interface: a blank screen with a short "prompt" indicating that some cryptic command is expected. A program can be made to present a more inviting interface only if the application programmer is willing to put a great deal of work into creating one.

Software organization in a PC running under DOS

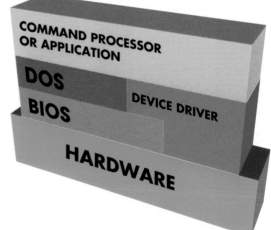

• The command processor is the DOS user interface. Most of it is unloaded from memory when an application is loaded.

• Several applications are in memory simultaneously. Some of these may be running in so-called *virtual DOS machines*, which allow you to run applications together that were designed to have a whole DOS machine to themselves.

Windows

• The command processor is used only to start up Windows.

APPLICATIONS
WINDOWS
DOS
BIOS
DEVICE DRIVER
HARDWARE

Some programs that run under DOS have very appealing user interfaces, but it's extremely rare that any two such programs from different publishers would have similarly functioning interfaces. To use a spreadsheet and a word processor, you have to learn how to use two different command sets. A *graphical user interface* (GUI, pronounced *gooey*) such as Windows (sometimes called an *operating environment*) can provide a solution to this problem and at the same time greatly simplify the programmer's task. A set of elements used to create a standard interface are pre-programmed for application programmers. Programmers then don't have to write the code for these elements, and users can benefit from a consistent interface from one program to the next.

The overwhelming success of Windows led Microsoft, its creator, to favor Windows development at the expense of DOS. The latest version, Windows 95, is a full operating system that doesn't even need MS-DOS. This should convince the last reluctant users to move to a graphical interface. However, for the foreseeable future all DOS programs will also be able to run under all versions of Windows. Compatibility will be maintained—devotees of the blank screen can sleep peacefully... for a while!

Device drivers

No system, be it DOS or Windows, has built into it the ability to control the entire range of available peripherals and expansion boards. To deal with this, extra software modules called *device drivers* can be added to your system to control unusual hardware. If you want to add a magnetic tape drive to your computer, or a full-page monitor or a removable disk drive, you have to install the corresponding device driver. The manufacturer usually provides this with the hardware. However, beware! A device driver may work only with specific hardware and software configurations. So the driver provided with, say, your network card may work only with that particular card and the current version of Windows. When you move to the next version of Windows, you'll have to find an updated driver on your own (though Windows often provides updated device drivers for common peripherals). If you can't get an updated device driver, you'll just have to junk the card. That's why you should stick to cards from well-established peripheral manufacturers, even if they cost a little more.

Almost all programs use numbers to identify their principal versions. The current version of DOS is 6. Windows is at version 3, with a new version coming soon. A major version change implies new functionality. Usually, the major version number followed by a dot and a number indicates a minor upgrade. Such a minor upgrade usually incorporates corrections and small improvements to the previous version. Thus, version 6.2 of DOS corrects some problems that were found in version 6.0. Version 3.1 of Windows provides improvements (essential to the user) over version 3.0. Even smaller revisions may be signaled by an appended letter or number. For example, version 2.0 might be slightly changed, becoming 2.0a, and Microsoft denoted slight changes to version 3.1 of Windows by adding another number (3.11). Now Microsoft is breaking with these long-standing numbering schemes by calling its new version of the product Windows 95.

Starting up a PC

When you turn on your PC, certain things must happen before you can start typing commands. You'll notice, among other things, that different messages are displayed on the screen and that the hard drive light blinks on and off. This activity is generated by a series of startup programs. The first program tests the hardware. After that, different components of the operating system are loaded into memory, along with the command interpreter. When operations aren't happening as they should, the PC's internal speaker is used to signal an error .

The PC's self-test

The first operation carried out by the computer when you turn it on is microprocessor reinitialization (among other things, the microprocessor's registers are all set to 0). Next, execution continues at address F000 in the BIOS. The BIOS starts with a test of the PC's components, called POST (power on self test). It's made up of the following procedures:

- Bus test

- Internal clock test

- Video display card test

- RAM test (the amount of memory is displayed on screen)

- Keyboard test

- Test to detect disk drives

- CMOS memory test. The configuration determined during the preceding tests is compared to the one stored in CMOS memory. If it doesn't match, an error message is displayed.

Once the test is over, the speaker emits a short beep. Absence of this signal, a long beep, or several successive beeps indicates an error.

Power on self test

- Video display card test

- Internal clock test

• The BIOS searches for a drive containing a disk it can read and loads into memory the contents of that disk's boot sector.

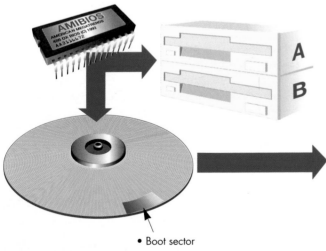

A

B

7000
- Program in the boot sector

- Boot sector

- CMOS memory test

Loading the disk operating system

If no problems were discovered in the startup tests, the BIOS checks drive A to see if it contains a floppy disk. If it does, the contents of that disk's boot sector are loaded into memory at a specific address. If there is no floppy disk in drive A, the BIOS tries to read the hard drive (usually drive C). Its boot sector is then loaded into memory. The boot sector of a formatted disk is always a program, no matter what else the disk contains. This program (often called a *bootstrap*) is then executed.

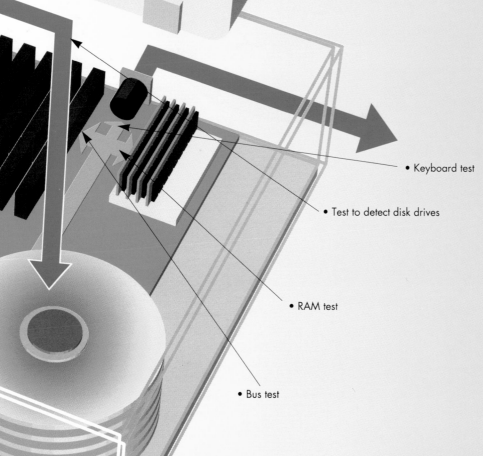

• Keyboard test

• Test to detect disk drives

• RAM test

• Bus test

If the disk isn't an operating system disk, its boot sector program simply displays a message to indicate that fact. If it does contain an operating system, the boot sector program looks on the disk for the file IO.SYS. This file contains part of the MS-DOS operating system. (In PC-DOS, this file is called IBMBIO.COM.) IO.SYS replaces the boot sector program in memory.

• The boot sector program loads IO.SYS and passes control to it.

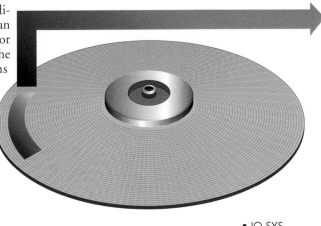

• IO.SYS

• IO.SYS loads MSDOS.SYS.

IO.SYS loads MSDOS.SYS into memory (IBMDOS.COM in the case of PC-DOS).

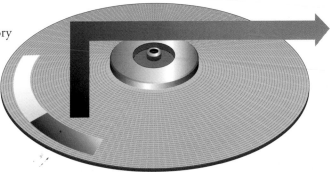

If you look at what's on your hard disk drive, you'll find the files CONFIG.SYS, AUTOEXEC.BAT (if it exists), and COMMAND.COM, but you won't find IO.SYS and MSDOS.SYS, which are "hidden." **A** *hidden* **file is simply a file that was given a special attribute so its name won't appear on the displayed list of files. IO.SYS and MSDOS.SYS also have the System (indicating they are part of the operating system) and Read Only attributes, which prevent them from being modified or erased. Don't be tempted to assign these attributes to CONFIG.SYS and AUTOEXEC.BAT, because these files usually need to be modified when you install new software and hardware. Instead, you should create a backup system floppy disk and copy CONFIG.SYS and AUTOEXEC.BAT to it.**

The program then looks in the root directory for a file called CONFIG.SYS. This file contains configuration instructions for DOS and instructions for loading device drivers for peripherals. If a CONFIG.SYS file exists (it almost always does), the instructions it contains are executed.

IO.SYS

MSDOS.SYS

Device drivers

• The instructions in CONFIG.SYS are executed.

COMMAND.COM, the command interpreter, is then loaded into memory and executed. It in turn looks in the root directory for another configuration file named AUTOEXEC.BAT. If AUTOEXEC.BAT exists, the instructions it contains are executed.

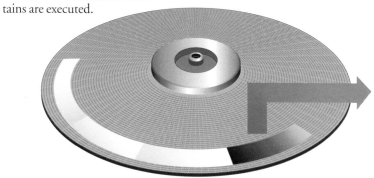

IO.SYS

MSDOS.SYS

Device drivers

COMMAND .COM

• COMMAND.COM, the command interpreter, is executed. It searches for AUTOEXEC.BAT and executes its instructions.

After the instructions in AUTOEXEC.BAT have been executed, the command interpreter displays the DOS prompt and waits for a command. However, if AUTOEXEC.BAT contains a command to launch an application, you'll see the DOS prompt only when you quit the application. That's what happens, for example, if your AUTOEXEC.BAT file contains the command WIN, which launches Windows.

Applications

The purpose of a computer is to run application software. Even if you are a programmer, you need programming tools, which are also applications. Application software is extremely varied and can help you in a myriad of diverse tasks. However, on PCs there are three major categories: word processors, spreadsheets, and databases. Other popular PC applications include programs for graphic design, page layout, digital photo retouching, computer assisted design (CAD), presentation graphics, and programs made for managing special databases—accounting, inventory management, invoicing, and so forth.

Word processing

A word processing program provides at least the following functions: text entry, text formatting, editing, storage, and printing. In fact, current word processors offer many more possibilities: tables, calculations based on tables, indexes, cross-references, tables of contents, text search and replacement, spelling and grammar checkers, access to a thesaurus, facilities for producing mass mailings, label printing, etc.

The basic principle of all word processors is very simple. Unlike typewritten text, text in a word processor exists independently of how it's formatted. Text can be entered quickly without worrying about line breaks or page breaks. The word processor takes care of laying out the lines and pages according to the margins and current paper size. If you later change these elements or even portions of the text itself, text formatting is adjusted correspondingly.

The amount of text that can be entered is obviously not limited to the size of the screen. The screen is only a window on the text. When the text gets to the bottom of the screen, the text scrolls up and the beginning disappears. Scrolling commands allow you to move the window over the text (or move the text behind the screen, depending on how you look at it).

How text scrolls in a word processor

• Scroll down command

• Scroll up command

• Text scrolls behind the screen.

The amount of text you can enter isn't limited by the amount of memory available on your computer but rather by the capacity of your disk drive. If memory is full, the program is able to store text on disk to free up memory for more text. This happens independently of the command that saves your work when you close the file. If you turn off your computer without saving your work, your work is lost. However, all word processors have features to protect you against this forgetfulness, as well as against power failures that could lead to the same result. These range from issuing warning messages reminding you to save your data to automatically saving the data at regular intervals.

Spreadsheets

Spreadsheet software is the application that established the personal computer. It provides a model of *cells* of data rectangularly arranged in rows and columns. In those cells, you can put numbers, text, or whatever you want. What makes spreadsheets so powerful is that you can create an equation in one cell whose computed value depends on the current contents of other cells. Here, cell A3 contains a formula that calculates the sum of the two cells above it. If the values in A1 and A2 are changed, the result in A3 is automatically recalculated. Furthermore, if the formula is copied to the following columns, it is automatically adjusted to perform the analogous computation for each new column.

How a spreadsheet works

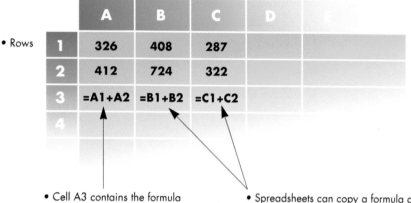

• Columns

• Rows

	A	B	C	D	E
1	326	408	287		
2	412	724	322		
3	=A1+A2	=B1+B2	=C1+C2		
4					

• Cell A3 contains the formula = A1 + A2. The result is maintained automatically.

• Spreadsheets can copy a formula and automatically adapt it to other columns.

How a relational database works

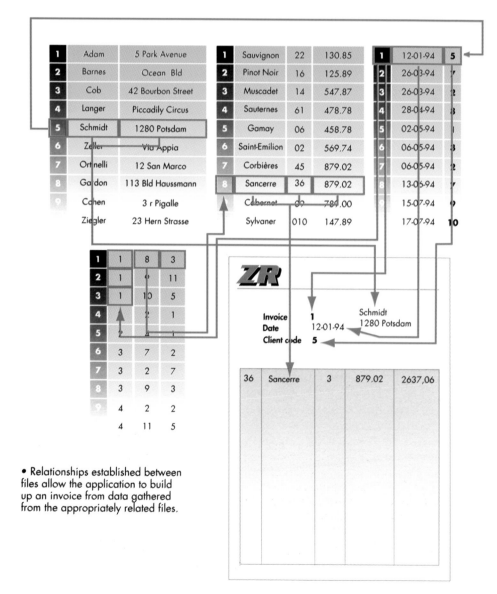

• Relationships established between files allow the application to build up an invoice from data gathered from the appropriately related files.

Databases

Computers are naturally adapted to databases. A database may consist of only one type of data (such a database is sometimes referred to as a *flat-file database*). A list of addresses is an example of such a database. The application can sort the addresses, find them easily, or select one or more according to a variety of criteria. For more complex database applications, such files can be related to one another. A database made up of several related files (or tables) of data is called a *relational database*. For example, let's look at a system of invoices. Each invoice includes the same elements: a date; an invoice number; the customer's address; and the part number, price, and description for each line item being invoiced. But when customers' addresses or parts prices change, you don't want to have to look up and input the correct data each time you create an invoice.

A relational database would include a customer file, a parts description file, a parts price file, and an invoice file. The invoice file then collects the data it needs for each invoice by using codes for the customer and part number that link to the appropriate file.

MULTIMEDIA

• What is multimedia ? 170

• Multimedia PC configuration 172

• A multimedia application 174

What is multimedia?

Nowadays, to be current, a PC must have *multimedia* capability. However, nobody can describe exactly what that means. Usually, a multimedia PC is defined as a computer that has a CD-ROM drive and a sound card. CD-ROM drives are the only widely available media with enough capacity to support the huge sound and graphics files used in multimedia applications. Technically, these applications could also be distributed on magnetic tapes or magneto-optical disks. But that's not economically feasible, because most people don't have these drives and the recording process is too involved. At this point, CD-ROM drives are simply the most economical way to distribute multimedia applications.

A multimedia application is an application that disseminates information through several media. But *medium* can mean two different things. It can be used to designate a *type of information:* text, images (fixed or animated), or sound. Looked at this way, we all have multimedia machines. Televisions and VCRs are the best examples. In fact, multimedia PCs produce exactly these types of information.

How a multimedia application works: an encyclopedia of birds

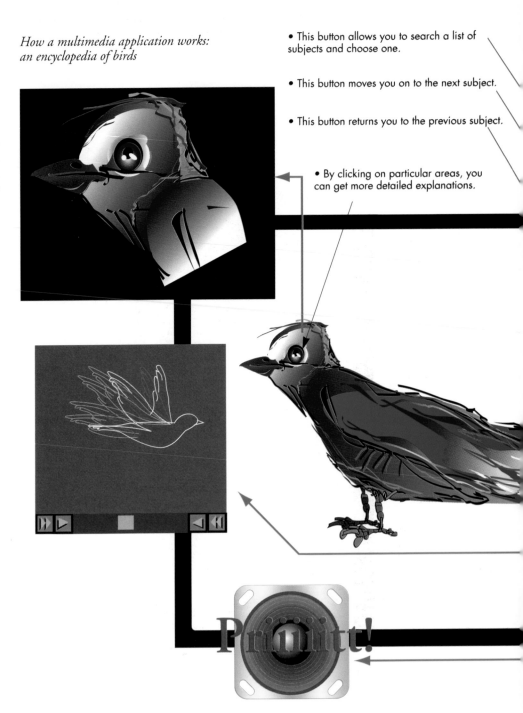

• This button allows you to search a list of subjects and choose one.

• This button moves you on to the next subject.

• This button returns you to the previous subject.

• By clicking on particular areas, you can get more detailed explanations.

Prüitt!

Medium can also refer to the physical material used to disseminate data. By that definition, a newspaper, a book, a record, a film, an audio or video cassette, and a telephone line are all media.

In fact, the only important thing to consider is whether a PC is able to run so-called multimedia applications. The definition of multimedia is then simple enough. To run multimedia applications distributed on CD-ROMs, a multimedia PC must have:

• A CD-ROM drive,

• A sound card compatible with the applications,

• Enough memory (a minimum of 4 MB, preferably 8 MB),

• The right software. This usually means DOS 5 (or higher) or Windows (version 3.1 or higher) and the necessary device drivers to use the CD-ROM drive and sound card. Required Windows extensions are usually bundled with the application and installed when the application is installed.

While it's not absolutely necessary, it is generally felt that a multimedia application must be interactive. This means that, unlike watching a video tape (which also produces animated images and sound), the user must also be able to interact with the program and so change what the program shows next.

• This button displays a text window describing the subject.

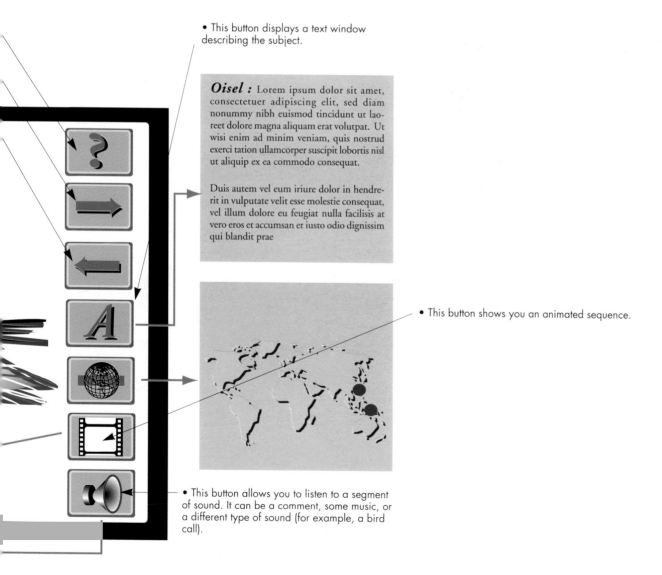

Oisel : Lorem ipsum dolor sit amet, consectetuer adipiscing elit, sed diam nonummy nibh euismod tincidunt ut laoreet dolore magna aliquam erat volutpat. Ut wisi enim ad minim veniam, quis nostrud exerci tation ullamcorper suscipit lobortis nisl ut aliquip ex ea commodo consequat.

Duis autem vel eum iriure dolor in hendrerit in vulputate velit esse molestie consequat, vel illum dolore eu feugiat nulla facilisis at vero eros et accumsan et iusto odio dignissim qui blandit prae

• This button shows you an animated sequence.

• This button allows you to listen to a segment of sound. It can be a comment, some music, or a different type of sound (for example, a bird call).

Multimedia PC configuration

If you are interested in multimedia applications, you must have a PC that is equipped to run such applications. In fact, few things are needed to transform a standard PC into a multimedia PC. If you have a standard PC, you can look into adding the necessary components. Most dealers offer more or less complete kits to make this transformation easy. The kits are usually made up of a CD-ROM drive, a sound card, a pair of speakers, and the cables necessary for installation. This kit will give you a multimedia PC if your PC has a fast enough CPU and enough memory. If not, you might have to upgrade your processor, add memory, or install Windows extensions.

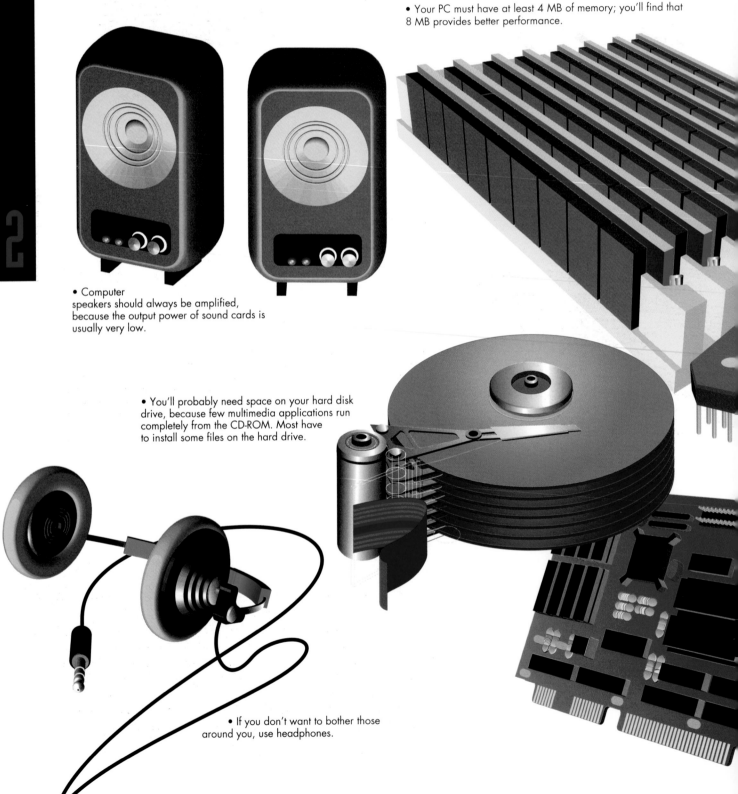

• Your PC must have at least 4 MB of memory; you'll find that 8 MB provides better performance.

• Computer speakers should always be amplified, because the output power of sound cards is usually very low.

• You'll probably need space on your hard disk drive, because few multimedia applications run completely from the CD-ROM. Most have to install some files on the hard drive.

• If you don't want to bother those around you, use headphones.

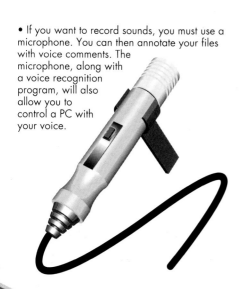

• If you want to record sounds, you must use a microphone. You can then annotate your files with voice comments. The microphone, along with a voice recognition program, will also allow you to control a PC with your voice.

• A compatible sound card that conforms to industry standards is essential. It has an interface for a CD-ROM drive, a joystick port, a microphone input jack, line input (to input from a tape recorder, for example), stereo output, and, ideally, a MIDI interface.

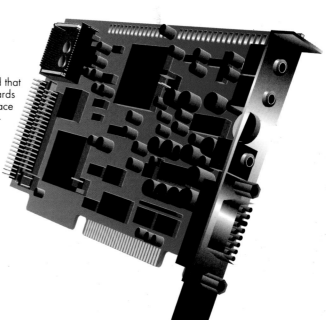

• You need an MPC-compatible CD-ROM drive. MPC compatibility requires an access time of less than one second and a minimum transfer rate of 150 KB per second, using less than 40 percent of the microprocessor's computing power. This means you must choose at least a double-speed drive. Typically, an MPC drive includes CD photo multisession capability, which allows you to view photographs created by special digital cameras.

• Your PC's processor must be at least a 486, preferably a DX.

To run multimedia applications, you'll need a number of multimedia extensions and special drivers, most of which are installed automatically when you install your sound card and CD-ROM drive. You must also have installed the CD-ROM MSCDEX.EXE driver. Some multimedia applications contain musical tracks and sound tracks that are played directly from the CD-ROM. To play these tracks, you must install an audio driver. However, many applications automatically install the necessary software elements if they are not already there.

A multimedia application

It is very difficult to provide in a book a good sense of a multimedia application. Here, we've chosen as an example *Multimedia Stravinsky,* from Microsoft, which offers a detailed analysis of this composer's major work, *The Rite of Spring.* The program plays the piece and provides an audio commentary, including a detailed analysis of its construction and the composition of the orchestra. Sections are dedicated to the life of Stravinsky, the work's genesis, and the Nijinsky choreography. When you are finished listening to (and looking at) all this, you can test your knowledge with a multiple choice quiz.

Introductory screen

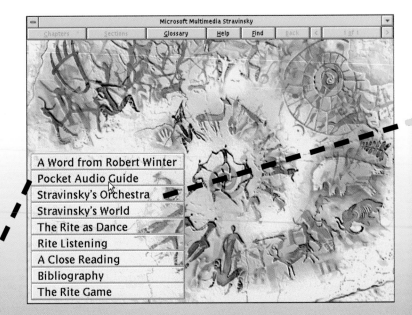

List of musical pieces

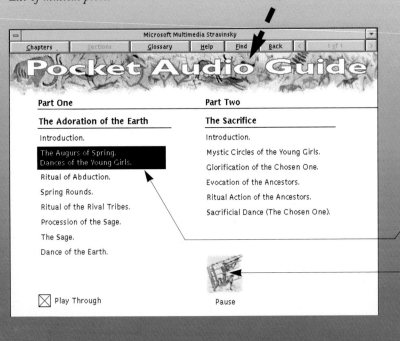

• Select a piece to listen to.

• Click here to pause the music.

The orchestra used by Stravinsky

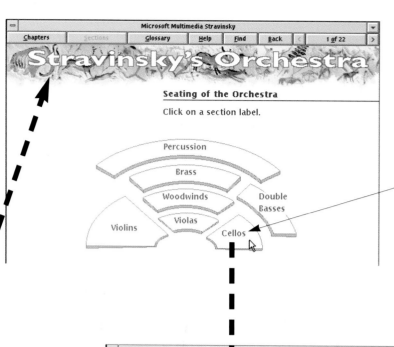

Seating of the Orchestra

Click on a section label.

Percussion
Brass
Woodwinds
Double Basses
Violas
Violins
Cellos

• Click here twice to see details of the string section.

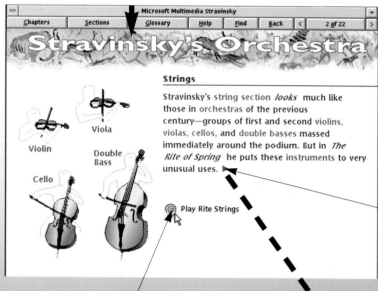

Strings

Stravinsky's string section *looks* much like those in orchestras of the previous century—groups of first and second violins, violas, cellos, and double basses massed immediately around the podium. But in *The Rite of Spring* he puts these instruments to very unusual uses. ►

Viola
Violin
Double Bass
Cello

Play Rite Strings

• Click here to see more.

• Click here to hear the sound of the string section.

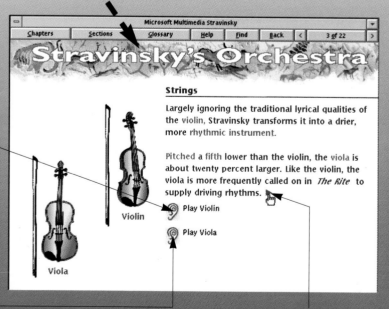

Strings

Largely ignoring the traditional lyrical qualities of the violin, Stravinsky transforms it into a drier, more rhythmic instrument.

Pitched a fifth lower than the violin, the viola is about twenty percent larger. Like the violin, the viola is more frequently called on in *The Rite* to supply driving rhythms.

Violin
Viola

Play Violin
Play Viola

• Click here to hear the violin.

• Click here to hear the viola.

• Click here to see more.

Microsoft Multimedia Stravinsky

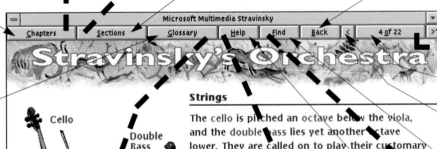

A Word from Robert Winter
Pocket Audio Guide
Stravinsky's Orchestra
Stravinsky's World
The Rite as Dance
Rite Listening
A Close Reading
Bibliography
The Rite Game

Chapters | Sections | Glossary | Help | Find | Back | < | 1 of 5 | >

• Click here to display the list of chapters.

Chapters | Sections | Glossary | Help | Find | Back | < | 4 of 22 | >

Stravinsky's Orchestra

Strings

The cello is pitched an octave below the viola, and the double bass lies yet another octave lower. They are called on to play their customary role of musical foundation far less frequently than they are called on to produce unusual sounds. ▶

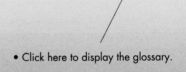

Cello

Double Bass

🎧 Play Cello

🎧 Play Double Bass

• Click here to display the glossary.

Rite Glossary

Type or select a word from the list   a tempo   ⬇

🔊 **A Tempo**

[ah Tehm-poh] Italian for "[back] in tempo," indicating a return to the original, or previous, tempo.

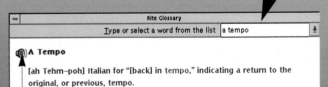

• Click here to hear pronunciation.

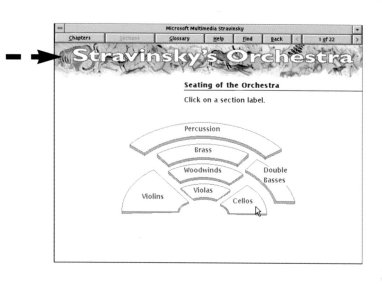

Seating of the Orchestra

Click on a section label.

• Click here to display the list of subjects.

• Click here to go back a page.

• Click here to display the next page.

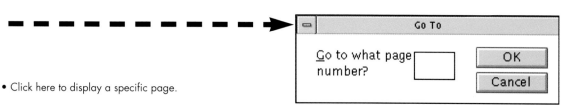

• Click here to display a specific page.

• Click here to display the previous page.

• Click here to find a subject.

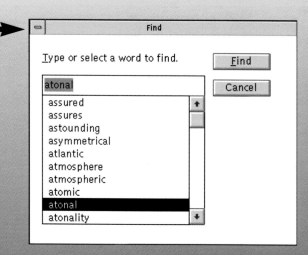

• Click here for help.

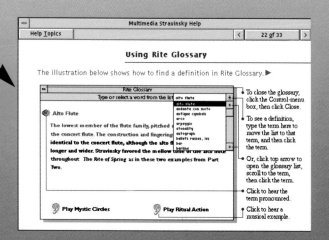

Note to the Reader: Boldfaced numbers indicate the principal discussion of a topic.

Numbers

3.5-inch floppy disks, 88
386 microprocessors, 20. *See also* microprocessors
486 microprocessors
    execution of instructions, 24–27
    installing memory for, 34
    jumpers and, 17
    overdrive chips for, 28
    overview of, **20–21**
487 SX math coprocessors, 17, 21, 28
8088 microprocessors, 20
8514/A video card, 100

A

access time
    for hard disk drives, 71
    for memory, 36, 43
active matrix monitors, 102, 103
additive synthesis, 134
addresses
    of data on hard disk drives, 63
    input/output (I/O) address, 57
    memory and, 34
    translating logical addresses into physical
        addresses, 23
allocation units, 72–73
ALUs (arithmetic/logic units), **23**, 25, 26
amplitude modulation screens, 139
analog joysticks, 116–117
animation, **104–105**
antistatic wrist bands, 43, 56
applications. *See also* programs; software
    database software, **167**
    multimedia
        applications, 170–171, 173, 174–177
    spreadsheet software, **167**
    word processors, 120, **166**

arcade games, 116–117
archiving data, **82–83**, 92–93
arithmetic/logic units (ALUs), **23**, 25, 26
aspect ratio, of monitors, 98
AT computers
    ISA bus and, 48
    Standard AT cases, 4
AUTOEXEC.BAT file, 164

B

back panel of PCs, **10–11**
backing up data, **82–83**, 92–93
bar code readers, **124**
bays, 6, 8
BIOS
    and accessing hard disk, 76–77
    cache BIOS, 44
    keyboard drivers and, 110–111
    overview of, **160**, 162, 163
    sector relocation and, 70
    upgrading, 44
bits
    defined, **20**
    kilobits, 31
    megabits, 31
    memory and, 30, 32, 34
bits per second (bps), 148
black screens, 138
boards. *See* interface cards
boot sector viruses, **86–87**
booting, 8, 43, **162–165**
    AUTOEXEC.BAT, 164
    COMMAND.COM, 164–165
    CONFIG.SYS, 164–165
    IBMBIO.COM, 164
    IO.SYS, 164
    loading DOS, **163–165**
    memory and, 43

MSDOS.SYS, 164
    POST (power on self test), 162
    rebooting, 8
bootstrap program, 163
bps (bits per second), 148
burning programs into chips, 44–45
bus interface unit, **23**, 26
bus mouse, 112
bus networks, **142–143**
buses, **46–51**
    bus controllers, 15, **46–47**
    defined, **46**
    EISA (Expanded Industry Standard
        Architecture) bus, **49**
    expansion slots for, 46–47
    ISA (Industry Standard Architecture) bu
    local bus
        hard disk drives and, 50
        local bus video cards, 52, 53, 101
        network interface cards and, 50
        overview of, **49**
    location of, 15
    MCA (Micro Channel Architecture) bus
    memory access time and, 36
    overview of, 46
    PCI (Peripheral Components Interconne
        bus, **51**
    PCMCIA bus, **51**
    types of, **48–51**
    VESA (Video Electronics Standards
        Association) bus, **50**
bytes, 30, 34

c

cache BIOS, 44
cache controller programs, 78
cache memory. *See also* memory
    configuring, 17
    disk caches and, **78–79**

and execution of instructions, **24–25**
and how microprocessors access
memory, **36–39**, 78–79
overview of, 15
versus RAM disks, **79**
read-ahead caching, 37
write-back caching, 39
write-through caching, 39
cache memory controller
and execution of instructions, 24, 25, **26–27**
and how microprocessors access
memory, 36–39
overview of, 15, **23**
caddies, for CD-ROMs, 91
cameras, digital, **125**
capacitive keys, 109
capacitors, memory and, 30, 32–33
cards. *See* interface cards
cases, **4–13**
back panel, **10–11**
bays, 6, 8
desktop (horizontal case) PCs
expandability of, 6
overview of, **4**
setting up, 5, 7
ergonomics and, **5**
expandability and, **6–7**
expansion slots
for buses, **46–47**
installing interface cards in, 56
location of, 10, 11, 15
front panel, **8–9**
hard disk light, 8
inside, **12–13**
mini-AT cases, 4
opening, 13
portable computers
expandability of, 6
handbook computers, 4
keyboards, 108
laptop computers, 4
microprocessors in, 18
notebook computers, 4
pointing devices for, 108, 114–115
sub-notebook computers, 4
types of, **4**
voltage selectors in, 11
ports
on input/output (I/O) cards, 54
joystick ports, 54, 55
overview of, 10
PS/2 mouse ports, 10, 112
power sockets, 10
power supplies, 3, 7, 10, 13
power switches, 8, 10
PS/2 mouse ports, 10, 112
reset button, 8, 9
security locks, 8
speakers, 13, 14, 172
Standard AT cases, 4
tower (vertical case) PCs, **4–5**, 6
turbo button, 8
types of, **4–5**
ventilation of, 5, 7, 10
voltage selector, 10, 11
CCD (charge-coupled device)
detectors, 120–121, 125
CD-ROM drives
CDs versus hard disks and floppy disks, 91
installing, 8
multimedia and, 170, 172–173
overview of, **90–91**
cells, in spreadsheet programs, 167
central processing units (CPUs). *See* microprocessors

CGA standard, 100
characters, optical character recognition
(OCR), 120, **122**
charge-coupled device (CCD)
detectors, 120–121, 125
chips. *See* microprocessors
CHKDSK command, DOS, 85
circuit boards. *See* motherboards
clock speed
memory and, 36
of microprocessors, 20
turbo button and, 8
clock speed multipliers, 22, 23
clocks
on motherboards, 15
"real time" clocks, 14
clusters
on floppy disks, 72
on hard disk drives, 72–73, 85
CMOS (complementary metal oxide semiconductor), **31**
collision detection, 142–143
color
additive synthesis, 134
color screens, 139
rendering on printers, **138–139**
subtractive synthesis, 134
three-color versus four-color printing, 134–135
color monitors, **96–97**. *See also* monitors
color printers, **134–135**
color scanners, 120
COMMAND.COM file, 164–165
communications, **148–151**. *See also* networks
baud rate, 148
bits per second (bps), 148
digital telephone networks, 149
error checking codes, 148
handshaking, 148
ISDN (Integrated Services Digital
Network), 149
modems and
acoustic modems, 149
fax modems, 150–151
internal and external modems, 149
on-line services, **151**
overview of, 148
protocols for, 148
remote access to local area networks, 151
transmission speeds, 148
wide area networks (WANs) and, 152
compact disk drives. *See* CD-ROM drives
complete image animation, 105
compression utilities, **75**
computer-generated image animation, 105
computers. *See* PCs
CONFIG.SYS file, 164–165
configuring
cache memory, 17
direct memory access channels (DMAs), 57
input/output (I/O) address, 57
interface cards, 57
interrupt request lines (IRQs), 57
motherboards, 14, 17
connecting motherboards to power supplies, 13
connectors
for keyboards, 10, 13
for mouse, 10
Y-cables, 13, 29
consoles. *See* cases
control and protection test units, 22
controllers. *See also* cache memory controller; disk
controllers
bus controllers, 15, 46–47

cache controller programs, 78
keyboard controllers, 14, 44, 110
converting logical addresses to physical
addresses, 23
cooling
computers, 5, 7, 10
overdrive chips, 28, 29
cost
of inkjet printers versus laser printers, 132
of mouse, 113
CPUs. *See* microprocessors
creating high-density disks from low-density
disks, 89
cross-linked files, 85
cylinders, 62, 63, 70

D

DACs (digital-to-analog converters), monitors
and, 98, 99
daisywheel printers, 128
DAT (digital audiotape), 93, 124
data compression utilities, **75**
data encoding, on hard disk drives, **67**
data security. *See* security
database software, **167**
daughterboards, 14. *See also* interface cards
decoding units, 22
dedicated servers, 154
deflection coils, 96–97
defragmenting hard disk drives, **75**
deleting
data on hard disk drives, 74
data loss and, 84
desktop (horizontal case) PCs. *See also* cases
expandability of, 6
overview of, **4**
setting up, 5, 7
device drivers
display drivers, 100, 101
keyboard drivers, 110–111
monitors and, 101
mouse drivers, 113
multimedia extensions and drivers, 173
overview of, **161**
differential backups, **83**
differential scrolling, video animation and, 105
digital audiotape (DAT), 93, 124
digital cameras, **125**
digital joysticks, **116–117**
digital telephone networks, **148–151**. *See also*
networks
baud rate, 148
bits per second (bps), 148
error checking codes, 148
fax modems and, 150–151
handshaking, 148
ISDN (Integrated Services Digital
Network), 149
modems and, 149
on-line services, 151
overview of, 148
protocols for, 148
remote access to local area networks, 151
transmission speeds, 148
using, 149
wide area networks (WANs) and, 152
digital-to-analog converters (DACs), monitors
and, 98, 99
digitized images, 120
digitizing pages of text, 120, 122
DIP switches, 17, 57
DIPs (dual in-line packages), 25

direct memory access channels (DMAs), 57
directories, 73
disk caches
  overview of, **78–79**
  and turning off PCs, 8
disk controllers, **70–71**. *See also* hard disk drives
  cache memory and, 78
  disk interface cards and, 53, 70
  IDE disk controllers, 70–71
  SCSI disk controllers, 70–71
disk doublers, 75
disk drives. *See* CD-ROM drives; floppy disk
  drives; hard disk drives
disk interface cards, 53, 70
diskettes, ejecting, 9
display adapters. *See* video cards
display drivers, 100, 101
display modes, of monitors, **99–101**
displays. *See* monitors
DMAs (direct memory access channels), 57
DOS. *See also* software
  and accessing hard disk, 76–77
  CHKDSK command, 85
  DOS sector numbers, 73
  FORMAT command, 85
  and formatting hard disk drives, 72–73
  loading, **163–165**
  overview of, **160**
  SCANDISK command, 85
dot pitch, of monitors, 96, 100
dot screens, 138
dot-matrix printers, **128–129**, 130
downloadable fonts, 131
DRAM (dynamic RAM), 30, **31**, 32–33
drivers. *See* device drivers
dual in-line packages (DIPs), 25

EGA standard, 100
EISA (Expanded Industry Standard Architecture)
  bus, 49
ejecting, diskettes, 9
electron guns, in monitors, 96–97
electronic mail (e-mail), **154**
entry neurons, 123
EPROM (erasable programmable read-only
  memory), 45
ergonomics, case design and, 5
error checking codes, 148
Ethernet networks, 54, 142
even parity, memory and, 35
executable-file viruses, **86–87**
exit neurons, 123
expandability of PCs, **6–7**
Expanded Industry Standard Architecture (EISA)
  bus, 49
expansion cards. *See* interface cards
expansion slots
  for buses, **46–47**
  installing interface cards in, 56
  location of, 10, 11, 15
  for ports, 54
extensions, multimedia, 173
external buses, microprocessors and, 20, 21

fax modems, **150–151**
fiber-optic networks, **157**
file allocation tables (FATs), **73–74**
file compression utilities, 75

file fragmentation, **75**
file servers, 154
files
  AUTOEXEC.BAT, 164
  COMMAND.COM, 164–165
  CONFIG.SYS, 164–165
  cross-linked files, 85
  IBMBIO.COM, 164
  IO.SYS, 164
  MSDOS.SYS, 164
film recorders, **136–137**
flat-file databases, 167
floating-point math units. *See* math coprocessors
floppy disk drives
  installing, 8, 13
  overview of, 2–3, 13, **89**
  stepper motors, 89
  and turning off PCs, 9
  write-protection and, 89
floppy disks
  versus CDs, 91
  clusters and sectors on, 72
  creating high-density disks from low-density
    disks, 89
  ejecting, 9
  overview of, **88**
  unformatting, 84, 85
  write-protecting, 88, 89
FM (frequency modulation) coding system, 67
fonts, **131**
FORMAT command, DOS, 85
formatting
  data loss and, 84–85
  hard disk drives, **72–73**
four-color printing, 134–135, 136
fragmentation of hard disk drives, **75**
frame grabber video cards, **125**
frequency modulation (FM) coding system, 67
frequency modulation screens, 139
front panel of PCs, **8–9**
full tower cases, 4

games, 116–117
geometry of hard disk drives, 63, 70–71
graphical user interfaces (GUIs), **161**
graphics cards. *See* video cards
graphics pads or tablets, **118–119**
grayscale and color rendering, **138–139**

handbook computers, 4. *See also* portable
  computers
handshaking, 148
hard disk drives, **60–81**
  access time, 71
  addresses of data on, 63
  allocation units, 72–73
  versus CDs, **91**
  clusters, 72–73, 85
  cylinders, 62, 63, 70
  data encoding, **67**
  defragmenting, **75**
  deleting data, 74
  disk caches, 9, **78–79**
  disk controllers
    cache memory and, 78
    disk interface cards and, 53, 70
    IDE disk controllers, 70–71
    SCSI disk controllers, 70–71

DOS sector numbers, 73
file allocation tables (FATs), 73–74
file compression utilities and, **75**
file fragmentation and, **75**
formatting, **72–73**
frequency modulation (FM) coding system, 67
geometry of, **63**, 70–71
hard disk light, 8
hardware caches, 78
high-level formatting, **72**
how microprocessors access, **76–77**
IDE disk controllers, 70–71
IDE disk drives, **70–71**, **80–81**
IDE interface cards, 53, 70–71
installing, 8, 13, **70–71**
  IDE hard disk drives, **80–81**
  SCSI hard disk drives, **81**
labels on, 64
landing zones, 65
linear speed of, 65, 68–69
local bus and, 50
logical drives, 72
low-level formatting, **72**
magneto-optical disks, **93**
versus memory, **30**
modified frequency modulation (MFM) coding
  system, 67
multimedia and, 172
overview of, 3, 13, 60
parking heads, **65**
partitioning, **72**
platters, 60–61
RAM (or virtual) disks, 79
read/write heads, 60, 61, 63, **64–65**, 70
reading data, **66**
reducing write current, **68–69**
removable hard disk cartridges, **92**, 124
root directory and, 73
run length limited (RLL) coding system, 67
SCSI disk controllers, 70–71
SCSI disk drives, **70–71**, **81**
SCSI interface cards, 53, 55, 70
sector relocation, **70**
sectors, 63, 70, 72–74
slack, 73
software caches, 78
ST 506 disk drives, 70
storage capacity of, **63**
structure of, **60–63**
tracks, 62, 65, 72
and turning off PCs, 9
virtual memory and, **40–41**
write precompensation, **69**
writing data, 66, 68–69
hardware caches, 78
heat sinks, 29
high-level formatting, **72**
horizontal (desktop) cases. *See also* cases
  expandability of, 6
  overview of, **4**
  setting up, 5, 7
horizontal frequency of monitors, 96

I/O. *See* input/output
IBM, 8514/A video card, 100
IBMBIO.COM file, 164
ICR (intelligent character recognition), 122
IDE disk controllers, 70–71
IDE disk drives
  installing, **80–81**
  overview of, 70–71

IDE interface cards, 53, 70–71
imagesetters, **136–137**
incremental backups, **83**
Industry Standard Architecture (ISA) bus, 48
inkjet printers, **132–133**
input devices. *See also* keyboards; microphones;
    mouse; pointing devices; sound cards
  bar code readers, **124**
  computers without keyboards, 108, **118–119**
  digital cameras, **125**
  frame grabber video cards, 125
  graphics pads or tablets, **118–119**
  lightpens, 115, **118–119**
  optical character recognition
      (OCR), 120, **122–123**
  scanners, **120–121**
  touch-sensitive screens, 115, **118–119**
  types of, 124
input/output (I/O) address, 57
input/output (I/O) cards, **54**
inside PCs, **12–13**
installing. *See also* upgrading
  CD-ROM drives, 8
  floppy disk drives, 8, 13
  hard disk drives, 8, 13, **70–71**
    IDE hard disk drives, **80–81**
    SCSI hard disk drives, **81**
  interface cards, 6, 14, **56–57**
  memory, 31, 34, **42–43**
  microprocessors, 28–29
  overdrive chips, 28–29
  SIMMs, 34, 42–43
instruction queues, 22
Integrated Services Digital Network (ISDN), 149
intelligent character recognition (ICR), 122
interactive multimedia, **171**
interface cards, **52–57.** *See also* ports
  for bus mouse, 112
  configuring, 57
  disk interface cards, 53
  expandability and, 6, 7
  versus expansion cards, **55**
  finding the right slot for, 56
  handling, 56
  IDE interface cards, 53, 70–71
  input/output (I/O) cards, **54**
  installing, 6, 14, **56–57**
  for joysticks, 117
  memory cards, 6
  modem cards, 6
  network interface cards
    bus networks and, 142
    local bus and, 50
    overview of, **54**
  overview of, 3, 6, 52
  SCSI interface cards, 53, 55, 70
  sound cards
    microphones and, **124–125**
    for multimedia applications, 170, 172, 173
    overview of, 6, 55
  video cards
    8514/A video card, 100
    display drivers and, 100
    on early PCs, 96
    frame grabber video cards, **125**
    local bus video cards, 52, 53, 101
    for Microsoft Windows, 52
    overview of, **52–53, 101**
interlacing, in monitors, 96
Internet, 153
interrupt request lines (IRQs), 57
IO.SYS file, 164

ISA (Industry Standard Architecture) bus, 48
ISDN (Integrated Services Digital Network), 149

J

joystick ports, 54, 55
joysticks, **116–117**
jumpers, 14, **17**

K

keyboard controllers, 14, 44, 110
keyboard drivers, 110–111
keyboards, **108–111**
  capacitative keys, 109
  computers without, 108, **118–119**
  connectors for, 10, 13
  how they communicate with PCs, **110–111**
  how they work, **109**
  layout of, **108**, 110
  numeric keypad, 108
  overview of, 3, 108
  for portable computers, 108
  scan codes, 110
  security locks and, 8
  switch-based keys, 109
kilobits, **31**

L

labels on hard disk drives, 64
landing zones, 65
lands, in CDs, 90
LANs. *See* local area networks (LANs)
laptop computers, 4. *See also* portable computers
laser printers. *See also* printers
  color printers, **134–135**
  versus inkjet printers, 132
  overview of, **130–131**
  speed of, 131
layout of keyboards, **108**, 110
LIF (Low Insertion Force) sockets, 29
lightpens, 115, **118–119**
linear speed, of hard disk drives, 65, 68–69
liquid crystal displays (LCDs), **102–103**
loading DOS, **163–165**
local area networks (LANs), **142–147.** *See also*
    networks
  bus networks, 142–143
  collision detection and, 142–143
  Ethernet networks, 54, 142
  remote access to, 151
  star networks, 146–147
  token ring networks, 144–145
local bus
  hard disk drives and, 50
  local bus video cards, 52, 53, 101
  network interface cards and, 50
  overview of, **49**
locks, 8
logical addresses, translating into physical
    addresses, 23
logical drives, 72
logical geometry of hard disk drives, 70–71
Low Insertion Force (LIF) sockets, 29
low-level formatting, **72**

M

magnetic tape, 93, 124
magneto-optical disks, **93**

main memory, 30
masks, in monitors, 96–97
mass storage memory, 30
math coprocessors
  486 SX microprocessors and, 22
  487 SX math coprocessors, 17, 21, 28
  arithmetic/logic units (ALUs) and, 23
  jumpers and, 17
  overview of, 20
matrix analysis for character recognition, 122
MCA (Micro Channel Architecture) bus, 49
megabits, **31**
memory, **30–45**
  access time, 36, 43
  addresses and, 34
  BIOS
    and accessing hard disk, 76–77
    cache BIOS, 44
    keyboard drivers and, 110–111
    overview of, **160**, 162, 163
    sector relocation and, 70
    upgrading, 44
  booting and, 43
  cache memory
    configuring, 17
    disk caches and, 78–79
    and execution of instructions, **24–25**
    and how microprocessors access
        memory, **36–39**, 78–79
    overview of, 15
    versus RAM disks, 79
    read-ahead caching, 37
    write-back caching, 39
    write-through caching, 39
  cache memory controller
    and execution of instructions, 24, 25, **26–27**
    and how microprocessors access
        memory, 36–39
    overview of, 15, **23**
  clock speed and, 36
  CMOS (complementary metal oxide semicon-
      ductor), **31**
  DIPs (dual in-line packages), 25
  even parity and, 35
  versus hard disk drives, 30
  how it works, **32–33**
  how microprocessors access
      memory, 22, 24–27, **36–39**
  installing, 31, 34, **42–43**
  memory banks, 31, 34
  multimedia and, 171, 172
  odd parity and, 35
  organization of, **34**
  overview of, 30
  parity bits, 31
  parity checking, **35**
  PCMCIA memory cards, 45
  populated memory banks, 31
  primary (main) versus secondary (mass storage)
      memory, 30
  RAM (random-access memory), 15, **30–31**
    disk caches and, 78
    DRAM (dynamic RAM), 30, **31**, 32–33
    location of, 15
    nonvolatile RAM, 45
    overview of, **30–31**
    RAM (or virtual) disks, **79**
    SRAM (static RAM), **31**, 33
    VRAM (video RAM), **31**, 42–43, 52, 99
  read-ahead caching, 37
  refresh circuits, 30, 32–33
  registers, 36
  ROM (read-only memory)
    burning programs into, 44–45

EPROM (erasable programmable read-only memory), 45
  location of, 15
  overview of, **44–45**
  PROM (programmable read-only memory), 45
  Shadow ROM, 44–45
SIMMs (single in-line memory modules)
  defined, **31**
  installing, 34, 42–43
  parity checking and, 35
transistors (capacitors) and, 30, 32–33
upgrading, **42–43**
virtual memory, **40–41**
words, 30, 32, 34
write-back caching, 39
write-through caching, 39
MFM (modified frequency modulation) coding system, 67
Micro Channel Architecture (MCA) bus, 49
microphones, **124–125**, 173
microprocessors, **18–29**. *See also* motherboards
  386 microprocessors, 20
  486 microprocessors
    execution of instructions, **24–27**
    installing memory for, 34
    jumpers and, 17
    overdrive chips for, 28
    overview of, **20–21**
  487 SX math coprocessors, 17, 21, 28
  8088 microprocessors, 20
  accessing hard disk drives, **76–77**
  architecture of, **22–23**
  arithmetic/logic units (ALUs), 23, 25, 26
  burning programs into, 44–45
  bus interface unit, **23**, 26
  cache memory
    controller, **23**, 24, 25, **26–27**, 36–39
  choosing a replacement processor, 28
  clock speed multipliers, 22, 23
  clock speed of, 20
  control and protection test units, 22
  decoding units, 22
  differences between, 20
  execution of basic instructions, 22, **24–27**, 36–39
  external buses and, 20, 21
  heat sinks, 29
  installing, **28–29**
  instruction queues, 22
  jumpers and, **17**
  keyboard drivers, 110
  Low Insertion Force (LIF) sockets, 29
  math coprocessors
    486 SX microprocessors and, 22
    487 SX math coprocessors, 17, 21, 28
    arithmetic/logic units (ALUs) and, 23
    jumpers and, 17
    overview of, 20
  memory access time and, 36
  multimedia and, 173
  overdrive chips
    for 486 microprocessors, 28
    cooling, 28, 29
    installing, **28–29**
    overview of, **21**
    Pentium overdrive chips, 21, 28
    sockets for, 14, 21
  overview of, 14, **18–19**
  P24T microprocessors, 21
  paging units, **23**, 24, 26
  Pentium microprocessors, 21, 28
  PGA (pin grid array) cases, 18
  in portable computers, 18

PQFP (plastic quad flat package) cases, 18, 19
pre-fetch units, **22**, 24, 25
read-ahead caching, 37
removing and inserting, 28, **29**
segmentation units, **23**, 24, 26
SQFP (small quad flat package) cases, 18
types of, 20–21
upgrading, 14, 21, **28–29**
wait states, 36
write-back caching, 39
write-through caching, 39
Zero Insertion Force (ZIF) sockets, 28, 29
Microsoft Windows. *See also* software
  and accessing hard disk, 76–77
  overview of, **161**
  video cards for, 52
mid-tower cases, 4
mini-AT cases, 4
mini-tower cases, 4
modems, **149–151**. *See also* communications
  acoustic modems, 149
  fax modems, 150–151
  internal and external modems, 149
  modem cards, 6
  on-line services and, 151
  and remote access to local area networks, 151
modified frequency modulation (MFM) coding system, 67
moiré effects, 139
monitors, **96–105**
  active matrix monitors, 102, 103
  aspect ratio, 98
  CGA standard, 100
  color monitors, **96–97**
  deflection coils, 96–97
  device drivers and, 101
  digital-to-analog converters (DACs) and, 98, 99
  display drivers, 100, 101
  display modes, **99–101**
  dot pitch and, 96, 100
  EGA standard, 100
  electron guns and, 96–97
  interlacing, 96
  liquid crystal displays (LCDs), **102–103**
  masks, 96–97
  overview of, 2–3, 96
  passive matrix monitors, 102, 103
  performance of, 100
  persistence and, 96, 103
  pixels and, 96, 98–99, 100, 102–103
  plugging into PCs, 10
  radiation safety standards, **96**
  refreshing, 96
  resolution of, 96, **98–101**
  scanning and, 96–97, 103
  Super VGA standard, 100
  touch-sensitive screens, 115, **118–119**
  vertical and horizontal frequencies of, 96
  VGA standards, 100
  video animation and, **104–105**
  video cards
    8514/A video card, 100
    display drivers and, 100
    on early PCs, 96
    frame grabber video cards, **125**
    local bus video cards, 52, 53, 101
    for Microsoft Windows, 52
    overview of, **52–53**, 101
  Video Electronics Standards Association (VESA), 50, 100
  video pages, 99
  VRAM (video RAM), **31**, 42–43, 52, 99

XGA standard, 100
morphological analysis for character recognition, 122
motherboards, **14–17**. *See also* microprocessors
  clocks, 15
  configuring, 14, 17
  connecting to power supplies, 13
  daughterboards, 14
  DIP switches, 17, 57
  jumpers, 14, **17**
  keyboard controllers, 14, 44, 110
  overview of, 2–3, 13
  parts of, **14–15**
  printed circuits on, **16**
  "real time" clocks, 14
  and upgrading microprocessors, 14, 21, 28
mouse, **112–115**
  bus mouse, 112

n

network interface cards
  bus networks and, 142
  local bus and, 50
  overview of, **54**
networks, **142–147**
  dedicated servers, 154
  digital telephone networks, **148–151**
    baud rate, 148
    bits per second (bps), 148
    error checking codes, 148
    fax modems and, 150–151
    handshaking, 148
    ISDN (Integrated Services Digital Network), 149
    modems and, 149
    on-line services, 151
    overview of, 148
    protocols for, 148
    remote access to local area networks, 151
    transmission speeds, 148
    using, 149
    wide area networks (WANs) and, 152
  electronic mail (e-mail), **154**
  fiber-optic networks, **157**
  file servers, 154
  future of, **156–157**
  Internet, 153
  local area networks (LANs), **142–147**
    bus networks, 142–143
    collision detection and, 142–143
    Ethernet networks, 54, 142
    remote access to, 151
    star networks, 146–147
    token ring networks, 144–145
  NSFnet, 153
  packet-switching networks, 153
  print servers, 154
  resource sharing on, **154**
  shared servers, 154
  site licenses and, 154
  telecommuting, **155**
  teleconferencing, **155**
  wide area networks (WANs), **152–153**
  wireless networks, **157**
neural networks for character recognition, 123
nonvolatile RAM, 45
notebook computers, 4. *See also* portable computers
NSFnet, 153
numeric keypad, 108
NumLock key, 108

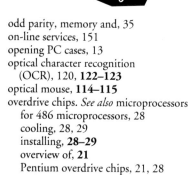

odd parity, memory and, 35
on-line services, 151
opening PC cases, 13
optical character recognition (OCR), 120, **122–123**
optical mouse, **114–115**
overdrive chips. *See also* microprocessors
    for 486 microprocessors, 28
    cooling, 28, 29
    installing, **28–29**
    overview of, **21**
    Pentium overdrive chips, 21, 28
    sockets for, 14, 21

P24T microprocessors, 21
packet-switching networks, 153
page description languages, 131
paging units, **23**, 24, 26
parallel mouse, 112
parallel ports, 54, 112
parity bits, 31
parity checking, **35**
parking hard disk drives, **65**
partitioning hard disk drives, **72**
passive matrix monitors, 102, 103
PCI network interface cards, 54
PCI (Peripheral Components Interconnect) bus, 51
PCMCIA bus, 51
PCMCIA cards
    expandability and, 6
    PCMCIA memory cards, 45
PCs. *See also* cases
    cooling, 5, 7, 10
    expandability of, **6–7**
    multimedia PCs, **171–173**
    overview of, **2–3**
    pen-based computers, 119
    performance of, **26–27**
    plugging monitors into, 10
    portable computers
        expandability of, 6
        handbook computers, 4
        keyboards, 108
        laptop computers, 4
        microprocessors in, 18
        notebook computers, 4
        pointing devices for, 108, 114–115
        sub-notebook computers, 4
        types of, **4**
        voltage selectors in, 11
    restarting, 8
    starting up, **162–165**
        AUTOEXEC.BAT, 164
        COMMAND.COM, 164–165
        CONFIG.SYS, 164–165
        IBMBIO.COM, 164
        IO.SYS, 164
        loading DOS, **163–165**
        memory and, 43
        MSDOS.SYS, 164
        POST (power on self test), 162
    turning off, 8, 9
    without keyboards, 108, **118–119**
pen-based computers, 119
Pentium microprocessors, 21, 28
performance. *See also* speed
    of monitors, 100
    of PCs, 26–27

of wide area networks (WANs), 152
Peripheral Components Interconnect (PCI) bus, 51
peripherals. *See also* CD-ROM drives; floppy disk drives; hard disk drives; input devices; mouse; pointing devices; printers
    device drivers and, 161
    expandability and, 6, 7
    sizes of, 13
persistence, in monitors, 96, 103
PGA (pin grid array) microprocessor cases, 18
physical geometry of hard disk drives, 70
pits, in CDs, 90
pixels, monitors and, 96, 98–99, 100, 102–103
plastic quad flat package (PQFP) microprocessor cases, 18, 19
platters, in hard disk drives, 60–61
Plug and Play, 51
pointers, video animation and, 104
pointing devices. *See also* input devices; mouse
    joysticks, **116–117**
    for laptop computers, 114–115
    lightpens, 115, **118–119**
populated memory banks, 31
portable computers
    expandability of, 6
    handbook computers, 4
    keyboards, 108
    laptop computers, 4
    microprocessors in, 18
    notebook computers, 4
    pointing devices for, 108, 114–115
    sub-notebook computers, 4
    types of, **4**
    voltage selectors in, 11
ports. *See also* interface cards
    on input/output (I/O) cards, 54
    joystick ports, 54, 55
    overview of, 10, 54
    parallel ports, 54, 112
    PS/2 mouse ports, 10, 112
    serial ports, 10, 54, 112
POST (power on self test), 162
PostScript, 131
power sockets, 10
power supplies, 3, 7, 10, 13
power switches, 8, 10
PQFP (plastic quad flat package) microprocessor cases, 18, 19
pre-fetch units, **22**, 24, 25
primary (main) memory, 30
print engines, 131
print servers, 154
printed circuits, on motherboards, **16**
printers, **128–139**
    daisywheel printers, 128
    dot-matrix printers, **128–129**, 130
    fonts and, 131
    grayscale and color rendering, **138–139**
    imagesetters and film recorders, **136–137**
    inkjet printers, **132–133**
    laser printers
        color printers, **134–135**
        versus inkjet printers, 132
        overview of, **130–131**
        speed of, 131
    overview of, 2, 128
    page description languages and, 131
processors. *See* microprocessors
programs. *See also* applications
    burning into chips, 44–45
    cache controller programs, 78
    PC performance and, 27

PROM (programmable read-only memory), 45
protocols, for telecommunications, 148
PS/2 mouse ports, 10, 112
punch cards, 108

QWERTY keyboard layout, 108

radiation safety standards, **96**
RAM (random-access memory)
    disk caches and, 78
    DRAM (dynamic RAM), 30, **31**, 32–33
    location of, 15
    nonvolatile RAM, 45
    overview of, **30–31**
    RAM (or virtual) disks, **79**
    SRAM (static RAM), **31**, 33
    VRAM (video RAM), **31**, 42–43, 52, 99
read/write heads, 60, 61, 63, **64–65**, 70
read-ahead caching, 37
reading data on hard disk drives, **66**
read-write memory. *See* RAM
"real time" clocks, 14
rebooting PCs, 8
reducing write current on hard disk drives, **68–69**
refresh circuits, 30, 32–33
refreshing monitors, 96
registers, memory, 36
relational databases, 167
relative addresses, translating into physical addresses, 23
remote access to local area networks, 151
removable hard disk cartridges, **92**, 124
removing microprocessors, 28, **29**
reset button, 8, 9
resolution
    of dot-matrix printers, 128
    of grayscale and color screens, 138
    of monitors, 96, **98–101**
    of scanners, 120
resource sharing on networks, **154**
restarting PCs, 8
The Rite of Spring (Stravinsky), 174–177
ROM (read-only memory)
    burning programs into, 44–45
    EPROM (erasable programmable read-only memory), 45
    location of, 15
    overview of, **44–45**
    PROM (programmable read-only memory), 45
    Shadow ROM, 44–45
root directory, 73
run length limited (RLL) coding system, 67

sampling, 124
scan codes for keyboards, 110
SCANDISK command, DOS, 85
scanners, **120–121**
scanning, in monitors, 96–97, 103
screens. *See also* monitors
    for grayscales and colors, 138–139
scrolling, video animation and, 104
SCSI disk controllers, 70–71
SCSI disk drives
    installing, **81**
    overview of, 70
SCSI interface cards, 53, 55, 70

secondary cache memory, 36–39
secondary (mass storage) memory, 30
sectors
    on CDs, 91
    on floppy disks, 72
    on hard disk drives, 63, 70, 72–74
    sector relocation on hard disk drives, **70**
security, **82–87**
    backing up data, **82–83**, 92–93
    common ways of losing data, 84
    cross-linked files, 85
    data confidentiality, 85
    security locks, 8
    viruses, **86–87**
segmentation units, **23**, 24, 26
serial mouse, 10, 112
serial ports, 10, 54, 112
service bureaus, 136–137
Shadow ROM, **44–45**
sharing resources on networks, **154**
SIMMs (single in-line memory modules). *See also*
    memory
    defined, **31**
    installing, 34, 42–43
    parity checking and, 35
simple animation, 104
site licenses, 154
size
    of hard disk drives, 63
    of peripherals, 13
slack, on hard disk drives, 73
slots. *See* expansion slots
small quad flat package (SQFP) microprocessor
    cases, 18
SMARTDRV.EXE program, 78
smoothing, scanners and, 120
software, **160–167**. *See also* programs
    applications, **166–167**
    BIOS
        and accessing hard disk, 76–77
        cache BIOS, 44
        keyboard drivers and, 110–111
        overview of, **160**, 162, 163
        sector relocation and, 70
        upgrading, 44
    bootstrap program, 163
    database software, **167**
    device drivers, **161**
    DOS
        and accessing hard disk, 76–77
        CHKDSK command, 85
        DOS sector numbers, 73
        FORMAT command, 85
        and formatting hard disk drives, 72–73
        loading, **163–165**
        overview of, **160**
        SCANDISK command, 85
    graphical user interfaces (GUIs), 161
    Microsoft Windows
        and accessing hard disk, 76–77
        overview of, **161**
        video cards for, 52
    programs
        burning into chips, 44–45
        PC performance and, 27
    site licenses, 154
    software caches, 78
    spreadsheet software, **167**
    and starting up PCs, **162–165**
        AUTOEXEC.BAT, 164
        COMMAND.COM, 164–165
        CONFIG.SYS, 164–165
        IBMBIO.COM, 164
        IO.SYS, 164

loading DOS, **163–165**
    memory and, 43
    MSDOS.SYS, 164
    POST (power on self test), 162
    versions of, 161
    word processing software, 120, **166**
sound cards
    microphones and, **124–125**
    for multimedia applications, 170, 172, 173
    overview of, 6, 55
SoundBlaster sound cards, 55
speakers, 13, 14, 172
speed. *See also* clock speed; performance
    of inkjet printers, 132
    of laser printers, 131
    linear speed of hard disk drives, 65, 68–69
    of PCs, 26–27
spreadsheet software, **167**
SQFP (small quad flat package) microprocessor
    cases, 18
SRAM (static RAM), **31**, 33
ST 506 hard disk drives, 70
Standard AT cases, 4
star networks, **146–147**
starting up PCs, **162–165**
    AUTOEXEC.BAT, 164
    COMMAND.COM, 164–165
    CONFIG.SYS, 164–165
    IBMBIO.COM, 164
    IO.SYS, 164
    loading DOS, **163–165**
    memory and, 43
    MSDOS.SYS, 164
    POST (power on self test), 162
static electricity, 43, 56
stepper motors, 89, 120
storage capacity of hard disk drives, **63**
Stravinsky, Igor, 174–177
sub-notebook computers, 4. *See also* portable
    computers
subtractive synthesis, 134
Super VGA standard, 100
switch-based keys, 109
system units. *See* cases

tape backups, 93
telecommunications. *See* communications
telecommuting, **155**
teleconferencing, **155**
telephone networks. *See* digital telephone net-
    works
text, optical character recognition
    (OCR), 120, **122–123**
three-color printing, 134
token ring networks, **144–145**
toner, for laser printers, 131
touch-sensitive screens, 115, **118–119**
tower (vertical case) PCs, **4–5**, 6
trackballs, 112, **114**
tracks, on hard disk drives, 62, 65, 72
transistors, memory and, 30, 32–33
translating logical addresses into physical
    addresses, 23
transmission speeds, 148
Trojan Horse viruses, **86**
TrueType fonts, 131
turbo button, 8
turning off PCs, 8, 9

unformatting floppy disks, 84, 85
upgrading. *See also* installing
    BIOS, 44
    memory, 42–43
    microprocessors, 14, 21, 28–29

vector fonts, 131
ventilation
    of computers, 5, 7, 10
    for overdrive chips, 28, 29
versions of software, 161
vertical case PCs, **4–5**, 6
vertical frequency, of monitors, 96
VESA (Video Electronics Standards Association)
    monitors and, 100
    VESA bus, 50
VGA standards, 100
video animation, **104–105**
video cards. *See also* interface cards; monitors
    8514/A video card, 100
    display drivers and, 100
    on early PCs, 96
    frame grabber video cards, **125**
    local bus video cards, 52, 53, 101
    for Microsoft Windows, 52
    overview of, **52–53**, **101**
video games, 116–117
video pages, 99
videotapes, 93, 124
virtual disks, **79**
virtual memory, **40–41**
viruses, **86–87**
voice recognition, 124
voltage selector, 10, 11
VRAM (video RAM), **31**, 42–43, 52, 99

wait states, 36
wide area networks (WANs), **152–153**
Windows. *See* Microsoft Windows
wireless networks, **157**
word processing software, 120, **166**
words, 30, 32, 34
wrist bands, antistatic, 43, 56
write current on hard disk drives, **68–69**
write precompensation, **69**
write-back caching, 39
write-protecting floppy disks, 88, 89
write-through caching, 39
writing data on hard disk drives, **66**, 68–69

XGA standard, 100

Y-cables, 13, 29

Zero Insertion Force (ZIF) sockets, 28, 29